THE
ECOLOGY
OF
RELIGION

THE
ECOLOGY
OF
RELIGION

From Writing to Religion
in the Study of Judaism

JACOB NEUSNER

Abingdon Press
Nashville

The Ecology of Religion: From Writing to Religion in the Study of
Judaism

This book is printed on acid-free paper.

Neusner, Jacob, 1932-
    The ecology of religion : from writing to religion in the study of
Judaism / Jacob Neusner.
    p. cm.
    Bibliography: p.
    Includes index.
    ISBN 0-687-11512-4
    1. Judaism—Study and teaching—Philosophy. 2. Religion—
Study and teaching—Philosophy. I. Title.
BM71.N46 1989   89-33141
296 .07—dc20   CIP

MANUFACTURED BY THE PARTHENON PRESS AT
NASHVILLE, TENNESSEE, UNITED STATES OF AMERICA

For

William Scott Green

a token of thanks
for
the events of
May 20 to 23, 1988

CONTENTS

Part Four

Matrix: *From Writing Through History to Religion*

THE
ECOLOGY
OF
RELIGION

I f we want to understand religion in times past, we have to learn how to read its writing and discern that religion. For most of what we know about religion before our own day comes to us in writing, in documents. The religions of the West—Judaism, Islam, and Christianity—all appeal to writing not only for information about their own past but also for authority for theology and norms alike (e.g., to the written as well as the oral Torah, to the Bible, and to the Quran). Accordingly, writing preserves and presents religion. All writing may be divided into two types: writing with named authors in a determinate time and place, and writing without clear evidence concerning who speaks where, when, and why. Describing a religious system out of writing bearing the names of authors allows immediate access to the time and circumstances in which the document came into being. But use of writing that does not identify the author and when and where the document came into being proves difficult. Here I address the problem of utilizing anonymous writings for the description, analysis, and interpretation of a religion.

Judaism forms the focus and supplies the example. The reason is that all of the authoritative writings of Judaism in its formative age are anonymous. There is not a single piece of religious writing in Judaism in late antiquity of which we know the name of an author, or where, when, why, and under what circumstances that author undertook to create that writing. In

11

my work over thirty years and two hundred volumes, I have devised methods for reading anonymous writings and on that basis describing, analyzing, and interpreting the religion presented by those writings. In this book I set forth some of the methods for the study of religion that comes to us in that very particular medium of discourse—hence, from writing to religion. I believe that these methods will prove fruitful for colleagues who study other religions and therefore for the entire field of the study of religion of a particular classification.

I wrote this book on the eve of my fifty-sixth birthday, making the move from earlier to later middle age. But this is not a summing up, in safe harbor, of a protracted journey, but merely a sighting on a voyage long in progress and without end in view—or wanted. Quite to the contrary, I am now moving in quite a different direction, away from the problem of documents entirely and onward to that larger and encompassing interest with which I began my career thirty-five years ago. I have always worked within the tradition of Max Weber and held his foundation writings for the social sciences to be as close to self-evident truth as in this mortal world we are apt to find. From my earliest reading of his writing in graduate school, I concluded that he asked all the right questions, but, by reason of an infirm grasp on the nature of literary evidence in particular, he produced answers resting on incorrect premises as to the character and use of writing. That explains why his stunningly apt questions—for example, on why one social world produced capitalism but another did not—yielded such hopelessly outdated and unreadable books as his *Ancient Judaism*. It is not only that the scale was too broad but also that the evidence was read as exemplary and illustrative, rather than closely analyzed in an inductive inquiry from detail to main point. After writing *Life of Yohanan ben Zakkai*, I found it necessary to rethink the usefulness of paradigms like spontaneity and routine, which I had swiped from Weber. For I found that book too pat and patterned, and even then, before I had grasped the critical program of historical scholarship, then and now utterly alien to the study of the history of the Jews and Judaism in ancient times, I knew that that book, despite its favorable reception, closed all roads backward.

For the next ten years I worked within the borrowed paradigms of history and of the history of religion, but the former I deemed trivial and inconsequential, and the latter I found insufficiently historical to produce answers of a more concrete and specific character than those of Weber. Historical study in its own terms seemed to me episodic and intellectually vacant. But history did provide the critical program that made all else possible, for it taught me to ask whether and how a source may be utilized in the construction of events. The approach of history of religion led upward to a level of generalization that, in my view, remained altogether too elevated for the nature of the sources. Not only so, but the sorts of generalizations then emerging from the history of religion (including anthropology and sociology) struck me as ineffably obvious, treating as null all the interesting questions of comparison and contrast, divergence and convergence. Still, history of religion instructed me on the basic requirements for the study of religion, and while the results seemed to me to violate the requirements of circumstance and context and to ignore divergence in the insistence upon convergence, still, history of religion became and remains the discipline with which I identify most of my work. But as this book makes clear, I propose to redefine history of religion along far more inductive lines than have been followed in a field of learning that finds both its power and its pathos in its tasks as a generalizing science. If I have opted for the focus on inductive study of detail, it is, after all, because I happily locate myself in what overseas critics have called the hypercritical American tradition of pragmatism and positivism. The same critics explain that there are things we know but cannot show. I owe them thanks for stating with great clarity precisely the point on which we most differ.

Returning to the sources in yet a third chapter of life, I simply reread them all, beginning to end, and retranslated most of them. The documentary method records in general terms what I did. Now, as I move back to Weber's program, it is on the foundation of the correct assessment of the character of the evidence. I can ask his questions once more, questions of rationality (which I call system) and of comparison. I answer them in the requisite detail, in the way in which he did not, and I do so with close attention to the fine contours of the landscape, as seen from above but near at hand, rather than—as with Weber and his continuators—through the haze from on high. Every critique of Weber's *Protestant Ethic and the Spirit of Capitalism* found troubling the lacunae of evidence not examined, generalizations attained to hastily. For the work of description, such as occupied Weber in his work on Judaism, India, and China, for example, I have corrected Weber's error regarding Judaism of generalizing too hastily and on the foundation of evidence read in an un-nuanced way. Accordingly, my reprise of Weber's program, in my *Economics of the Mishnah, Politics of Judaism,* and *Philosophy of Judaism* (the first done, the next two in progress) will form the first stage in this fourth chapter of my life. In these works I set forth what I conceive to be the applied rationality and practical reason of the Judaism of the initial statement. What must follow—I now speak of the 1990s—will be parallel studies of the same systemic rationality in the Judaism of the second phase. The comparison of the one with the other then should tell us—but why proceed into the twenty-first century?

With every major project I have found myself anxious about coming to the end of an idea or a problem. Where, I wondered, would my next idea emerge, and how should I find a new problem? But the answer has always come from within. My own dissatisfaction with the results formed sufficient stimulus, and I have not run out of ideas and, if truth be told, no longer worry that I might. Every book, every project, forms a review and critique of the one before and also the motivation for the one beyond. Here I explain why.

This first and only methods book of mine comes in the aftermath of some two hundred scholarly monographs, books, translations, studies, and synthetic statements, which are catalogued in the bibliography. In them I have translated the canonical writings and then set forth the religious system of the Judaism of the dual Torah, variously called normative, talmudic (for its principal literary evidence), rabbinic (for the honorific of its holy men), classical, or simply "Judaism." I have developed a theory of how, on the basis of acutely detailed written evidence, to formulate the description, analysis, and interpretation of a religion. Accordingly, the purpose of this book is to give a secure grounding in the documentary theory of describing a religion, specifically the system of formative Judaism. That theory on transforming writing into religion has until now been worked out only inductively and in detail through books of mine that have embodied and expressed it. My stress is on the analysis of discourse as a route into the framing of the social world formed by a religious system. The modes of discourse encompass rhetoric, the patterning of language, and logic, the composition of mutually intelligible exchanges of ideas in fully articulated language made up of words and sentences that follow a public syntax.

The particular stimulus for writing this methods book derives from two sources. First, the idea of my writing a "methods book" originally came from my old friend and then editor at Abingdon Press, Dr. Davis Perkins. When he joined Abingdon after years of valued service at Fortress Press, I told him that I wanted to write a book for him in his new office. He suggested what ultimately became this book. My fondness for Davis Perkins does not account for my interest in his project; rather, it comes from my respect for his professionalism and my desire to learn from working with him.

Second, it was not I but Professor William Scott Green who saw in some of my books what is, in fact, a sustained methodological inquiry. While the book, as it turns out, is quite different from what he and I originally discussed, he was the one who saw things whole and directed my attention to what might be done, and, moreover, he talked with me about this book as it evolved to its final form. But I originally asked for his help because of a very particular occasion.

The proximate necessity for undertaking the book was precipitated in May and June, 1988, by a National Endowment for the Humanities Summer Seminar for College Teachers at Brown University, which I gave in June, July, and August 1988. I had the notion of teaching colleagues in the study of religion what I think I have learned about the study of religious systems. The idea was inchoate, but I had the conception that the systemic study of religion offered a method that might be adapted for the study of other Judaisms beside the Judaism of the dual Torah in late antiquity, and even for the description, analysis, and interpretation of other religions altogether. When much to my surprise the application succeeded in the 1987–1988 competition, I faced the necessity of setting forth not merely results but my methods. These had been, if occasionally articulated, essentially intuitive responses to the character of a particular corpus of evidence and the (self-imposed) insistence on inductively reading that evidence.

I also presented the chapters to my twelve colleagues in the NEH summer seminar at Brown University in 1988 and enjoyed the benefit of their stimulating discussion. These generous colleagues are as follows: Professors Eugene Gallagher, Gary Phillips, Carroll Pastner, Aaron Milavec, Barry Crawford, Paul Livermore, Stefan Davies, C. Thomas McCullough, Frank Trombley, Ricky Johnson, Merrill Miller, and David Bossman.

As I do in all intellectual and scholarly projects, I quite naturally consulted Professor Green, Chair of the Department of Religious and Classical Studies at the University of Rochester, not only because he is partner in so many projects of mine, but also because, as editor of the *Journal of the American Academy of Religion,* he has an unmatched grasp of the field of the academic study of religion in our day. In response to my inquiry he contributed the initial outline of the seminar (revised, of course, in consultation with the colleagues of the NEH seminar), which in the nature of things also became the basic design for the book. His outline for the seminar program in its principal parts is now the organization of this book. Once he laid matters out as he did, everything seemed "obvious," and I began to view the corpus of my work in the systematic way in which I am now able to present it.

I am uncommonly happy to express my indebtedness and thanks to Dr. Perkins and to Professor Green, surely the best editors anyone can hope to have.

The dedication of this book responds to yet another act of both wit and also supererogatory kindness. I wish William Scott Green students as astute, as thoughtful, and also as generous and intellectually helpful to him as he is to me. I am uncommonly grateful that he is part of my life, and I his.

Jacob Neusner

PROLOGUE

T he purpose in moving from writing to religion, the goal of
my documentary method for the study of Judaism, is to
investigate through the case of Judaism what I call *the ecology of
religion* (hence the title of this book). By this term I mean the
interplay between a religious system and the social world that
gives to that system its shape and meaning. When we understand
a religious system in the context of its social order, we grasp
whatever in this world we are likely to understand about religion
in the shaping of the civilization of humanity. And no other
generative force in civilization has exceeded in power and effect
the formative force of religion. Accordingly, in this method I
have meant to exemplify in a very particular setting the larger
problem of how to relate the content of a religion to its context,
religious conviction to social culture, and above all, social
change, which is public and general, to symbol change, which is
particular and invariably distinctive to its setting. At stake in the
study of the ecology of religion is whether and how religion
forms an independent variable in the shaping of civilization.

In the framing of my method I draw upon a metaphor from
natural sciences for the study of religion. My inquiry, then,
concerns whether, in the analysis of the interrelated components
of civilization, religion constitutes a singular constituent of the
whole. Ecology is a branch of science concerned with the
interrelationships of organisms and their environments. By

17

"ecology of" I mean the study of the interrelationship between a particular, religious way of viewing the world and living life, and the historical, social, and especially political situation of the people who view the world and live life in accord with the teachings of their religion. The Jews have formed ongoing groups, existing over time in various places and hence describing, analyzing, and interpreting in context a Judaism does not conclude the work of studying the ecology of Judaism as exemplar of the ecology of religion. An ongoing social entity, after all, yields more than a single system, but the ecology of the social entity in its indicative traits requires attention not only for its change but also for its enduring qualities.

Turning writing into religion defines the task of all who propose to understand the religious life through other than its most acutely contemporary evidences. For, prior to our own day, writing forms the paramount medium by which we are informed about the sustaining conceptions of the sacred (worked out in a social entity's world view, way of life, and definition of itself), that altogether define a religion. When we know the names and historical contexts of writers of these evidences, the work is hard enough. But the task is made exceedingly difficult when, as in the case of ancient Judaisms, we do not know anything about the writers. Then we have to identify the evidence for their circumstance and concern, their modes of thought and manner of framing the world, only in what they have made and set forth for us.

Moving backward from what people say and how they say it to what they are thinking and why they are reflecting as they are, is what I believe I know how to do. For I have had to study a religion contained in writings that at no point indicate the names, times, circumstances, or critical concerns of their authors. I believe that my methods will prove interesting to anyone who wishes to study religion, for books without named authors convey much of what we know about many religions, not only Judaism. But let us begin with the religion that provides the occasion for the methodological study undertaken here and then explain the method and program of this book.

Here I chart an intellectual adventure of thirty-five years. I do so in hope that others, reading different writings to describe other religions, may make the same journey. For I have worked out methods of reading documents in such a way as to discern, within written evidence, the religious system that an authorship proposes in some way to address or to reshape. That is what I mean to set forth here. My method proposes to explain how, through written sources in particular, to find evidence for the inner structure, the imagination and world-framing, world-conceiving mentality, of a religious system, a Judaism. While the method has evolved from inductive studies of documents and inquiries into their interrelationships, it may be spelled out in a way accessible to those who do not find the motivation or interest to read the some two hundred books of mine in which I have shaped it in acute detail. Accordingly, I lay out in this book the main lines of the methods I have devised for the study of the written evidence of religion. I want to set forth *how*, in quest of an understanding of the particular Judaism that took shape in the first seven centuries and has predominated ever since, I have read written evidence and so produced an account of a religion in its formative age. This is therefore a book that concerns method, specifically the method of reading writing and describing, analyzing, and interpreting religion. The book will succeed if readers derive from what I have done their own ways of reading the documents of other religions.

Whatever I put forth in these pages is for exemplary purposes. Obviously, I review discussions scattered in prior writings. But here I present a fresh and cogent statement, framed in terms of the requirements to define and illustrate a particular method in studying a religion through its writings. It follows that while I refer to and, of course, draw upon results of research already completed, my purpose is not simply to write the précis of a life's work, which cannot and need not be done. Nor, all the more so, do I propose to undertake an intellectual autobiography, which I cannot conceive to be useful or interesting to anyone. It is, rather, to set out as clearly as I can what I deem to be the main lines of that part of my method for the study of religion that utilizes written sources in the description of the religious system that is contained within those sources. Others, working on not only the same sources on which I have concentrated but other religious traditions and their writing altogether, can adapt my methods for their own use.

In offering a methods book, I take the logical next step in a career devoted to the study of religion through the case of Judaism. I have spent my life studying a literature not widely accessible in the humanities and social sciences. I have aimed to make that literature useful to specialists in a variety of fields within the academic study of religion as well as in ancient history and culture and Near and Middle Eastern studies. My work has concerned the exemplary classics of Judaism and how they form a cogent statement. These classical writings, which form the canon of a particular statement of Judaism, the Judaism of the dual Torah, oral and written, defined the Judaism in the context of which both Christendom and Islam took shape. The circumstances of the formation of the writings that comprised that Judaic canon in the formative epoch of Western civilization, the issues important to its framers in that exemplary age, the kind of writings they produced, their modes of mediating change and responding to crisis, the power of the Judaism they shaped to define the life of Israel, the Jewish people, and to endure through the whole of the history of the West and Middle East alike—these form the center of my interest. And these are no small concerns, for they encompass what I conceive to be the critical issues of Western civilization, so far as these issues encompass Judaism and Israel, the Jewish people, so far as Judaism and that utopian Israel participate in the civilization of the West.

But I claim that all students of all religions address the task that I have taken up, which is to speak of a religion as exemplary of the genus religion, and to seek issues of general intelligibility in what is held to be particular and special. The reason is that if we wish to study not only religions but *religion*, not only the species but the *genus*, then we shall have to seek to generalize, just as do anthropologists who describe a village but also ask about humanity *in nuce*, just as do sociologists who formulate hypotheses of social action and explanation of that action and test the hypotheses against the data of diverse social entities. The academic study of religion draws upon written evidence and correctly insists upon the close reading of that evidence. But the purpose of the reading draws learning beyond the limits of the text and even of the canonical context thereof, since in the end we read the document because we want to describe, analyze, and interpret the religion to which the document attests.

The emphasis on documents is for two reasons. First, documentary evidence by definition is written evidence, and the evidence of the particular Judaism treated here for its formative period is entirely in writing. The synagogue art that has come to light from the same period hardly correlates with rabbinic writings on the same themes, let alone with rabbinic rules governing the use of iconic art in the holy life of Israel, the Jewish people. Hence, if we propose to describe that Judaism, we have to develop methods for transforming writing into religion, that is to say, for reading texts and extracting the religious structure and system to which those texts testify. Second, a document by definition is not fragmentary but a whole and complete statement, and, as will become clear, my emphasis is on the reading of documents wholly and in their entirety, rather than on selecting bits and pieces of this and that for the composition of a picture of a religious system drawn within lines dictated from without. I therefore aim to teach for the case of Judaism how to conceive and analyze a religious system through written evidence.

In my career I have translated (or retranslated, where necessary) and reread for historical purposes the classic documents of the Judaism that took shape in the first through sixth centuries c.e. and that has predominated since then. These documents—the Mishnah, the Tosefta, the Midrash-compilations assigned to late antiquity, the two Talmuds and related writings—represent the collective statement and consensus of authorships and show us how those authorships proposed to make a statement to their situation—and about the human condition. These documents by definition are public and speak of a social world, for no document is credibly assigned to a single author (hence "authorship"), and, more important still, all are preserved because they are deemed canonical and authoritative. That is why I have claimed not only to study the documents of ancient sages of Judaism but also to speak of the social world that they imagined and invented, that is, to describe out of their documents their Judaism.

The documentary approach to the description of a religious system focuses, as the name indicates, upon the reading of whole documents. Prior to the present time, there were two other modes of reading these writings, neither of which yielded results useful for the study of religion. The more common was, and is, anti-intellectual. It is the exegetical-philological method, which tells us about the meanings of words and phrases but does not read words and phrases as sentences containing meaning. The second is anti-historical in that it reads sentences out of all context. Ignoring the limits of documents and therewith the definitive power of historical context and social circumstance, all books on "Judaism" (or "classical," "Rabbinic," "Talmudic" Judaism) before my work have promiscuously cited all writings deemed canonical in constructing composite pictures of the theology or law of that Judaism, severally and jointly, so telling us about Judaism all at once and in the aggregate. That anti-historical, narrowly theological, apologetic approach has lost all standing in the study of the history of Christianity of the same time and place, for most scholars of the history of Christianity understand the diversity and contextual differentiation exhibited by the classical Christian writers. But by contrast, ignoring the documentary origin of statements, the received pictures of Judaism have been presented as uniform and unitary theological and legal facts that originated each in its own document, that is to say, in its distinctive time and place, and each as part of a documentary context, possibly also of a distinct system of its own. I have corrected the errors of both methods.

Against the narrowly exegetical-philological reading of texts, I have insisted that documents testify not only to lexicography but also to religion. Against the theological and harmonizing reading of sentences out of documentary context, I have insisted that each document be read in its own terms, as a statement—if it constituted such a statement—*of* a Judaism, or, at least, *to*, and so in behalf of, a Judaism. It follows that each theological and legal fact was to be interpreted, to begin with, in relationship to the other theological and legal facts among which it found its original location. These negative principles of method set the stage for the methodological program spelled out in this book.

The upshot of my documentary method is now spread

through a variety of books. These are listed in the bibliography at the end of this book. The result of the reading of documents as whole but discrete statements, as I believe we can readily demonstrate defined their original character, is exemplified (but only that) in such works of mine as *Judaism: The Evidence of the Mishnah, Judaism and Society: The Evidence of the Yerushalmi, Judaism and Scripture: The Evidence of Leviticus Rabbah,* as well as *Judaism and Story: The Evidence of The Fathers According to Rabbi Nathan.*

In this way I have described the principal documents of the Judaism of the dual Torah, each in its own terms and context. I have further undertaken a set of comparative studies of two or more documents, showing the points in common as well as the contrasts between and among them. This protracted work is represented by systematic accounts of the Mishnah, tractate Avot, the Tosefta, Sifra, Sifré to Numbers, the Yerushalmi, Genesis Rabbah, Leviticus Rabbah, Pesiqta deRab Kahana, The Fathers According to Rabbi Nathan, the Bavli, Pesiqta Rabbati, and various other writings. In all of this work I have proposed to examine one by one and then in groups of affines the main components of the dual Torah. I have wished to place each into its own setting and so to attempt to trace the unfolding of the dual Torah in its historical manifestations. In the later stages of the work, I have attempted to address the question of how some or even all of the particular documents form a general statement. In this way I have developed the documentary approach to the study of a religious system, a Judaism that in its main outlines I set forth in the present book. In chapter 1 I place the method into its context within the study of religion and in the discussion of text, context, and matrix. In chapter 2 I lay out principal modes of documentary analysis, that is, the sorts of evidence I have shown we must identify and analyze. Then, in the successive parts of the book, I spell out how the method works, with sizable examples. Readers who want a definition of the Judaism under study here and a brief account of its writings will find both in the Appendix.

PART ONE

The Theory:
An Overview of the Method of Documentary Analysis

CHAPTER ONE

From Writing to Religion: A Religious System as a Theory of Society

The story of civilization is written by religion, which so forms attitudes and viewpoints as to move nations and societies to act in one way, rather than some other. It is important for people to know what they believe God wants of them, what he approves or disapproves of, rewards or punishes, how he tells them to live and what to do together. Whether the consequent deeds are private and individual or public and social, Heaven's dictates inform and enthuse humanity in society. Since, moreover, the social world forms the matrix for the individual and family, it is the power of religion to define and inform society that matters in framing the story of civilization. For social continuities define the range of choice for individual and family alike. Accordingly, if we propose to describe religion, to analyze its traits and effects, and to interpret its character as the formative force in civilization, we ask about the social world framed and formed by religion. At stake in the answer is the understanding of how humanity forms society, creates culture, sustains civilization. That understanding comes to us when we grasp the way religion informs society, frames the possibilities of culture, and defines what it means to live in civilization.

When we ask about religion and society, what we want to know about religion in particular is how to describe, analyze, and interpret the social world that a religious system sets forth. The way in which a religion conceives humanity to organize itself, the structures of society and the divisions of the social order, the tasks of the group and the responsibilities of the family and the individual within the larger group—these social issues find resolution in a religion's theory of the whole and of the parts within the whole. Accordingly, it is that theory of the whole that focuses our attention and demands our sustained inquiry if we propose to explain to ourselves the social order of civilization. Prior to our own day and even now, with the exception of some limited circumstances, it was and is religion that has presented that theory of the whole. If we want to grasp all together and all at once an account of all the world, the group within the world, the family within the group, the individual within the family—that theory that has situated everything and everyone in its proper place, we turn to religion.

For the whole then continues to be held together, in particular, by reason of the social imagination of religion. That act of shared imagination concerning the social world comprises the mentality, the world view, and above all, the world-defining view that religion sets forth to link heaven to earth. It holds all together and all at once, in proper balance, proportion, and composition. Accordingly, to make sense of civilization as humanity has known it for the brief moment in which humanity has formed the consciousness to want to know itself, religion takes center stage. Its sense of things, its explanations, its modes of sorting things out and placing all things into perspective— these acts of imagination define and dictate the traits of those social worlds that have endured over time.

Accordingly, in trying to make sense of civilization we propose to ask ourselves how religion forms and informs social worlds. The answer comes not from the study of sociology and anthropology but rather from the study of religion as a world-defining force and fact, an independent variable. For the question of civilization as now framed requires answers not from the facts of society but from the fantasies of humanity imagining, thinking, wondering. The attitudes and viewpoints that impart shape and structure to the social life come out of the imaginative life. Because people believe things, they do things, define their lives and give them up, for instance. True, we may describe a society by appeal to diverse indicative traits. But if we hope to make sense of that society and explain what holds it together, imparts purpose and cogency to the whole, gives to the parts symmetry and balance, and makes society social and enduring, we turn from the facts of sociology to the fantasies of faith. That is where we find the (to the outsider) nonsense that (to the engaged person) makes sense of the realities of everyday society. This is not to claim that religion stands over against and separate from the social world that appeals to religion. Rather, it is to judge that religion forms the source of motivation and the court of appeal for justification, because religion sets forth the account and explanation for how things are and ought to be: for what God wants. Explaining the parts and making them whole and coherent, religion then stands for the power of imagination to account for reality. And, as everyone knows, the inner eye shapes vision, and imagination dictates how history is made and people make their lives.

Wanting to know how and why the story of civilization is written by religion, we naturally find our way to the study of religion. What we want to investigate is the power of religion to so form attitudes and viewpoints as to move nations and societies to act as they do—however that is. But when we take up the study of religion, we find ourselves bound by the limitations of the sorts of evidence to which, over time and in the present, we gain access. The evidence, first of all, concerns not religion but religions. Religion, after all, does not exist in abstract form except in the mind of the academic scholar of religion. Religion in the world exists only as religions, one by one. We then propose to generalize about religion out of the data of religions. And religions moreover testify to their qualities not in generalities but in concrete kinds of evidence. They speak through diverse media, for diverse purposes, to diverse issues. Religions come to concrete expression in many ways. To study one religion or set of religions, we require knowledge of philosophy; to investigate another, we need to know the possibilities of the theater; a third will require us to know about visual arts, a fourth about music, a fifth about dance, a sixth about storytelling. As many religions as there are, so many are the modes of paramount expression (hence the types of evidence) that demand analysis.

Still, among the varieties of data for the study of religions and therefore of religion, the evidence for religions in times past falls into two fundamental classifications: written and other-than-written, therefore religion with an accessible past as against religion with only an eternal present, whenever, wherever, that present takes place. A religion that we know only in its non-written forms speaks eloquently through art, dance, music, theater, storytelling. But the voice is forever one we hear, like music before the age of recording, heard once for all, only in the here and now of the moment of performance, and then never again. Recording preserved the record of the performance, with distortion to be sure, but in such a way that the performance could be re-presented. Religions that mean to emerge out of the distant past come to us only in writing, the counterpart to recorded music. Writing is what preserves, in the language and idiom of another time to be sure, whatever art, dance, music, theater, or storytelling in that other age yielded for formulation and preservation.

Without a written record, we may examine and appreciate the artifacts of culture, whether high or material, speculating on what people may have meant by making this amphora or that sculpture. But we can never go beyond our encounter, shaped wholly in our own acutely contemporary categories, with an ever-silent past. We know how we respond. We cannot know what the artist, long ago, meant. When, by contrast, we have writing and have deciphered it, we join the artifact with intelligible thought and gain access to a world beyond and before our own. Without the record of notes or the counterpart thereof, music happens only once. Without a way of recording gesture, the dance, spontaneous or invented, is preserved in mere imagination and frail memory, therefore for only a brief spell indeed. Without language, religion persists in a silent and mute world, inviting speculation but never satisfying curiosity.

To study religion in the present world, we have ample media other than the written ones. When we propose to study religions and therefore also religion in the here and now, we have readily accessible information and know precisely how to collect, organize, and interpret it. The social sciences, particularly sociology and anthropology, exercise the power to describe, analyze, and interpret what they see in today's society. Anthropologists visiting remote societies need no writing to tell them what they see, and, by astutely framing questions and reflecting upon the answers, they frame theories of religions and religion. Sociologists collecting data about attitudes, beliefs, and behavior consult the evidence of the palpable social world at hand. By interpreting the facts of that world, they too set forth theories of religions in the societies that they study. But once we move away from our present, we no longer find it possible to consult the textbook of a living society. Seeking the histories of religions and the history of religion in the civilization of humankind, we are constrained to turn to books that come to us in only a single medium, writing.

True, from archaeology, if only adventitiously, we derive facts about religions and religion in times past. But we find coherence and sense, evidence for religions in their contexts and for religion in the context of humanity, only in writing preserved by an ongoing community that wants to have a history and that values its past and appeals to its authority—and therefore has written down what it wants to know and by clear and deliberate policy wants us to know, too. Therefore that writing is of a very particular kind. It is writing that uses only words formed into sentences supposed to make sense by appeal to a syntax people in ages unimagined by the writers are supposed to be able to grasp and understand—and to want to comprehend. For it is best through the written word that we gain access to remote ages, and it is through writing that those distant ages' intellectuals, sages, and writers proposed to deliver their message: from never-never-land to whom it may concern—not a very precise message. Writing then forms evidence of a very particular kind, different from all other kinds of evidence concerning religion because it gives us access to a determinate time and place before and (ordinarily) quite different from our own, in a form of a well-defined character different from the forms of contemporary thought and expression.

All other evidence reaching us from other ages than our own speaks to us only within our thought and understanding. Non-verbal evidence communicates only in our language, no one else's and therefore through mere anachronism places us into a closed circle of acutely contemporary solecism. Monuments without inscriptions that we can read—the Mayan in the Yucatan before the recent past and cities without signposts, Zimbabwe for example—tell us little more than *that* they were there. They do not tell us much about what they were, though they do not stand wholly mute. Such information as they do give, however, is incoherent and adventitious. From these silent stones no account of religion as attitude and emotion, as ineffable conviction yielding concrete action, is to be heard. Now that we have learned to read the Mayan glyphs and elsewhere uncovered written records, however trivial, we have reentered their realm of history and so know something of what happened. We regain the vast ranges of their religion and therefore know why things happened. Books convey what monuments do not, must as—for sensibility and emotion, for example—monuments preserve what books cannot record. Monuments uninterpreted leave us wholly within our own imaginations. Books by themselves tell us only what their authors wanted us to know.

But the issue in the study of religion is very specific. Books of an ancient world, one remote from our own, teach us not what happened then but how people who wrote books wanted their contemporaries and continuators to think about what happened. That sort of learning about religion leads us deep into the imagination, concerning society and the social world, of people who wrote a given book and people who valued and preserved that book and put it together with other such books to form a canon of truth: the scheme of a social world as it should be. It is, therefore, precisely this aspect of religion that makes religion important: its power to frame society and define culture, its force as a social fact, its capacity to define the world that people share and sustain together. The very thing that makes religion a critical and definitive power in civilization, its standing as an independent variable in the making of social worlds, is that to which writing attests with particular force. For writing by definition comprises a social action, and the preservation of writing, the identification of writings as authoritative and worth saving, copying, handing on, teaching, and learning—these form social decisions and therefore attest to the social standing of a writing. So far as we propose to study religion in its capacity to frame civilization, we require not only writing but also the means for making sense of the writing that we have.

Along with canonical writings we should want evidence concerning those who read those writings and acted on their basis to make a world. Only knowing what people thought tells us about imagination, not about the reality that formed and tempered imagination. Knowing about imagination yields no trivial data, however. It reveals the (ultimately) decisive facts of a social system as first invented, then effected. When we remember that Christianity, Buddhism, and Islam have defined the history of the West, the East, and the global belt in between, we recognize the simple and descriptive character of the claim that if we wish to make sense of civilization, we turn to the social world imagined by religion and realized by believers. And the power of religion, whether vast in extent, such as the Christian, Buddhist, or Islamic, or vast only in influence and in temporal continuity, such as the Judaic, in our own day easily finds its emblem in a catalogue of geographic names: the Middle East, Ireland, Poland, India, Sri Lanka, and so forth.

These observations, mere commonplaces concerning the character of religion in society, carry us to the particular problem I address in the methods I have devised for the study of religion through the study of a religion, a Judaism in particular. I have worked out ways of reading documents and developing a conception of the religious system upon which those documents draw or to which they refer. This is a method that focuses upon the smallest details of writing and moves inductively outward from syntax and grammar, repetition and recurrent pattern. It is a method that allows us to characterize whole writings, not merely cite them, and to see all together and all at once what a given authorship—the person or persons responsible for the final form and closure of a piece of writing—wishes to say as its fundamental message. That message is the religion that I claim to derive from a piece of writing. I claim to show how to study a religion that is attested only by written evidence, books written down in the formative time of that religion and preserved thereafter by the choice of the continuators and heirs of that same religion and in institutions that saw themselves as continuous with the original institutions of that religion. This accounts for the problem at hand, and it further explains why I believe that my methods also serve in the study of other religions that are attested principally or only by written documents in a sizable corpus.

Before proceeding, let me offer definitions for terms that

have already made their appearance and that appear throughout. By a religious system I understand three things that are one:

1. Ethos: a world view that by reference to the intersection of the supernatural and the natural worlds accounts for how things are and puts them together into a cogent and harmonious picture;
2. Ethics: a way of life that expresses in concrete actions the world view and that is explained by that world view;
3. Ethnos: a social group for which the world view accounts and that is defined as an entity by a way of life through which it gives expression in the everyday world to its world view.

A religious system is one that appeals to a deity or deities as the principal power. A Judaic system is a religious system—ethos, ethics, ethnos—that identifies the Hebrew Scriptures or "Old Testament" as a principal component of its canon. A Judaism, then, comprises not merely a theory—a book—distinct from social reality but an explanation for the group (again, "Israel") that gives social form to the system and an account of the distinctive way of life of that group. A Judaism is not a book, and no social group took shape because people read a book and agreed that God had revealed what the book said they should do. A Judaism, that is, a Judaic system, derives from and focuses upon a social entity, a group of Jews who (in their minds at least) constitute not *an* Israel but *Israel*.

With these definitions in mind, I return to the argument at hand. My claim is that writing is social and that the world view of a document, the way of life premised therein, the social entity to whom the document is meant to speak, forms not merely a personal and individual statement but one that bears meaning for two or more persons: a social entity, one that is supposed by an authorship to see the world in a certain way, and to live by a certain set of rules. This is what forms the religion yielded by the writing. But why do I claim that from writing we may recover religion? It is because when we read the writing as evidence of religion, we gain access not only to the proposition set forth by the writing but also to the system that makes the writing cogent. My premise is that in the documents of the religion at hand we may uncover the main beams and supporting intellectual structures of religion. By this I mean shared and public thought, mode and outcome as well, concerning the way of life, world view, and social entity of those who join in discourse within the writing. And that mode of thought, as much as the result of thinking, emerges in the documents and in their use of language. The limits of language form the limits of world; within the arts of language we may claim to discern a world view.

If, therefore, we want to understand how the intellectuals of a social entity—responsible for the writings of a religion—make sense of things, we have to examine the language they used in order to speak sensibly. That language presents the evidence on how people both reach *and convey* conclusions of consequence. When, for example, we can understand how people discern the relationship between one fact, that is, one sentence, and another and, further, how they set forth conclusions to be drawn from this relationship or connection, we know not only what they think but, from the character of the connection, how they think. So God lives in the syntax of cogent thought and intelligible statement of thought, and Judaism is the statement of process, yielding propositions as well. The propositions vary from document to document, but the process, which characterizes all documents, uniformly imposes its connections and ubiquitously generates its conclusions. That matter of process grasped, we know how the mind of that social entity frames the propositions that it proposes as its system and the foundation of its order.

Accordingly, writing reveals the shared and public logic of intelligible discourse, the premise of self-evident comprehension and, above all, the intangible sensibility that makes connections between one thing and something else and yields conclusions transcending them both. These social realities are what hold together many minds in one community of shared and mutually intelligible speech that, in the aggregate, we may call society—in our instance, the society of Judaism or the "Israel" at hand. The evidence for that shared intellect, that mind in common, therefore comes to us in how people speak to one another, in the connections each makes between two or more sentences, and in the connections all make with one another. The formation of a shared intellect, the making of a mind in common—these derive from process and connection.

And it is in writing that we gain access to the syntax and grammar of thought and expression, to the epiphenomena of the religious system preserved in this medium and in no other.

When we can trace through the writings of a given social entity the unfolding of modes of thought, identifying the choices afforded to intellectuals by those received modes of thought, we may fairly claim to know how a social entity, in its enduring cultural heritage, has made up its mind. In other words, we may know its social system, conveyed through its religion. That social entity, in the case of the authorships of the documents deemed canonical by the Judaism that took shape between the first and the seventh centuries, called the Judaism of the dual Torah, comprises a textual community.[1] By that I mean that the authorships which, all together, stand behind writings deemed to form not merely a compilation or a library of writings but a coherent canon of authoritative law and theology. This textual community is amply documented by the canonical writings of the Judaism of the dual Torah. Its writings carry us deep within its processes of thought, the ways in which it makes connections between one thing and another and makes of the two something new again. That textual community made up Judaism, and its principal writings for close to two millennia educated Jews' minds. At stake, therefore, in reading books and describing religion is the framing of that world of private thought and public conscience, individual intellect and public sensibility, that Jews comprised in Judaism.

From these general remarks let us proceed to the definition of the specific terms of this discussion. While I claim to speak of "religion" in general, I refer throughout to a particular religion, the Judaism of the dual Torah, oral and written, as it is represented by *writing,* and I propose to show how to translate this writing into religion. The canon, or writing, treated here is a huge one in volume. It comprises the Mishnah, an oral law code of sixty-three tractates and more than five hundred chapters, and two Talmuds, amplifications of the Mishnah, the one of thirty-nine tractates, the other of thirty-seven. The written Torah (speaking within the mythic language of the system)

---

1. I owe this term to Brian Stock, *The Implications of Literacy* (Princeton: Princeton University Press 1985).

comprises the Hebrew Scriptures. Corresponding to the two Talmuds that serve the Mishnah are nearly a dozen Midrash-compilations devoted to the amplification of those Scriptures, covering Exodus, Leviticus, Numbers, Deuteronomy, and other matters as well. The writings of the Judaism of the dual Torah therefore comprise a large corpus of law and Scriptural exegesis, collectively deemed "the oral Torah," and the Hebrew Scriptures ("Old Testament") called, in the Judaism at hand, "the written Torah," which together constitute God's revelation to Moses at Mount Sinai. These writings appeal to a religious system—the intellectual composition comprising a way of life, a world view, and an address to a defined social entity that in the case of a Judaism is an "Israel." All this together forms the theory of the holy society at hand. I should claim that any religious system must encompass these three components: ethos, ethics, and ethnos; that is, it must address a particular social entity. The system becomes systemic when the three components form a tightly fitting account—at least in theory—of a coherent social group.

The reason why we read holy writing as religion, that is to say, as a *social* statement of the transcendent life of a holy community, is simple and draws us back to the commonplace observations with which I commenced. Religion is something people do together, something they do to accomplish shared goals. Hence, religion is a social fact, and the artifacts of religion (texts, drawings, dances, and music, for example) form components of a shared and therefore a social system. Religion encompasses a shared world view, explains a shared way of life, identifies the social entity of those that realize the one and live by the other; it forms the integrating power that makes a single statement out of politics and economics, as much as out of the individual's life cycle and the communal calendar that distinguishes one season from another and marks a day as holy. In order to study such a protean and encompassing definitive element of the social system, I need to be able to describe it and to do that I have to know what data will serve my inquiry. To answer that question, as I have now made clear, I ask three simple questions: What is the world view of a religion? What is the way of life of a religion? What is the social entity to which the world view is addressed and that realizes or embodies the way of life? The answers to these questions in hand can be described as religious system.

Writings such as those in the Judaic canon of the dual Torah have been selected by the framers of a religious system and, read all together, are deemed to make a cogent and important statement of a system, a Judaism. I call that encompassing, canonical, written picture a "religious system" when it is composed of the three necessary components that relate to the questions asked above: an account of a world view, a prescription of a corresponding way of life, and a definition of the social entity that finds definition in the one and description in the other. When those three fundamental components fit together, they sustain one another in explaining the whole of a social order, hence constituting the theoretical account of a system. Systems defined in this way work out a cogent picture of *how* things are correctly to be sorted out and fitted together, of *why* things are done in one way rather than in some other, and of *who* they are that do and understand matters in this particular way. When, as is commonly the case, people involve God as the foundation for their world view, maintaining that their way of life corresponds to what God wants of them, projecting their social entity in a particular relationship to God, then we have a religious system. When, finally, a religious system appeals as an important part of its authoritative literature or canon to the Hebrew Scriptures of ancient Israel (or the "Old Testament") we have a Judaism.

In analyzing a religious system, I have a further intellectual labor. It is to find a way of holding together the three components of a religious system—ethos, ethics, ethnos. This can be done by a hypothesis that reads these components as elements of an answer to a question. If I can propose a single encompassing statement that constitutes the system's recurrent message and judgment, then I can claim to know the answer to the question of cogency and coherence. From that knowledge I can make a good guess at the question to which the answer responds. And then I can test my proposed hypotheses through the evidence at hand. Once I have come to a theory on the description of the system—ethos, ethics, social entity—and the analysis of that system—urgent question, compelling answer—I reach the state of interpretation, at which, of course, the comparison of system to system forms the elementary stage in the study of the systems of the religious life. That, sum and substance, frames a theory of the academic study of religion that derives strength from both the humanities' powers of a close reading of a single, very particular document and the culture that produced that document and also the social sciences' powers of theoretical explanation of the whole. I should find in the humanities the account of the species, in the social sciences the theory of the genus.

Systems begin in the social entity, whether one or two persons or two hundred or ten thousand—there, and not in their canonical writings, or even in their politics, both of which come only afterward. The social group, however formed, frames the system, the *religion*. The system then defines its canon of holy *writings* within and addresses the larger setting without. But in the nature of the evidence, we describe systems from their end products, the writings. We have then to work our way back from written canon to social system, for the canon neither is nor creates the system. The canonical writings speak in particular to those who can hear, that is, to the members of the community who, on account of that perspicacity of hearing, constitute the social entity or systemic community. The community then comprises that social group, the system of which is recapitulated by the selected canon. The group's exegesis of the canon in terms of the everyday imparts to the system the power to sustain the community in a reciprocal and self-nourishing process. The community through its exegesis then imposes continuity and unity on whatever is in its canon.

We cannot account for the origin of a successful system, on the basis of the writings of a religious system, but we can explain its power to persist. It is a symbolic transaction in which social change comes to expression in symbol-change. That symbolic transaction, specifically, takes place in its exegesis of the systemic canon, which in literary terms constitutes the social entity's statement of itself. So the texts recapitulate the system, or in the language of my title, the writing recapitulates the religion, not the other way around. The system comes before the texts and defines the canon. That does not make the writing less important. On the contrary, the exegesis of the canon forms that ongoing social action that sustains the whole. A system does not recapitulate its texts, but selects and orders them. A religious system imputes to them as a whole cogency, what their original authorships have not expressed in and through the parts. A religious system expresses its deepest logic through its texts, and they also frame that fit that joins system to circumstance.

The issue of the success or failure of a system by itself proves impertinent to the analysis of a system but, of course, necessary to our interpretation of it. A system on its own is like a language. A language produces communication through rules of syntax and verbal arrangement. That paradigm serves full well however many people speak the language or however long the language serves. Two people who understand each other form a language-community, even, and especially, if no one understands them. In the same way, religions address the living, constitute societies, frame and compose cultures. For however long, at whatever moment in historic time, a religious system always grows up in the perpetual present, an artifact of its day, whether today or a long-ago time. The only appropriate tense for a religious system is the present. A religious system always *is*, whatever it was, whatever it will be. Why so? Because its traits address a condition of humanity in society, a circumstance of an hour—however brief or protracted the hour and the circumstance.

When we ask that a religious system speak to a society with a message of the *is* and the *ought* and with a meaning for the everyday, we focus on the power of that system to hold the whole together: the society the system addresses, the individuals who compose the society, and the ordinary lives they lead, in ascending order of consequence. This system then forms a whole structure that will secure for the system either an extended or an ephemeral span of life. But the system, for however long it lasts, serves. It is this focus on the eternal present that justifies my interest in analyzing why a system works, when it does, and why it may also cease to work (lose self-evidence, be bereft of its "Israel," for example). The phrase *the history of a system* presents us with an oxymoron. Systems endure—and their classic texts with them—in that eternal present that they create. They evoke precedent, but they do not have a history.

A system relates to context but, as I have stressed, exists in an enduring moment (which, to be sure, changes all the time). We capture the system in a moment; the worm consumes it an hour later. That is the way of mortality, whether for us one by one or for the works of humanity in society. But systemic analysis and interpretation requires us to ask questions of history and comparison; mere description of structure and cogency will not suffice. So in this exercise we undertake first description (that is, the text), then analysis (that is, the context), and finally interpretation (that is, the matrix in which a system has its being).

In the study of religion we move from literary evidence to a theory about the nature of the religious world that produced the evidence in hand and thence to setting forth hypotheses of general intelligibility about religion. For reading a text in its context and as a statement of a larger matrix of meaning, I propose to ask larger questions of systemic description of a religious system represented by the particular text and its encompassing canon. What is to be done to achieve this goal?

First, I place a document on display in its own terms, examining the text in its full particularity and immediacy by describing it from three perspectives: rhetoric, logic, and topic (the standard program of modern literary criticism). Reading documents one by one represents a new approach in the study of a Judaism. Ordinarily, scholars have composed studies by citing sayings attributed to diverse authorities, without regard to the place in which these sayings occur. They have assumed that the sayings really were said by those to whom they are attributed, and in consequence, the generative category is not the document but the named authority. But if we do not assume that the documentary lines are irrelevant and that the attributions are everywhere to be taken at face value, then the point of origin—the document—defines the study.

Second, I seek to move from the text to that larger context suggested by the traits of rhetoric, logic, and topic by comparing one text to others of its class and asking how these recurrent points of emphasis, those critical issues and generative tensions, draw attention from the limits of the text to the social world that the text's authorship proposed to address. Here, too, the notion that a document exhibits traits paritcular to itself is new with my work, although some scholars have episodically noted traits of rhetoric distinctive to a given document, and on the surface, differences as to topic—observed but not explained—have been noted. Hence, the movement from text to context and how it is effected represents a fresh initiative on my part.

Finally, so far as I can, I want to find my way outward toward the matrix in which a variety of texts find their place. In this third stage I want to move from the world of intellectuals to the world they proposed to shape and create. That inquiry defines as its generative question how the social world formed by the texts as a whole proposes to define and respond to a powerful and urgent question; that is, I want to read the canonical writings as response to critical and urgent questions. Relating documents to their larger political settings is not a commonplace, and moreover, doing so in detail—with attention to the traits of logic, rhetoric, and topic—is still less familiar.

I recognize that in moving beyond specific texts into the larger world view they endeavor to present, I may be thought to cross the border from the humanistic study of classical texts to the social-scientific or anthropological reading of those same texts. I therefore emphasize that I take most seriously the particularity and specificity of each document—its program, its aesthetics, its logic. I do not propose to commit upon a classic writing an act of reductionism, reading a work of humanistic meaning merely as a sociological artifact. And further, as between Weber and his critics, I take my place with Weber in maintaining that ideas, in their context and circumstance, constitute what sociologists call independent variables, not only responding to issues of society but framing and giving definition to those larger issues. In this way I take my stand in the systemic reading of the classic writings of Judaism in its formative age with those who insist upon the ultimate rationality of discourse.

In its ideal form the academic study of religion unites the strength of the social sciences and the power of the humanities. In a less ideal form it offers out of the humanities statements of incomprehensible specificity or out of the social sciences generalizations of stupefying vacuity, beyond all testing (if indeed not surpassing all comprehension), based on a skewed sample of evidence, the probative character of which no one even can assess. From the Renaissance onward, philological and literary studies have developed methods for the analysis of the texts of religion that call upon rich erudition to make sense of detail. But this very particularity of the humanistic method, which is its strength, also makes the work of generalization parlous. Humanistic study of religion yields explanation of words and phrases but silence about the larger questions of the method and meaning of religion; of religion as formative force in human society. The writing affords only slight access to the religion that generated the writing.

From the nineteenth century onward, social sciences have taught much about the study of religion. But in the nature of things, these sciences take up the evidence of material society in the here and now, finding difficult the reading of (merely) written evidence. Anyone who has tried to follow Max Weber in detail, for instance, in his *Ancient Judaism,* knows how one of the greatest social scientists failed to master the least of the rules for the reading of documents. And from Weber to the present we look in vain for social scientists able to make sustained and important use of the written evidence for religion. The social-scientific account of religion then draws sparsely upon the writing that, for all religion before the acutely contemporary kind, forms the principal corpus of evidence. How then to move from writing, in the reading of which humanistic study excels, to religion, in the description of which social-scientific study rightly predominates?

How do I propose to describe, analyze, and interpret not documents but the religious system that defines the intellectual structure of those documents, on the basis of literary evidence? There is no easy way of securing the benefits of both social science and humanistic learning for the academic study of religion, standing as it does on the margins between sociology and philology, economics and text study, history and philosophy. Requiring the gifts of two quite distinct, if intersecting, realms of learning, the academic study of religion has yet to frame its demands to each. In order to address this problem, I have been trying through the study of written evidence to form a theory of how to study a religion in accord with a program of generalization serving religion in general, that is to say, to study one religion as I might any other religion. It goes without saying that everything I do rests upon the particularities of one age, the formative one, and of one religion, the Judaism of the dual Torah. But by setting forth the basic initiatives I have worked out, I hope to offer some methods of common utility.

This book deals in particular with the problem of a religion viewed as a statement of a social system, one that is laid out by a set of documents. While I work out of the sources of formative Judaism, from the first seven centuries, C.E., I believe that anyone interested in making the move from the study of the holy writings of a religion to the description, analysis, and interpretation of the religious system and structure of that religion should find my methods suggestive and even useful.

Yet another perspective shapes our vision of the whole. I have shown that a text locates itself in a three-dimensional world of relationships. First, a document by definition stands autonomous, making a statement of its own. It may refer to a variety of other writings, but so far as a document proves coherent and cogent, it is to be read completely and as a whole. Second, a document in the canon selected by the system of the Judaism of the dual Torah also proves connected to other writings. The universal connection, of course, is to the Hebrew Scriptures, a connection that is self-evident and that is the premise of all writing in all Judaisms. But in the library of the Judaism of the dual Torah, authorships of documents draw upon the writings of prior authorships, with the result that there is the second dimension by which we take the measure of a writing, and that is its connection with other writings. Ordinarily, connections are indicated through explicit signals that some other writing is being quoted—for instance, the nearly ubiquitous "as it is said." Other such signals take the form of a shift in language, for example, from Aramaic to Hebrew in the Talmuds, or an incomplete allusion to a prior writing, for example, to a verse of Scripture or to a sentence of the Mishnah, as in a Midrash-compilation in respect to Scripture or as in the Tosefta and the Talmuds in relationship to the Mishnah. Third, all documents as a matter of hypothesis are meant to be continuous with all other documents; that is to say, from a theological perspective all writings within a given religion make a single, seamless statement. These three dimensions—autonomy, connection, and continuity—correspond to the classifications already set forth of text, context, and matrix, and they are so represented in the organization of this book.

Hence, I lay out not a single method but a variety of methods and perspectives on the writings of the Judaism of the dual Torah, seen as text, in context, and within matrix, perceived as autonomous, as connected with other writings, and as continuous with an entire canon. This multiple vision is set forth in four concrete scholarly aspects:

1. Text: how to identify the distinguishing literary traits of a document, read autonomously, shown through study of a rabbinic document (part 2);
2. Text: how to describe a document wholly by appealing to traits of rhetoric, logic, and topic (part 2);
3. Context: how to write history and describe religion (that is, the religious system) on the basis of single documents that intersect (part 3);
4. Matrix: how, through the comparison and contrast of documents of a single canon, to use the "documentary theory" for synthetic, usually diachronic, analyses of rabbinic Judaism and of the larger context in which all Judaisms are located (part 4).

This program, which moves from text/autonomy to context/ connection and ends with matrix/continuity, then accounts for the plan of the book as a whole, which is simple and encompassing.

So far as we study not only religions, one by one, but religion as a fundamental trait of humanity and society, the effort to adapt and to generalize is critical. Thus I turn now to the documentary method itself—autonomous text, texts connected in context, texts formed into a continuity in the nourishing matrix of an enduring human circumstance of history and society. I begin with the fundamental points of analysis of any text, the traits that indicate whether and how a given piece of writing forms a coherent, autonomous statement: rhetoric, logic, topic.

CHAPTER TWO

The Documentary Method in the
Systemic Study of Religion

When we can describe the mind of a social entity by sorting out the rules governing how diverse authorships reach discrete and disparate conclusions, then we can claim to understand how the mind of a society of like-minded people is formed. For then we gain access to those generative rules of culture and regulations of system that succeeding generations receive in the family and village from infancy and transmit to an unknowable future. Attitudes shift. Values and beliefs change. One generation's immutable truths travel to the coming age as commonplace truths, banalities, or nonsense. But processes of reflection about the sense of things endure like oceans and mountains. My premise, that religions form social worlds and do so through the power of their rational thought, therefore requires me to identify the evidence for how thought comes to concrete expression so that we can analyze it.

I find the data in writing, and only in writing. For it is writing that both reaches us as a result of processes of an intellectual character and preserves evidences of the distinct character of those processes in their own day. We may admire and respond to the art of an ancient synagogue, but we cannot reconstruct the modes and processes of thought of the artist. All we have are the attitudes and responses dictated by our own time. But in traits of writing we can identify the way in which the author or authorship long ago proposed to compose and communicate thought. How artists create only they know, but how authorships frame and write their thoughts testifies to the way in which their minds work. Grammar and syntax attest to intellect, and the afterlife of what authorships write attests to the social setting in which they write, that is, to the way in which the minds of others in their setting work. After all, we have access to the writings of ancient times only because successive generations through their authoritative institutions granted us that access. These two facts—first, the possibility of working our way back from writing to system and, second, the opportunity of working our way outward from writing to the social reception of writing—form the foundations of my work. That explains why the modes of thought paramount in the canonical writings of the Judaism of the dual Torah in its formative age are what I propose to describe, analyze, and interpret. The reason why I think I can do so is that we have in the canonical writings of Judaism from the first through the seventh century ample evidence of the results of how people have thought deeply and abstractly, as well as concrete evidences in language of the conduct of thought. Accordingly, from the language people used to say what they were thinking, I propose to move backward to the processes of thought encapsulated in that language.

Now, whose processes of thought are subject to analysis, and for whom does a piece of writing, a document, speak? To respond to that question, I have invoked the word "an authorship," meaning the consensus that a document repre-sents, rather than "an author." It is, I maintain, the system of an authorship that a document preserved in a social setting expresses (and that, by definition, is how all Judaisms preserved their writings). An authorship may not actually have written all the materials it has assembled; it may have picked and chosen from among available resources, like single paragraphs or even whole chapters (to use, anachronistically, divisions of writing familiar to us). The document testifies to taste and judgment, program and system. True, it may also testify to capacities for making things up and writing them down as well. But that is not a primary consideration, for however obvious the evidence that a document forms a composite of already formed and framed materials, it is the document as a cogent statement that we analyze. Its sources, if any, can be shown to serve the purpose of the final authorship—redactors, compositors, or writers, it hardly matters—and that not merely by appeal to premise. The demonstration invariably lies in the answer to the question, why has this authorship used this item in the place it has, for the purpose it has, and with the effect it has achieved? Since the question ordinarily finds its answer in an appeal to the purpose of the writing as a whole, it follows that the principal focus of analysis is the document's use of prior materials, rather than the character or provenance of those already available materials.

Accordingly, I call the framers of a document that found its way into the canon of the Judaism of the dual Torah (and by definition, all documents in hand fall into the classification of canon) "an authorship." That collectivity—from one to an indeterminate number of persons, flourishing for from ten minutes to five hundred or a thousand years—determined and then followed fixed and public rules of orderly discourse that govern a given book's rhetoric, logic, and topic. These fixed rules, seen all together, permit us to describe the intent and program of those responsible for this writing: the authorship. Received in a canonical process of transmission under the auspices of a religious system, a rabbinic writing enjoys authority and status within that canon and system. Hence, it is deemed to speak not for a private person but for a community and to represent and contribute to the consensus of that community. No document has a named author, for such a designation would deprive the document of all standing and authority. Accordingly, a piece of writing is represented on the surface as the statement of a consensus.

In considering any piece of writing, therefore, we have to ask whether this writing exhibits a cogent character and shows conformity to laws and regularities, that is, whether it derives from a considered set of decisions of a rhetorical, logical, and topical order. If it does, then as a matter of definition it derives from an authorship, a collectivity that stands behind the consensus exhibited in this particular writing. If I find no regularities and indications of an orderly program, then I may fairly claim that this writing is different from one that speaks in behalf of people who have made rules or adopted them for the inclusion of fresh ideas of their own. It belongs in a classification not of a composition but of a scrapbook, a mishmash of this and that which fell together we know not how.

All of the documents that together constitute the canon of the Judaism of the dual Torah as defined down to the Bavli do indeed exhibit rules of public discourse—rhetoric, logic, topic—though, of course, the rules revealed by one do not conform to those followed by another. Therefore, I have now to examine, first, the rhetorical conventions of an authorship, second, the logical modes by which they proposed to convey intelligible thought, and, third, the topical, propositional, or thematic range they identified as urgent. This third point of analyzing a piece of writing attends to the argumentation in behalf of its proposition, its kinds of evidence, and its manner of marshaling this evidence. If there is a connection—whether in rhetoric, logic, or topic—between one thing and something else, for instance, I want to ask what makes the connection self-evident, so that one thing fits with some other and another thing does not. The authors of the canonical writings of the Judaism of the formative age mastered the requirements of applied reason and practical logic. But that means they also were masters of intellect and logical acumen. And, in the nature of things, they also produced a literature that enjoyed extraordinary power to sustain attention and compel interest not in the time of the writing alone but for two thousand years thereafter—no mean achievement.

The bridge from proposition, that is, *what* people think, to process, *how* they think, therefore is built of modes of discourse preserved and transmitted in writing. Discourse thus refers to the way in which statements are made so that the connections are intelligible and cogent to others. To describe the modes of discourse that attest to modes of thought in the deep structure of mind, we ask not only how the conclusions are put on display but also about the sense of language. Accordingly, it is in a cogent argument concerning a proposition that the mind becomes social, that is to say, incarnate, and mind incarnate is what I mean by system. The reader may wonder whether my insistence on the analysis of regularities of rhetoric, logic, and topic is sustained in the literary evidence at hand. For even though, as a matter of theory, one concedes my points on the social power of intellectual process, still the evidence subject to analysis must permit inquiry into these specified traits.

As a matter of fact, I did my work inductively, finding in the evidence regularities that led me to reflect on the larger issues of order and structure in society that I have already set forth. In nearly all the canonical writings of the Judaism of the dual Torah, ideas are conveyed in highly formalized modes of composition. Fixed literary structures (that is, rhetoric) dictate to the authorships of nearly all documents the repertoire of choices available for saying what they wish to say. What this means is that individual preferences, for instance, personal modes of forming sentences, rarely come into play. Thoughts are set forth in a few well-defined ways and not in the myriad diverse ways that could be found in less formalized literature. This fact vastly facilitates the comparison of one document to another, since the range of rhetorical choices is limited to the forms and literary structures paramount in the documents subject to description and analytical comparison.

Once we have defined a form or rhetorical pattern or structure, we know whether or not it is present by appealing to some few facts that are readily accessible to the naked eye. Consequently, there can be irrefutable proof that one set of forms or literary structures, and not another, predominates in a given document, and that proof can even be used in statistically describing the total number of units of thought subject to description and the proportion of those units of thought that fall into the several defined categories of form or structure, as against the proportion of those that do not. Defining these rhetorical conventions therefore sets forth the first step in describing the documents, one by one, and then comparing them to one another. Only when we have established the distinctive traits of documents by appeal to such external matters, in which matters of taste and judgment do not figure, do we move on to substantive differences of topic and even proposition.

Let me proceed to some simple definitions, beginning with language for rhetorical analysis. A *form* or *literary structure* comprises a set of rules that dictate those recurrent conventions of expression, organization, or proportion—the grammar and syntax of thought and expression—that occur invariably in the ordinary patterning of language and also are *extrinsic* to the message of the author. The conventions at hand bear none of the particular burden of the author's message, so they are not

idiosyncratic but systemic and public. A form or literary
structure or language-pattern of syntax and grammar imposes
upon the individual writer a limited set of choices about how he
will convey whatever message he has in mind. Or the formal
convention will limit an editor or redactor to an equally
circumscribed set of alternatives about how to arrange received
materials. These conventions then form a substrata of the
literary culture that preserves and expresses the particularities
of the system at hand.

One example of a formal convention will illustrate. It concerns
the representation of a dispute, that is, different opinions on a
given problem. The form will ordinarily be as follows:

> As to problem X
> Rabbi A says . . .
> Rabbi B says . . .

This is, of course, hardly the only way of expressing a
disagreement. Different opinions may simply be juxtaposed.
The disagreement need not be highlighted at all. But, in the
Mishnah, when the authorship wishes to show us how a given
problem is susceptible to more than a single solution, it will
resort to the form just now given. Not only that, but it will very
often frame the opinions of the two authorities in matching
language, using the same words with or without the negative, the
same words but in different order, words with the same number
of syllables, and similar efforts at imposing acute balance. This is
an example of the highly conventional and stereotypic language
that characterizes Mishnaic discourse.

When we can define the form or literary structures, we can
also ask about the program of thought—recurrent modes of
analysis and exercises of conflict and resolution—that dictates
the content of the commentary. For how I think and what the
syntax of my language and thought permits me to say dictates
what I shall think and why I shall think it. How are we to
recognize the presence of such structures? On the basis of forms
that merely appear to be patterned or extrinsic to particular
meaning and so entirely formal, we cannot allege that we have in
hand a fixed form or literary structure. Such a judgment would
prove subjective. Nor shall we benefit from bringing to the text

at hand recurrent syntactic or grammatical patterns shown in *other* texts, even of the same canon of literature, to define conventions for communicating ideas. Quite to the contrary, we find guidance in a simple principle: *A text has to define its own structures for us.*

Patterning of language is readily discerned, for in general, authors resort repeatedly and exclusively to one severely circumscribed set of literary conventions. These patterns, we shall soon see, not only dictate formal syntax and principles of composition but also define the deep structure of logical analysis and the modes of proof for particular propositions of argument. On the basis of inductive evidence alone, therefore, a document will testify that its authors adhere to a fixed canon of literary forms. That canon of forms shows that forms guide the authors to the propositions for or against which they choose to argue: It shows the program of the book, not only its plan. If demonstrably present, these forms present an author or editor with a few choices on how ideas are to be organized and expressed in intelligible—and therefore public—compositions. So internal evidence alone testifies to the form or literary structures of a given text.

In form-analysis (or the study of rhetoric) the adjective "recurrent" obviously constitutes a redundancy when joined to the noun "structure" or "pattern." For we cannot know that we have a structure if the text under analysis does not repeatedly resort to the presentation of its message through a disciplined structure entirely external to its message on any given point. Forms or literary structures or patterns find definition in entirely formal and objective facts, and that is why anyone may replicate the results of form-analysis carried on inductively in any rabbinic writing.[1]

Second in order of analysis is the logic of a document. I use the simple word "logic" to stand for the principle of intelligibility and cogency of thought and the expression of thought in public

---

1. Replicate, but also improve upon those results. All of my form-analytical work has been carried on with attention only to the most gross and crude traits of language patterning. Refinement will show many more patterns and a much more subtle and intricate sense for implicit structure—poetic structure, I should claim—than I have found it necessary to display for the purpose of my sustained and encompassing demonstration of the traits of the literature as a whole. Now that this work is done, a second generation of form-analysis can render it obsolete.

discourse. Logic is what joins one sentence to the next and forms the whole into paragraphs of meaning, intelligible propositions, each with its place and sense in a still larger, accessible system. Because of logic, one mind connects to another, public discourse becomes possible, debate on issues of general intelligibility takes place, and an *anthology* of statements about a single subject becomes a *composition* of theorems about that subject. What people think—exegesis in accord with a fixed hermeneutic of the system—knows no limit. How they think makes all the difference.

If the strict conventions of forms and literary structures make their mark on the very surface of documents, the inquiry into the logics of cogent discourse carries us to the depths of the structures of thought of those same documents. For rhetoric dictates the palpable and visible arrangement of words, whereas logic dictates the possibilities of thought: the ineffable determination of why thought arranged or set forth in one way makes sense, in another way nonsense. And yet whether we explore the extrinsic traits of formal expression or the most profound layers of intelligible discourse and coherent thought that hold sentences together and form of them all propositions or presentations that can be understood, we produce a single result. It is that each document's authorship does make choices. Choosing modes of cogent discourse and coherent thought involves a repertoire that is exceedingly limited. Options in rhetoric by contrast prove quite diverse. But the work of comparison and contrast in both sorts of choices proves entirely feasible, since with regard to both rhetoric and logic we are required to compare fixed and external traits. There is no appeal to subjective taste and judgment.

Now let me explain what is at issue when I speak of "logic."[2] We begin with the conception of "cogent discourse." People wish not only to frame but also to communicate their ideas, and when they make propositions for others' attention, they do so only by appealing to shared conventions of thought. To be understood by others, the one who frames ideas has to compose thought in

---

2. I review ideas worked out elsewhere, in particular in my *Making of the Mind of Judaism* (Atlanta: Scholars Press for Brown Judaic Studies, 1987), *Sifré to Deuteronomy, An Introduction* (Atlanta: Scholars Press for Brown Judaic Studies, 1987), and *Formation of the Jewish Intellect* (Atlanta: Scholars Press for Brown Judaic Studies, 1988).

ways that others understand. This understanding requires in particular a shared conception of the connections between one fact and another. When we know and can describe the character of those connections, which can be quite diverse, we point to what I designate as the logics of intelligible discourse for a given group. Such logics can serve an entire culture or only two people who form a social entity of some sort; in our case, they serve our authorship. For that authorship presents statements, whether or not aimed at constituting propositions, to reach others and make sense to them. Such intelligible expression must evoke a shared logic, so that others make the same connections that, to the authorship, prove self-evident. It is that repertoire of logics that makes the thought of one "person," our authorship, intelligible to some other person(s).

In concrete terms, this means that one sentence—in modes of intelligible discourse familiar to us—not only stands beside but generates another; a consequent statement follows from a prior one. We share a sense of connection, pertinence, relevance—the aptness of joining thought A to thought B to produce proposition 1. These (only by way of example) form intelligible discourses, turning facts into statements of meaning and consequence. To conduct intelligible discourse, therefore, people make two or more statements that, in the world in which they say their piece, are deemed self-evidently to hang together and form a proposition understood by someone else in that same world. It is the matter of self-evident cogency and intelligibility in the document at hand that now gains our attention.

In studies of other documents of the canon of the Judaism of the dual Torah, I have identified four different logics by which two or more sentences are deemed to cohere and to constitute a statement of consequence and intelligibility. One is familiar to us as philosophical logic; the second is equally familiar as the logic of cogent discourse attained through narrative. These two, self-evidently, are logics of a propositional order, evoking a logic of a philosophical character. The third is not propositional, and as a matter of fact, it also is not ordinarily familiar to us at all. It is a mode of joining two or more statements—sentences—not on the foundation of meaning or sense or proposition but on the foundation of a different order altogether. Specifically, unrelated propositions are associated via a common text, to which both statements are made to refer. The fourth mode of coherent discourse, distinct from the prior three, establishes connections at the most abstract and profound level of thought, which is through highly methodical analysis of many things in a single way. Like the third logic, it also is not propositional, though it yields its encompassing truths of order, proportion, structure, and self-evidence.

We turn first to the two familiar modes of turning two sentences into a coherent statement of one weight and meaning, both of which not only connect the two sentences, forming them into a whole, but also present a statement that in meaning and intelligible proposition transcends the sum of the parts.

The logic of propositional cogency: The first logic, most familiar to the Western world, establishes propositions that rest upon philosophical bases, for example, through the proposal of a thesis and the composition of a list of facts that prove the thesis. This mode of scientific expression through the classification of data may be called the science of making lists *(Listenwissenschaft)*. It was frequently used by philosophers in antiquity and works in a familiar way. Its issue is one of connection, of the relationship between one fact and another. When we set up as a sequence two or more facts and claim out of that sequence to make a proposition different from and transcending the facts at hand, we join the two sentences or facts in the philosophical logic of cogent discourse that is most common in our own setting. We may also call this the logic of propositional discourse. We demonstrate propositions in a variety of ways, appealing both to a repertoire of probative facts and to a set of accepted modes of argument. In this way we engage in a kind of discourse that gains its logic from what, in general, we may call philosophy: the rigorous analysis and testing of propositions against the canons of an accepted reason.

Philosophy accomplishes the miracle of making the whole more—or less—than the sum of the parts. In the simple language I have used up to now, philosophy shows the connections between fact 1 and fact 2, in such a way as to yield proposition A. We begin with the irrefutable fact; our issue is not how facts gain their facticity but rather how from givens people construct propositions or make statements that are deemed sense and not nonsense or gibberish. So the problem is to explain the connections between and among facts, so accounting for the conclusions people draw, on the one side, or the acceptable associations people tolerate, on the other, in the exchange of language and thought.

Propositional logic also may be syllogistic, as shown in this variant on a famous syllogistic argument:

1. All Greeks are philosophers.
2. Demosthenes is a Greek.
3. Therefore Demosthenes is a philosopher.

At issue is not mere facticity but rather the *connections* between facts. The problem to be analyzed here is therefore how one thing follows from something else or how one thing generates something else. The sentences 1, 2, and 3 of our example, standing entirely by themselves, convey not a proposition but merely statements of facts, which may or may not be true and which may or may not bear sense and meaning beyond themselves. Sentence 1 and sentence 2 by themselves state facts but announce no proposition. But the logic of syllogistic discourse joins the two into sentence 3, which indeed does constitute a proposition and also shows the linkage between sentence 1 and sentence 2.

No less familiar to us is yet another way of carrying on cogent discourse through propositional logic, which is to offer a proposition, lay out the axioms, present the proofs, and test the proposition against contrary argument. The demonstration of propositions we generally know as *Listenwissenschaft* compels us to reach a given conclusion based on evidence and argument. These probative facts adduced in evidence for a proposition may derive from the classification of data. A catalogue of facts, for example, may be so composed that, through the regularities and indicative traits of the entries, the catalogue yields a proposition. A list of parallel items points to a simple conclusion, which may or may not be given at the end of the catalogue. All of the catalogued facts are taken to bear self-evident connections to one another, established by those pertinent shared traits implicit in the composition of the list, therefore also bearing meaning and pointing through the weight of evidence to an inescapable conclusion. The discrete facts then join together because of some trait common to them all. This is a mode of classification of facts to lead to an identification of what the facts have in common and an explanation of their meaning. These and other modes of philosophical argument are entirely familiar to us all. In calling all of them "philosophical," I mean only to distinguish them from the other three logics we shall presently examine.

Teleological or narrative cogency: This brings us to the second, equally familiar logic of cogent discourse, which is narrative or, as I shall explain, teleological in character. This second way of stating and demonstrating a proposition resorts to narrative (itself subject to a taxonomy of its own) both to establish and to explain connections between naked facts. A proposition (whether or not it is stated explicitly) may be set forth and demonstrated by showing through the telling of a tale (of a variety of kinds, e.g., historical, fictional, parabolic, and the like) that a sequence of events, real or imagined, reveals the ineluctable truth of a given proposition. The logic of connection demonstrated through narrative, rather than philosophy, is simply stated. It is connection attained and explained by invoking some mode of narrative in which a sequence of events, is understood to yield a proposition. That sequence both states and establishes a proposition in a way different from the philosophical and argumentative mode of propositional discourse. Whether or not the generalization is stated in so many words rarely matters, because the power of well-crafted narrative is to make an explicit drawing of the moral unnecessary.

This second logic is one of narrative that sees cogency in purpose and regards the necessary order of events as causative. This kind of logic or intelligibility of connection is attained through teleology: the claim of purpose, therefore cause, in the garb of a story of what happened because it had to happen. Narrative conveys a proposition through the setting forth of happenings in a framework of inevitability, in a sequence that makes a point, that is, establishes not merely the facts of what happens, but the teleology that explains those facts. Then we speak not only of events—our naked facts—but of their relationship. We claim to account for that relationship teleologically, in the purposive sequence and necessary order of happenings. In due course we shall see how various kinds of narratives serve to convey highly intelligible and persuasive propositions.

The logical cogency of fixed association: We come to the third, and the one genuinely odd, mode of discourse in many documents in the canon of the Judaism of the dual Torah. I call it the logic of fixed association, in which distinct facts or sentences or thoughts are held together without actually joining into sequential and coherent propositions of any kind. It is so alien to our Western modes of thought that I present an illustrative case that derives from Sifré to Deuteronomy. What we have in the example is a sequence of absolutely unrelated sentences, made up in each instance of a clause of a verse, followed by a phrase of amplification. Nothing links one sentence (completed thought) to the ones before or after. Yet the compositors show us that these sentences that are represented side by side with sentences that do form large compositions, are linked one to the next by connections that we can readily discern. That seems to me to indicate that our authorship conceives one mode of connecting sentences to form a counterpart to another.

The fixed-association mode of discourse serves to sustain a commentary to a book of the Bible, for it appeals to cogency between and among discrete sentences to a verse of Scripture. The negative criteria of the logic of fixed association are, first, that the sentences, two or more, do not all together yield a statement that transcends the sum of the parts. Fixed-association compositions, moreover, do not gain cogency through statements of propositions. The sentences are cogent, but the cogency derives from a source other than shared propositions or participation in an argument yielding a shared proposition. Accordingly, the fixed association derives from a "text" outside of the composition at hand, and yet this text is known to, and even taken for granted by, the composition at hand. This "text" may be a list of names; it may be a received document or portion thereof. But it is given, and its cogency is the single prevailing premise that otherwise unrelated facts belong together in some sort of established sequence and order. For fine examples of cogent discourse that rests solely upon fixed associations, I refer to this simple instance.

Sifré to Deuteronomy CLXXVIII:III

1. A. ". . . the prophet has uttered it presumptuously:"
    B. One is liable for acting presumptuously, and one is not
       liable for acting in error.

2. A. ". . . do not stand in dread of him:"
    B. Do not hesitate to hold him guilty as charged.

Each numbered unit forms a single declarative sentence.
number 1 makes a distinction important only in legal theory, and
number 2 simply exhorts people to enforce the law. Nothing
joins number 1 to number 2 except that both rest upon clauses of
the same verse. The compositor of the passage took for granted
that this fixed association validated his joining number 1 to
number 2.

The logic of fixed association will join together sentences that
are connected not in theme, let alone in proposition, but solely in
the *name* of the authority who said them. Here are instances in
The Fathers, chapter 1:

12. Hillel and Shammai received [the Torah] from them.
Hillel says: Be disciples of Aaron, loving peace and pursuing
grace, loving people and drawing them near to the Torah.
13. He would say [in Aramaic]: A name made great is a name
destroyed, and one who does not add, subtracts. And who does
not learn is liable to death. And the one who uses the crown,
passes away.
14. He would say: If I am not for myself, who is for me? And
when I am for myself, what am I? And if not now, when?

Nothing joins the several statements assigned to Hillel, no
common theme, assuredly no single syllogism to be proven on
the basis of facts that are adduced. The Mishnah contains a tiny
proportion of materials joined solely by reason of the name(s) of
authorities, for example, tractate Eduyyot; the Yerushalmi and
Bavli have some sizable compositions in which only the name
and not the theme or (all the more so) the proposition serves to
link one sentence to another.

Now, to show the difference between appeal to a name alone
for cogency and use of a shared theme or even a proposition, let
me point to a composition (also from The Fathers) in which

three sayings make essentially the same point, which is to listen and shut up:

> **1:17.** Simeon his son says: All my life I grew up among the sages, and I found nothing better for a person [the body] than silence. And not the learning is the thing, but the doing. And whoever talks too much causes sin.

The difference now is clear. Overall, we shall look in vain for evidence that, by making a single point or even discussing a single theme, or even by joining together names of authorities in some sort of fixed order, the framers of the document found cogency between two or among three or more sentences. The generally prevailing logic will assemble diverse, thematically only loosely connected, sayings, which join together merely because the same authority is supposed to have said them—an extreme but not uncommon way of connecting one thing with someone else.

The third logic therefore rests upon this premise: *An established sequence of words joins whatever is attached to those words into a set of cogent statements, even though it does not form of those statements propositions of any kind, implicit or explicit.* The established sequence of words may be made up of names always associated with one another. It may be made up of a received text, with deep meanings of its own, such as a verse or a clause of Scripture. It may be made up of the sequence of holy days or synagogue lections, which are assumed to be known by everyone and so to connect on their own. The fixed association of these words, whether names, formulas such as verses of Scripture, or lists of facts, serves to link otherwise unrelated statements to one another and to form of them all not a proposition but *an entirely intelligible sequence of connected or related sentences.*

How, then, does the logic of cogent discourse supplied by fixed association accomplish its goal? In the sample we have cited, we find side by side a sequence of sentences that bear no relationship or connection at all between one another. These discrete sentences have come before us in "commentary-form," for instance:

> "Clause 1:" "This means A."
> "Clause 2:" "This refers to Q."

Nothing joins A and Q. Indeed, had I used symbols out of different classifications altogether, for example, A, a letter of an alphabet, and #, which stands for something other than a sound of an alphabet, the picture would have been still clearer. Nothing joins A to Q or A to # except that clause 2 follows clause 1. The upshot is that no proposition links A to Q or A to #, and so far as there is a connection between A and Q or A and #, it is not propositional. Then is there a connection at all? I think the authorship of the document that set forth matters as they did assumes that there is a connection. For there clearly is—at the very least—an order in the text (that is, "clause 1" is prior to "clause 2," that out of clauses 1 and 2 does form an intelligible statement, that is, two connected, not merely adjacent, sentences.

This third way in which two or more sentences are deemed, in the canonical literature of Judaism, to constitute a more than random, episodic sequence of unrelated allegations, A, X, Q, C, and so on, on its own, out of context, yields gibberish—no proposition, no sense, no joining between two sentences, no implicit connection accessible without considerable labor of access. But this third way can see cogent discourse even where there is no proposition at all, and even where the relationship between sentence A and sentence X does not derive from the interplay among the propositions at hand. It is hard for us even to imagine nonpropositional yet intelligible discourse, outside the realm of feeling or inchoate attitude, and yet, as we shall see, before us is a principle of intelligible discourse that is entirely routine, clearly assumed to be comprehensible, and utterly accessible. This third logic rests on a premise of education—that is, of prior discourse attained through processes of learning a logic not as easily accessible to us as the logics of philosophy and narrative.

What holds the whole together? It is knowledge shared among those to whom this writing is addressed, hence the "fixed" part of "fixed association," as distinct from (mere) free association. Cogency is social, therefore not ever the product of private, free association, any more than form ever permits an individual manner of expressing ideas. Connection here rests on the premise of education or what we may call the system and structure of a textual community (using the phrase in no technical sense). That premise derives from prior discourse attained through processes of learning; it is not a logic readily accessible, as are the logics of philosophy and narrative, but one that comes only through the training of the mind, through learning the terms that are fixed in their associations with one another. Our authorship assumes that the discrete sentences will form an intelligible statement (even with an unarticulated proposition, though that need not detain us) in which sentence A joins sentence B to say something important, even though that statement is not conveyed by what A says and what B says. For these sentences to form connected statements, we have then to know that these names bear meaning, in their facticity of course but also in the order in which they occur, in the conglomerates which they comprise.

I have dwelt on this logic for two reasons. First, the logic of fixed association proves paramount in joining thought to thought in certain documents. Second, that same logic serves effectively when what one intends is simply to string together essentially discrete units of completed thought. An encyclopedia of well-crafted articles need not appeal for large-scale coherence to the alphabetical order of topics. It can also utilize the coherence supplied by the topics dictated by a received canon, for example, a chapter of Scripture.

The cogency of methodical-analytical logic: The fourth logic of intelligible discourse is discourse in which one analytical method applies to many sentences, with the result that many discrete and diverse sentences are shown to constitute a single conceptual structure. A variety of explanations and amplifications, topically and propositionally unrelated, will be joined in a methodical way to produce a broadly applicable conclusion that many things really conform to a single pattern or structure. Such methodologically coherent analysis imposes upon a variety of data a structure that is external to all of the data yet that imposes connection between and among facts or sentences. The connection consists in the recurrent order, repeated balance, and replicated meaning of all the facts, seen in the aggregate. This is commonly done by asking the same question of many things and producing a single result many times.

Methodical analysis may be conducted by addressing a set of fixed questions, or by imposing a sequence of stable procedures on a vast variety of data. What may emerge is not a proposition, or even a sequence of facts formerly unconnected but now connected, but a different mode of cogency, one that derives from showing that many things follow a single rule or may be interpreted in a single way. It is the intelligible proposition that is general and not particular, that imposes upon the whole a sense of understanding and comprehension, even though the parts of the whole do not join together. What happens in this mode of discourse is that we turn the particular into the general, the case into a rule, and if I had to point to one overall purpose of the authorships of Sifra and Sifré to Deuteronomy, it is to turn the cases of the books of Leviticus and Deuteronomy into rules that conform, overall, to the way in which the Mishnah presents its rules: logically, topically, as a set of philosophically defensible generalizations.

From the generally less familiar issue of the logics of cogent discourse, we come, finally, to the well-known task of analyzing the topical or propositional character of a piece of writing. At issue in the description and analysis of the topical program of a document is a deceptively simple question. We ask what subject an authorship has chosen to discuss, and, more important, what are the propositions concerning that subject that an authorship has chosen to set forth. We may describe a document's topic and the generative problematic of the topic—the thing the authorship wants to know and say about that topic—but then we must correlate the topical program with the rhetorical and logical traits of a piece of writing. When we know how an authorship has chosen among a repertoire of modes of expression and thought a distinctive manner of patterning language and a singular means of conducting cogent and intelligible discourse, we may then ask about the correspondence between medium of expression and of thought and the message conveyed.

All parties share the same ground, namely, that outlined by Scripture. But if we assume that because everyone reads the same revelation, therefore any party to public discourse will set forth a message congruent with that of any other party to the same discourse, we are misled. The first consideration in defining the program of discourse calls attention to the centrality of Scripture. Can we not simply list the verses discussed by an authorship to determine the topical progam of that authorship? All examples of the classification of writing under consideration sustain a dialogue with Scripture, so, on the face of matters, the topic of each document ought to derive from revelation. But knowing that all authorships in common address Scripture, viewed as God's revelation to Israel, does not allow us to predict the topical program of any particular writing.

One example makes the basic point in a compelling way. Two authorships read the book of Leviticus. The one produced Leviticus Rabbah, the other, Sifra. The topical programs of those two authorships bear no interesting resemblances. Indeed, they scarcely intersect. The authorship of Sifra pursued the topical program of Scripture verse by verse, beginning to end, in 272 chapters. The counterpart compilers of Leviticus Rabbah discuss thirty-seven verses of Leviticus and set forth thirty-seven propositions. So knowing that Scripture defines a program of subjects and may even set forth propositions for inquiry does not provide great enlightenment. That is why the comparison and contrast of topical programs and specific propositions as set forth by diverse authorships proves illuminating. And when we come to Sifra, we identify only with great difficulty the topical program of that authorship so far as that program transcends the successive verses of the book of Leviticus; no sustained polemic particular to the comments on the verses presents itself.

When, in the case of the two Midrash-compilations addressed to the book of Leviticus, we ask about the components of a topical program, we should like to know whether an authorship has focused upon the topics of that book or upon some other list of topics altogether. Specifically, the book of Leviticus is concerned with sacrifice and the cult; the sanctity of Israel and, in particular, of its priestly caste; the distributive economics of the Temple effected through the disposition of crops and land; and the like. Are these the principal foci of discussion? In addressing these topics an author can introduce a wholly different program, for example, allegorically reading one thing in terms of something else. Then the exposition of the topics of the book of Leviticus will enjoy only slight attention. A different topical program will attach itself to the book of Leviticus, from the range of subjects which that book covers. In the case of the book of Leviticus, a set of historical questions of a salvific character can take the place of the inquiry into cultic questions concerning sanctification with which the priestly writers originally dealt. That example may not be restated in terms pertinent to a variety of documents. In more general terms, an authorship may follow the topical program of the biblical writing on which it chooses to comment, or it may well treat that program as a pretext for discourse on entirely other matters. Therein lies one complexity of topical analysis.

But there is yet another source of puzzlement. An authorship may treat a topic but present no propositions that we can identify. That is to say, the authorship may simply paraphrase, clarify, and generate some secondary considerations, without expressing any systematic interest in saying more than the text says in its own terms and language. In commenting on words and phrases, for instance, no important propositions may emerge. The topical program of a document may prove not even an expansion or disquisition upon themes of Leviticus but simply a repetition and paraphrase of the topical program of that book.

Our survey of the logics of cogent discourse has already produced yet another possibility. An authorship may address a variety of topics in a single way. Then, while it has no topical program distinctive to itself, it does convey the particular message that it has chosen to set forth. When an authorship repeatedly asks a single question in the confrontation with diverse data, it does so in such a way as to treat no identified subject matter at all. Rather, the authorship aims to prove various encompassing principles that are not particular to any theme but, rather, constitute generative of modes of thought as these apply to every theme. The associated logic, of course, is the logic of analytical-methodical discourse. In that context, while we find it difficult to claim that a given document follows a topical program at all, the document nonetheless does set forth a message and may be shown to intend to demonstrate a clear-cut proposition. The authorship presents propositions *illustrated by its treatment of a variety of subjects,* all of them incidental to what is really at stake in the discourse and its sustained argument.

The description of the topical program of a document begins in finding the answers to these questions:

1. Does the document at hand deliver a particular message and viewpoint, or does it merely serve as a repository for diverse received materials?
2. Does the authorship deliver its message, its choices as to form and meaning, or merely transmit someone else's?

To broaden the issue, let me unpack secondary questions. First, do we have a cogent statement or a mere scrapbook? Comparing one compilation to another yields the correct way of finding the answer. A document may serve solely as a convenient repository of prior sayings and stories, available materials that will have served equally well (or poorly) wherever they took up their final location. A composition may exhibit a viewpoint, a purpose of authorship distinctive to its framers or collectors and arrangers. Such a characteristic literary purpose would be so powerfully particular to one authorship that nearly everything at hand can be shown to have been (re)shaped for the ultimate purpose of the authorship at hand. These, then, are collectors and arrangers who demand the title of authors. Context and circumstance then form the prior condition of inquiry.

Through the description of the traits of rhetoric, logic, and topic of a document read autonomously, I work my way back from the way in which people compose their cogent and persuasive statements to the mind, the intellect, the religious system composed of way of life, world view, and address to a defined social entity, that teaches them not only or mainly *what* to think but also *how* to think. My claim is that the religious system, an abstraction, finds form in a fully exposed manner of reaching and demonstrating a particular statement of sense. In the canonical writings of the Judaism studied here for exemplary purposes, that is to say, the Judaism of the dual Torah that has constituted normative Judaism from the seventh century to the present day, the system of Judaism finds realization. That system takes form in the framing of a proposition, complete in exposition, from beginning statement through middle demonstration and argumentation to end conclusion and the drawing of consequences. The documentary method therefore inquires into the systemic formation through analyzing the evidence of writing, by which I mean the joining of sentence to sentence into an intelligible, cogent, proportioned composition, a documentary statement. Now to apply the method to principal documents of the Judaism of the dual Torah, we turn to the analysis of texts seen as autonomous statements, standing entirely on their own.

PART TWO

Text:
The Autonomous Statement

CHAPTER THREE

Reading Norms,
Discerning System

The claim that we may describe documents wholly and completely, treating them as autonomous statements, rests upon a simple premise. It is that whatever the broader context, whether intellectual or social, a piece of writing demonstrably stands on its own and may be read in terms defined by a single authorship. Writings may be differentiated from one another, each expressing choices effected by an authorship, all displaying marks of internal cogency of language and cogent discourse, of rhetoric and logic, which define the indicative criteria of a document. Choices made by an authorship, not adventitious or happenstance characteristics, then mark a piece of writing as freestanding, internally coherent, autonomous, and intelligible in its own terms and discourse. If I can show that various documents exhibit well-crafted choices governing how things are expressed, I have a strong claim that these documents, each in its own terms, come to us from authorships that have made and carried out decisions to say things in one particular way and to set forth propositions in a cogent manner through a logic that dictates their connection, coherence, and cogency. When, furthermore, we can demonstrate that the formal traits of language and of logic correspond to the propositional program of an authorship, we have very sound reason indeed for insisting that this particular piece of writing realizes a plan as to rhetoric and logic, and a program as to topic and proposition. That is to say, we have shown that a piece of writing constitutes a document and accomplishes public discourse, which, as I proposed in chapters 1 and 2, characterize the writings of the Judaism of the dual Torah. On that basis, appealing to concrete traits of rhetoric and logic, I claim to translate *writing into religion.*

Since, after Scripture, the Mishnah comprises the initial document of the Judaism of the dual Torah, we begin with the description of the rhetoric and logic of that writing. (In chapter 10 we turn to the account of the system, seen in its historical context, of the Mishnah's authorship.) Our task is to demonstrate that the Mishnah's authorship imparted to the document as a whole coherent traits of formalization of language and also paramount characteristics of cogent discourse. We have then to show that another authorship made other choices as to rhetoric and logic when it composed a different document altogether, one that is connected with, and therefore may be legitimately contrasted to, the Mishnah.

Let us start, in our rhetorical description of the Mishnah as a piece of writing, with the simple question of how the document is organized. Examining internal evidence alone, we want to know whether the authorship has presented its statement autonomously or contingently, that is, as a sustained statement in its own terms or as a commentary suspended from someone else's writing. Further, what program of discourse, thematic and propositional or amplificatory and exegetical, has guided the organization of the writing? These are questions anyone can answer in reading any document, simply by making an outline of the topics covered by the writing and asking where and how the authorship has identified and laid out these topics.

In the case of the Mishnah, the answer is straightforward. The document presents its discourses as thematic expositions, with beginnings, middles, and endings, and principles and secondary developments thereof. Accordingly, even if we had manuscripts from antiquity lacking all punctuation and marks of sentences, paragraphs, chapters, and tractates, internal evidence alone would tell us the major divisions of the document. For throughout the Mishnah the preferred mode of layout is through themes, spelled out along the lines of the logic embedded in those themes.

The Mishnah is divided up into six principal divisions, each expounding a single immense topic. The tractates of each division furthermore take up subtopics of the principal theme. The chapters then unfold along the lines of what was to the framers the logic of the necessary dissection of the division. While that mode of organization may appear to be necessary or "self-evident", we should notice that there are three other modes of organization found within the document. One of them is to collect diverse sayings around the name of a given authority. (The whole of tractate Eduyyot is organized in that way.) A second mode is to express a given basic principle through diverse topics, for example, a fundamental rule cutting across many areas of law, stated in one place through all of the diverse types of law through which the rule or principle may be expressed. A third mode is to take a striking language pattern and collect sayings on diverse topics that conform to the given language pattern. But faced with these possible ways of organizing materials, the framers of the Mishnah chose to adhere to a highly disciplined thematic-logical principle of organization.

In antiquity, paragraphing and punctuation were not commonly used. Long columns of words would contain a text, and the student of the text had the task of breaking up those columns into tractates, chapters, sentences, and large and small sense-units. Now, if we had the entire Mishnah in a single immense scroll and spread the scroll out on the ground—perhaps the length of a football field!—we should have no difficulty at all discovering the point, on the five-yard line, at which the first tractate ends and the second begins, and so on down the field to the opposite goal. For from Berakhot at the beginning to Uqsin at the end, the breaking points practically jump up from the ground like white lines of lime denoting the changes of principal topic. So the criterion of division, internal to the document and not merely imposed by copyists and printers, is thematic. That is, the tractates are readily distinguishable from one another since each treats a distinct topic. So if Mishnah were to be copied out in a long scroll without the significance of lines of demarcation among the several tractates, the opening pericope of each tractate would leave no doubt that one topic had been completed and a new one undertaken.

The same is true within the tractates. Intermediate divisions of these principal divisions (we might call them chapters of books) are to be discerned on the basis of internal evidence, through the confluence of theme and form. That is to say, a given intermediate division of a tractate (a chapter) will be marked by a particular, recurrent, formal pattern in accord with which sentences are constructed, and also by a particular and distinct theme, to which these sentences are addressed. When a new theme commences, a fresh formal pattern will be used. Within the intermediate divisions, we are able to recognize the components, or smallest whole units of thought (or cognitive units), because there will be a recurrent pattern of sentence structure within the unit and a shifting at the commencement of the next theme. Each point at which the recurrent pattern commences marks the beginning of a new cognitive unit. In general, an intermediate division will contain a carefully enumerated sequence of exempla of cognitive units, in the established formal pattern, commonly in groups of three or five or multiples of three or five. A single rhetorical pattern will govern the whole set of topical instances of a logical proposition. When the logical-topical program changes, the rhetorical pattern will change, too. So the mnemonics of the Mishnah and the foundations of its discourse rest throughout on the confluence of manifest rhetoric, deep logic, and articulated topic.

The Mishnah's authorship took as its mode of expression not the statement of generalization but the implicit communication of generalization only through grouped examples of a common rule, which rule would rarely be articulated. While utilizing propositional logic, that is a subtle mode of discourse indeed, and, joined to the intent of memorization and oral transmission, it represents an extraordinary compliment to the proposed audience of the document. The technology of mnemonics, therefore, forms the surface of a deep texture of thought about communication. These fundamental traits tell us two important facts about our authorship. First, it proposed to make an autonomous, freestanding statement, which did not appeal to some other writing for order and proportion. Rather, it treated the topics of its choice within an autonomous logic dictated by the requirements of those topics. Specifically, it exhibits the sense that a given topic has its own inner tension and generates its own program of thought and exposition. Second, the authorship's freestanding statement was set forth in a highly systematic and rhetorically careful way. Since the exposition bore the burden of clarifying itself, unable to appeal to some other document for structure and cogency, the formulation of that exposition would have to exhibit those signals of sense— beginnings, middles, endings—that instructed the reader on how to follow the whole. These traits will strike us as consequential only when we take up other writings of the same set, in which discourse is not propositional and the formalization of language is not critical to the exposition at all.

Let me summarize the criteria of formalization and organization of the Mishnah. The first of the two criteria that derive from the nature of the principal divisions themselves is the theme. It is along thematic lines that the redactors organized vast bodies of materials into principal divisions, or tractates. These fundamental themes themselves were subdivided into smaller conceptual units. The principal divisions treat their themes in units indicated by the sequential unfolding of their inner logical structure. The second fundamental criterion is the literary character, the syntactical and grammatical pattern, that differentiates and characterizes a sequence of primitive (that is, undifferentiable, indivisible) units of thought. Normally, when the subject changes, the mode of expression, the formal patterning of language, will change as well. From the basic traits of large-scale organization, which appeal to the characteristics of subject matter, we turn to the way in which sentences and paragraphs are put together. By a "paragraph" (a term drawn from our modern vocabulary) I mean a completed exposition of thought, the setting forth of a proposition wholly and completely, now without regard to the larger function, for example, in a sustained discourse of argument or proposition, served by that thought. Two or more lapidary statements, for instance, allegations as to fact, will make up such a sustained cognitive unit. The cognitive units in the Mishnah in particular resort to a remarkably limited repertoire of formulary patterns, and the document as a whole exhibits remarkable formal uniformity.

The authorship of the Mishnah manages to say whatever it wants in one of the following ways:

1. The simple declarative sentence, in which the subject, verb, and predicate are syntactically tightly joined to one another: *He who does so and so is such and such;*
2. The duplicated subject, in which the subject of the sentence is stated twice: *He who does so and so, lo, he is such and such;*
3. Mild apocopation, in which the subject of the sentence is cut off from the verb, which refers to its own subject and not the one with which the sentence commences: *He who does so and so . . . , it [the thing he has done] is such and such;*
4. Extreme apocopation, in which a series of clauses is presented, none of them tightly joined to what precedes or follows, and all of them cut off from the predicate of the sentence: *He who does so and so . . . , it [the thing he has done] is such and such . . . , it is a matter of doubt whether . . . or whether . . . lo, it [referring to nothing in the antecedent, apocopated clauses of the subject of the sentence] is so and so. . . .*
5. In addition to these formulary patterns, in which the distinctive formulary traits are effected through variations in the relationship between the subject and the predicate of the sentence, or in which the subject itself is given a distinctive development, there is yet a fifth. In this last one we have a contrastive complex predicate, in which case we may have two sentences, independent of each other yet clearly formulated so as to stand in acute balance with each other in the predicate: *He who does . . . is unclean, and he who does not . . . is clean.*

Is it possible that "a simple declarative sentence" may be asked to serve as a formulary pattern, alongside the rather distinctive and unusual constructions that follow? By itself, a tightly constructed sentence consisting of subject verb, and complement, in which the verb refers to the subject and the complement to the verb, hardly exhibits traits of particular formal interest. Yet a sequence of such sentences, built along the same gross grammatical lines, may well exhibit a clear-cut and distinctive pattern. And here the mnemonics of the document enter into consideration. The Mishnah is not a generalizing document; it makes its points by repeating several cases that yield the same, ordinarily unarticulated, general principle. Accordingly, the Mishnah, as I said, utilizes sets of three or five repetitions of cases to make a single point. Now when we see that three or five "simple declarative sentences" take up one principle or problem, and that, when the principle or problem shifts, a quite distinctive formal pattern will be utilized, we realize that the "simple declarative sentence" has served the formulator of the unit of thought as aptly as did apocopation, a dispute, or another more obviously distinctive form or formal pattern. The contrastive predicate is one example; the Mishnah contains many more.

The important point of differentiation, particularly for the simple declarative sentence, appears in the interplay between theme and form. It is there that we see a single pattern recurring in a long sequence of sentences as, for example, *the X which has lost its Y is unclean because of its Z, and the Z which has lost its Y is unclean because of its X.* Another example will be a long sequence of highly developed sentences, laden with relative clauses and other explanatory matter, in which a single syntactical pattern will govern the articulation of three or six or nine exempla. That sequence will be followed by one terse, repeated sentence pattern: *X is so and so, Y is such and such, Z is thus and so.* The former group will treat one principle or theme, the latter some other. There can be no doubt, therefore, that the declarative sentence in recurrent patterns is, in its way, just as carefully formalized as a sequence of severely apocopated sentences or of contrastive predicates or duplicated subjects. None of the Mishnah's secondary and amplificatory companions—the Tosefta, the Talmud of the Land of Israel or Yerushalmi, the Talmud of Babylonia or Bavli—exhibits the same tight rhetorical cogency.

The reason for the patterning of rhetoric becomes apparent when we appreciate the effect of doing so. It is to facilitate memorizing the document. Exactly how does the formulation of the document facilitate remembering its exact words? The answer to that question derives from the smallest whole units of discourse, the cognitive units, defined as groups of sentences that make a point completely and entirely on their own, which become intelligible on three bases: logical, topical, and rhetorical. What I am going to prove is simple: It is the confluence of logic, topic, and rhetoric that generates at the deepest structure of the Mishnah's language a set of mnemonic patterns. These

mnemonics serve by definition to facilitate the easy memorization of the text of the Mishnah.

First, to define the matter: What marks the smallest whole unit
of discourse—a handful of sentences—is that the several
sentences of which it is composed are unintelligible or not wholly
intelligible by themselves, but are entirely intelligible when seen
as a group. The smallest whole unit of discourse in the Mishnah
invariably constitutes a syllogism, that is, a statement of a
proposition, in which a condition or question, the protasis, finds
resolution in a rule or answer, the apodosis. "If such and such is
the case, then so and so is the rule"—that is the characteristic
cognitive structure of the Mishnah's smallest whole unit of
thought or discourse. Even if that statement were made up of
two or three or even five declarative sentences, it is only when the
proposition is fully exposed, both protasis and apodosis, that the
declarative sentences reach the level of full and complete
expression, that is, of sense and intelligibility.

For the purpose of making this point clear, let me take up a
brief example, drawn from Mishnah-tractate Sanhedrin chapter
2, paragraphs 1 and 2 (hence M. Sanhedrin 2:1-2).

[1] A. *A high priest judges, and [others] judge him;*
[2] B. *gives testimony, and [others] give testimony about him;*
[3] C. *performs the rite of removing the shoe [Deut. 25:7-9], and*
   [others] perform the rite of removing the shoe with his wife.
[4] D. *[Others] enter levirate marriage with his wife, but he does*
   not enter into levirate marriage,
   E. *because he is prohibited to marry a widow.*

Thus far we have simple declarative sentences—subject, verb.
Now the syntax shifts to conditional sentences or other qualified
statements.

F. [If] he suffers a death [in his family], he does not
   follow the bier.
G. "But when [the bearers of the bier] are not visible, he
   is visible; when they are visible, he is not.
H. "And he goes with them to the city gate," the words of
   R. Meir.
I. R. Judah says, "He never leaves the sanctuary,

J.   "since it says, '*Nor shall he go out of the sanctuary*' (Lev. 21:12)."

K.   And when he gives comfort to others

L.   the accepted practice is for all the people to pass one after another, and the appointed [prefect of the priests] stands between him and the people.

M.   And when he receives consolation from others,

N.   all the people say to him, "Let us be your atonement."

O.   And he says to them, "May you be blessed by Heaven."

P.   And when they provide him with the funeral meal,

Q.   all the people sit on the ground, while he sits on a stool.

(M. Sanhedrin 2:1)

I have emphasized the simple declarative sentence because of the match to follow. But we shall see other correspondences, for example, the "and when . . ." type.

[1]   A.   *The king does not judge, and [others] do not judge him;*

[2]   B.   *does not give testimony, and [others] do not give testimony about him;*

[3]   C.   *does not perform the rite of removing the shoe, and others do not perform the rite of removing the shoe with his wife;*

[4]   D.   *does not enter into levirate marriage, nor [do his brothers] enter levirate marriage with his wife.*

E.   R. Judah says, "If he wanted to perform the rite of removing the shoe or to enter into levirate marriage, his memory is a blessing."

F.   They said to him, "They pay no attention to him [if he expressed the wish to do so]."

G.   [Others] do not marry his widow.

H.   R. Judah says, "A king may marry the widow of a king.

I.   "For so we find in the case of David, that he married the widow of Saul,

J.   "For it is said, 'And I gave you your master's house and your master's wives into your embrace' (2 Sam. 12:8)."

(M. Sanhedrin 2:2)

Now if we wish to ask what point emerges in the carefully crafted details before us, we do not have far to go to find the answer. It is that the high priest and the king form a single genus but two distinct species, and the variations between the species form a single set of taxonomic indicators. The one is like the other in these ways, unlike the other in those ways. Does that information yield a proposition? Without doubt. Does the proposition generate further propositions, so that it constitutes a syllogism? Without doubt. How so? The remainder of the passage shows us the secondary amplification and discussion of the implication of the established principle, and that principle proves generative of further syllogisms, proposed and debated in the secondary details of the passage. We now have a clear picture of the unit of discourse and its rhetorical components as well as its syllogistic character.

The language of the apodosis and protasis of the Mishnah's smallest whole units of discourse is framed in formal, mnemonic patterns. They follow a few simple rules. These rules, once known, apply nearly everywhere and form stunning evidence for the document's cogency. They permit anyone to reconstruct, out of a few key phrases, an entire cognitive unit, and even to complete intermediate units of discourse. Working downward from the surface, therefore, anyone can penetrate into the deeper layers of meaning of the Mishnah. Then and at the same time, while discovering the principle behind the cases, one can easily memorize the whole by mastering the recurrent rhetorical pattern dictating the expression of the cogent set of cases. For it is easy to note the shift from one rhetorical pattern to another and to follow the repeated cases, articulated in the new pattern downward to its logical substrate. So syllogistic propositions, in the Mishnah's authors' hands, come to full expression not only in *what* people wish to state but also in *how* they choose to say it. The limits of rhetoric define the arena of topical articulation. Once we ask what three or five joined, topical propositions have in common, we state the logic and can therefore propose the syllogism that is shared among them all.

The analysis of the Mishnah's linguistic formalization requires brief attention to the forms not only of cognitive units ("paragraphs") but also of sentences (smallest whole units of thought). The smallest whole unit of discourse is made up of fixed, recurrent formulas, clichés, patterns, or little phrases, out of which whole pericopes, or large elements in pericopes, for

example, complete sayings, are constructed. Small units of
tradition, while constitutive of pericopes, do not generate new
sayings or legal problems, as do apothegmatic formulas. An
example of part of a pericope (smallest whole unit of thought)
composed primarily of recurrent formulas is as follows:

> *A basket of fruit intended for the Sabbath*
> House of Shammai declare exempt
> *And* the House of Hillel declare liable.

The italicized words are not fixed formulas. "And" is redactional; the formulation of the statement of the problem does not
follow a pattern. The "House" sentences, by contrast, are
formed of fixed, recurrent phrases, which occur in numerous
pericopes. Similarly: "House of Shammai say . . . House of Hillel
say . . ." are fixed small units, whether or not the predicate
matches; when it balances, we have a larger unit of tradition
composed of two small units. By definition these small formulas
cannot be random, or they would not constitute formulas. Such
small units are whole words, not syntactical or grammatical
particles. They also are not mere redactional devices used to join
together discrete pericopes in the later processes of collection
and organization, such as connecting words, editorial conventions, formulaic introductions to Scriptures, and other redactional clichés.

Some of the patterning or formalization of language serves in
the expression of the proposition at hand. The pattern, then, is
internal to the idea that is expressed, and it predominates in the
linguistic formalization of that idea. If this pattern recurs for two
or more cognitive units, then we have a formulary trait internal
to the pattern of language of each element in a subdivision. Each
and every cognitive unit within said subdivision will express its
particular concept or thought in conformity with this common
pattern, which therefore is to be designated as internal to the
whole. The recurrent pattern of syntax or language is
redactional, in that what is to be expressed is the work of those
responsible for both the formulary and formalized character
and the cognitive substance of the subdivision in all of its parts
and as a whole. The following illustrates the formulary pattern
just now described:

8:1 B. The House of Shammai *say, "One blesses over the* [1] day, *and afterward one blesses over the* [2] wine."

C. And the House of Hillel *say, "One blesses over the* [2] wine, *and afterward one blesses over the* [1] day."

8:2 A. The House of Shammai say, "They wash [1] the hands and afterward mix [2] the cup."

And the House of Hillel say, "They mix [2] the cup and afterward wash [1] the hands." . . .

8:4 A. The House of Shammai say, "They clean [1] the house, and afterward they wash [2] the hands."

And the House of Hillel say, "They wash [2] the hands, and afterward they clean [1] the house."

(M. Berakhot 8:1, 2, 4)

Here we have a highly coherent theme ("concerning the meal") and a rigidly adhered to formulary pattern, 1, 2, versus 2, 1.

The formal pattern may also stand external to the idea that is expressed and superficial, and that occurs chiefly at the outset of a cognitive unit. The arrangement of words of said unit will ignore this external formulary trait. What is to be said can be, and is, stated without regard to the superficial trait shared among several cognitive units. Indeed, we may readily discern that the formulary trait of a seies of cognitive units is external to the formulation of all of them, simply because each cognitive unit goes its own way, stating its ideas in its own form or formulary pattern, without any regard whatsoever for the formal traits of other units to which it is joined. The joining—the shared language or formulary or formal pattern—is therefore external to the several units. An example of a unit presenting a coherent theme but lacking a coherent formulary pattern derives from the passage of tracate Sanhedrin cited above.

The Mishnah's formal traits of rhetoric indicate that the document has been formulated all at once and not in an incremental, linear process extending into a remote (mythic) past (e.g., to Sinai). These traits, common to a series of distinct cognitive units, are redactional, because they are imposed at that point at which someone intended to join together discrete (finished) units on a given theme. The varieties of traits particular to the discrete units and the diversity of authorities cited therein, including masters of two or three or even four strata from the turn of the first century to the end of the second, make it highly improbable that the several units were formulated in a common pattern and then preserved until, later on, still further units, on the same theme and in the same pattern, were worked out and added. The entire indifference, moreover, to the historical order of authorities and the concentration on the logical unfolding of a given theme or problem without reference to the sequence of authorities confirms the supposition that formulation and redaction go forward together. The principal framework of formulation and formalization in the Mishnah is the intermediate division rather than the cognitive unit. The least-formalized formulary pattern, the simple declarative sentence, turns out to yield many examples of acute formalization, in which a single distinctive pattern is imposed upon two or more cognitive units. While an intermediate division of a tractate may be composed of several such conglomerates of cognitive units, it is rare indeed for cognitive units formally to stand wholly by themselves. Normally, cognitive units share formal or formulary traits with others to which they are juxtaposed and whose theme they share. This is why the principal unit of formulary formalization is the intermediate division and not the cognitive unit.

So much for the form-analysis of the Mishnah. What about the logic of cogent discourse?

The Mishnah's logic of cogent discourse establishes propositions that rest upon philosophical bases, for example, through the proposal of a thesis and the composition of a list of facts that prove the thesis (e.g., through shared traits of a taxonomic order). The Mishnah presents rules and treats stories (inclusive of history) as incidental and of merely taxonomic interest. Its logic is propositional, and its intellect does its work through a vast labor of classification, comparison, and contrast, generating governing rules and generalizations. A simple contrasting case shows us that the stakes are very high. For that purpose, let us turn to a document our authorship knew well, namely, the written Torah.

The Pentateuch appeals to a logic of cogent discourse different from the Mishnah's. It is the cogency imparted by teleology, that is, a logic that provides an account of how things were in order to explain how things are and to set forth how they should be, with the tabernacle in the wilderness as the model for (and modeled after) the Temple in Jerusalem. The Mishnah speaks in a continuing present tense, saying only how things are, indifferent to the *were* and the *will-be*. The Pentateuch focuses upon self-conscious "Israel," saying who they were and what they must become to overcome who they now are. The Mishnah understands by "Israel" as much the individual as the nation and identifies as its principal actors, the heroes of its narrative, not the family become a nation but the priest and the householder, the woman and the slave, the adult and the child, and other castes and categories of persons within an inward-looking, established, fully landed community. Given the Mishnah's interest in classifications and categories, and, therefore, in systematic hierarchization of an orderly world, one can hardly find odd that (re)definition of the subject matter and problematic of the systemic social entity.

We may briefly dwell on this matter of difference in the prevailing logic, because the contrast allows us to see how one document will appeal to one logic, another to a different logic. While the Pentateuch appeals to the logic of teleology to draw together and make sense of facts, so making connections by appeal to the end and drawing conclusions concerning the purpose of things, The Mishnah's authorship knows only the philosophical logic of syllogism, the rule-making logic of lists. The pentateuchal logic reached concrete expression in narrative, which served to point to the direction and goal of matters, and hence of history. Accordingly, those authors, when putting together diverse materials, so shaped everything as to form of it all as continuous a narrative as they could construct, and through that "history" that they made up, they delivered their message and also portrayed that message as cogent and compelling. While the pentateuchal writers were theologians of history, the Mishnah's aimed at composing a natural philosophy for supernatural, holy Israel. Like good Aristotelians, they would uncover the components of the rules by comparison and contrast, showing the rule for one thing by finding out how it compared with like things and contrasted with the unlike.[1]

---

1. Compare G. E. R. Lloyd, *Polarity and Analogy. Two Types of Argumentation in Early Greek Thought* (Cambridge: Cambridge University Press, 1966). But the core-logic of *Listenwissenschaft* extends back to Sumerian times.

Then, in their view, the unknown would become known, conforming to the rule of the like thing and also to the opposite of the rule governing the unlike thing.

That purpose is accomplished in particular through list making, which places on display the data of the like and the unlike and then conveys the rule implicitly. It is this resort to list making that accounts for the rhetorical stress on groups of examples of a common principle. Once a series is established, the authorship assumes, the governing rule will be perceived. That explains why, in exposing the interior logic of its authorship's intellect, the Mishnah had to be a book of lists, with the implicit order, the nomothetic traits of a monothetic order, dictating the ordinarily unstated general and encompassing rule.

And all this why? It is in order to make a single statement, endless times over, and to repeat in a mass of tangled detail precisely the same fundamental judgment. The Mishnah in its way is as blatantly repetitious in its fundamental statement as is the Pentateuch. But the power of the pentateuchal authorship, denied to that of the Mishnah, lies in its capacity always to be heard, to create sound by resonance of the surfaces of things. The Pentateuch is fundamentally a popular and accessible piece of writing. By contrast, the Mishnah's writers spoke into the depths, anticipating a more acute hearing than they ever would receive. So the repetitions of Scripture reinforce the message, while the endlessly repeated paradigm of the Mishnah sits too deeply in the structure of the system to gain hearing from the ear that lacks acuity or to attain visibility to the untutored eye. So much for the logic.

Given the subtlety of intellect of the Mishnah's authorship, we cannot find it surprising that the systemic message speaks not only in what is said but also in what is omitted. The framers of the Mishnah appeal solely to the traits of things.[2] The logical basis of coherent speech and discourse in the Mishnah then derives from *Listenwissenschaft*. That mode of thought defines ways of proving propositions through classification and so establishing a set of shared traits that form a rule that compels us to reach a given conclusion. Probative facts derive from the

---

2. The authorship of Sifra by contrast insists that by themselves, the traits of things do not settle anything.

classification of data, all of which point in one direction and not in another. A catalogue of facts, for example, may be so composed that, through the regularities and indicative traits of the entries, the catalogue yields a proposition. A list of parallel items points to a simple conclusion; the conclusion may or may not be given at the end of the catalogue, but the catalogue—by definition—is pointed. All of the catalogued facts are taken to bear self-evident connections to one another, established by those pertinent shared traits implicit in the composition of the list and therefore also bearing meaning and pointing through the weight of evidence to an inescapable conclusion. The discrete facts then join together because of traits common to them all. This is a mode of classification of facts that leads to an identification of what the facts have in common and—it goes without saying—an explanation of their meaning. This and other modes of philosophical argument are entirely familiar to us all. In calling all of them "philosophical," I mean only to distinguish them from the other three logics we shall presently examine. Now we see how fundamental was Sifra's authorship's insistence that Scripture, not things viewed on their own, dictates the classification of things.

The diverse topical program of the Mishnah, time and again making the same points on the centrality of order, works itself out in a single logic of cogent discourse, one that seeks the rule that governs diverse cases. And, as we now see, that logic states within its interior structure the fundamental point of the document as a whole. The correspondence of logic to system here, as in the Pentateuch viewed overall, hardly presents surprises. Seeing how the logic does its work within the document, therefore, need not detain us for very long. Two pericopes of the Mishnah show us the logic that joins fact to fact, sentence to sentence, in a cogent proposition, or, in our terms, a paragraph that makes a statement. To see how this intellect does its work, we return to familiar materials, those in which we have already discerned formalization of speech. We come first to Mishnah-tractate Berakhot, chapter 8, to see list making in its simplest form, and then to Mishnah-tractate Sanhedrin, chapter 2, to see the more subtle way in which list making yields a powerfully argued philosophical theorem. In the first of our two abstracts we have a list, carefully formulated, in which the announcement at the outset tells us what is catalogued, and in which careful mnemonic devices so arrange matters that we may readily remember the conflicting opinions. So in formal terms we have a list that means to facilitate memorization. But in substantive terms the purpose of the list and its message(s) is not set forth, and only ample exegesis will succeed in spelling out what is at stake. Here is an instance of a Mishnah-passage that demands an exegesis not supplied by the Mishnah's authorship.

8:1. A.   These are the things which are between the House of Shammai and the House of Hillel in [regard to] the meal:
[1]   B.   The House of Shammai say, "One blesses over the day, and afterward one blesses over the wine."
And the House of Hillel say, "One blesses over the wine, and afterward one blesses over the day."
[2]   **8:2.** A.   The House of Shammai say, "They wash the hands and afterward mix the cup."
And the House of Hillel say, "They mix the cup and afterward wash the hands."
[3]   **8:3.** A.   The House of Shammai say, "He dries his hands on the cloth and lays it on the table."
And the House of Hillel say, "On the pillow."
[4]   **8:4.** A.   The House of Shammai say, "They clean the house, and afterward they wash the hands."
And the House of Hillel say, "They wash the hands, and afterward they clean the house."
[5]   **8:5.** A.   The House of Shammai say, "Light, and food, and spices, and *Havdalah.*"
And the House of Hillel say, "Light, and spices, and food, and *Havdalah.*"
[6]   B.   The House of Shammai say, "Who created the light of the fire."
And the House of Hillel say, "Who creates the lights of the fire."
(M. Berahkot, chap. 8)

As we recall, the mnemonic serving the list does its work by the simple reversal of items. If authority A has the order 1, 2, then authority B will give 2, 1. Only entry [3] breaks that pattern. What is at stake in the making of the list is hardly transparent, and why day/wine versus wine/day, with parallel constructions such as clean/wash versus wash/clean, yields a general principle, the authorship does not indicate. All we know at this point, therefore, is that we deal with list makers. But how lists work to communicate principles awaits exemplification.

The next extract allows us much more explicitly to identify the *and* and the *equal* of Mishnaic discourse, showing us through the making of connections and the drawing of conclusions the propositional and essentially philosophical mind that animates the Mishnah. In the following passage, drawn from Mishnah-tractate Sanhedrin, chapter 2, the authorship wishes to say that Israel has two heads, one of state (the king), the other of cult (the high priest), and that these two offices are nearly wholly congruent with one another, with a few differences based on the particular traits of each. Broadly speaking, therefore, our exercise is one of setting forth the genus and the species. The genus is head of holy Israel. The species are king and high priest. Here are the traits in common and the differences, and the exercise is fully exposed for what it is, an inquiry into the rules that govern, the points of regularity and order, in this minor matter of political structure. My outline, imposed in boldface type, states the important point in each setting. We deal with Mishnah-tractate Sanhedrin, chapter 2:

1. The rules of the high priest: subject to the law, marital rites, conduct in bereavement

2:1. A. A high priest judges, and [others] judge him;

B. gives testimony, and [others] give testimony about him;

C. performs the rite of removing the shoe [Deut. 25:7-9], and [others] perform the rite of removing the shoe with his wife.

D. [Others] enter levirate marriage with his wife, but he does not enter into levirate marriage,

E. because he is prohibited to marry a widow.

F. [If] he suffers a death [in his family], he does not follow the bier.

G. "But when [the bearers of the bier] are not visible, he is visible; when they are visible, he is not.

H. "And he goes with them to the city gate," the words of R. Meir.

I. R. Judah says, "He never leaves the sanctuary,

J. "since it says, '*Nor shall he go out of the sanctuary*' (Lev. 21:12)."

K. And when he gives comfort to others

L. the accepted practice is for all the people to pass one after another, and the appointed [prefect of the priests] stands between him and the people.

M. And when he receives consolation from others,

N. all the people say to him, "Let us be your atonement."

O. And he says to them, "May you be blessed by Heaven."

P. And when they provide him with the funeral meal,

Q. all the people sit on the ground, while he sits on a stool.

2. The rules of the king: not subject to the law, marital rites, conduct in bereavement

2:2. A. The king does not judge, and [others] do not judge him;

B. does not give testimony, and [others] do not give testimony about him;

C. does not perform the rite of removing the shoe, and others do not perform the rite of removing the shoe with his wife;

D. does not enter into levirate marriage, nor [do his brother] enter levirate marriage with his wife.

E. R. Judah says, "If he wanted to perform the rite of removing the shoe or to enter into levirate marriage, his memory is a blessing."

F. They said to him, "They pay no attention to him [if he expressed the wish to do so]."

G. [Others] do not marry his widow.

H. R. Judah says, "A king may marry the widow of a king.

I. "For so we find in the case of David, that he married the widow of Saul,

J. "For it is said, '*And I gave you your master's house and your master's wives into your embrace*' (2 Sam. 12:8)."

2:3. A. [If] [the king] suffers a death in his family, he does not leave the gate of his palace.

B. R. Judah says, "If he wants to go out after the bier, he goes out,

C. "for thus we find in the case of David, that he went out after the bier of Abner,

D. "since it is said, '*And King David followed the bier*' (2 Sam. 3:31)."

E. They said to him, "This action was only to appease the people."

F. And when they provide him with the funeral meal, all the people sit on the ground, while he sits on a couch.

3. **Special rules pertinent to the king because of his calling**

2:4. A. [The king] calls out [the army to wage] a war fought by choice on the instructions of a court of seventy-one.

B. He [may exercise the right to] open a road for himself, and [others] may not stop him.

C. The royal road has no required measure.

D. All the people plunder and lay before him [what they have grabbed], and he takes the first portion.

E. *"He should not multiply wives to himself"* (Deut. 17:17)—only eighteen.

F. R. Judah says, "He may have as many as he wants, so long as they *do not entice him* [to abandon the Lord (Deut. 7:4)]."

G. R. Simeon says, "Even if there is only one who entices him [to abandon the Lord]—lo, this one should not marry her."

H. If so, why is it said, "He should not multiply wives to himself "?

I. Even though they should be like Abigail [1 Sam. 25:3].

J. *"He should not multiply horses to himself"* (Deut. 17:16)—only enough for his chariot.

K. *"Neither shall he greatly multiply to himself silver and gold"* (Deut. 17:16)—only enough to pay his army.

L. *"And he writes out a scroll of the Torah for himself"* (Deut. 17:17)

M. When he goes to war, he takes it out with him; when he comes back, he brings it back with him; when he is in session in court, it is with him; when he is reclining, it is before him,

N. as it is said, *"And it shall be with him, and he shall read in it all the days of his life"* (Deut. 17:19).

2:5.   A.   [Others may] not ride on his horse, sit on his throne, handle his scepter.

B.   And [others may] not watch him while he is getting a haircut, or while he is nude, or in the bath-house,

C.   since it is said, *"You shall surely set him as king over you"* (Deut. 17:15)—that reverence for him will be upon you.

The subordination of Scripture to the classification scheme is self-evident. Scripture supplies facts. The traits of things—kings, high priests—dictate categories on their own, without Scripture's dictate.

The philosophical cast of mind is amply revealed in this essay, which in concrete terms effects a taxonomy, a study of the genus, national leader, and its two species, king and high priest, as to how are they alike, not alike, and what accounts for the differences. The premise is that national leaders are alike and follow the same rule, except where they differ and follow the opposite rule from one another. But that premise also is subject to the proof effected by the survey of the data consisting of concrete rules, those systemically inert facts that here come to life for the purposes of establishing a proposition. By itself, the fact that, for example, others may not ride on the king's horse bears the burden of no systemic proposition. In the context of an argument constructed for nomothetic, taxonomic purposes, the same fact is active and weighty. The whole depends upon three premises: (1) the importance of comparison and contrast, with the supposition that (2) like follows like, and the unlike follows the opposite rule, and (3) when we classify, we also hierarchize, which yields the argument from hierarchical classification: If this, which is the lesser, follows rule X, then that, which is the greater, surely should follow rule X. And that is the whole sum and substance of the logic of *Listenwissenschaft* as the Mishnah applies that logic in a practical way.

If I had to specify a single mode of thought that established connections between one fact and another, it would be the search for points in common and therefore also points of contrast. We seek connection between fact and fact, sentence and sentence, in the subtle and balanced rhetoric of the Mishnah by comparing and contrasting two things that are like and not alike. At the logical level, too, the Mishnah falls into the category of familiar philosophical thought. Once we seek regularities, we propose rules. What is like one thing falls under its rule, and what is not like it falls under the opposite rule. Accordingly, as to the species of the genus, insofar as they are alike, they share the same rule. So far as they are not alike, each follows a rule contrary to that governing the other. So the work of analysis is what produces connection, and therefore the drawing of conclusions derives from comparison and contrast. The proposition, then, that forms the conclusion concerns the essential likeness of the two offices, except where they are different, but the subterranean premise is that we can explain both likeness and difference by appeal to a principle of fundamental order and unity. To make these observations concrete, we turn to the case at hand. The important contrast comes at the outset. The high priest and the king fall into a single genus, but speciation, based on traits particular to the king, then distingiushes the one from the other. All of this exercise is conducted essentially independently of Scripture; the classifications derive from the system and are viewed as autonomous constructs; traits of things define classifications and dictate what is like and what is unlike.

The creation of pattern through grammatical relationship of syntactical elements, more than through concrete sounds, matches the formation of statements of principles solely through cases. Both the rhetoric and the logic of the Mishnah point toward a single premise concerning the social world to which the authorship imagined they addressed themselves. The tight union of rhetoric and logic tells us that the people who memorized conceptions reduced to these particular forms were capable of extraordinarily abstract perception. Hearing peculiarities of word order in quite diverse cognitive contexts, their ears and minds perceived regularities of grammatical arrangement, repeated functional variations of utilization of diverse words, and grasped from such subtleties syntactical patterns not imposed or expressed by recurrent external phenomena and autonomous of particular meanings. And the authorship assumed that its "Israel," the world to which it spoke, would perceive out of language the meaning and message they meant to convey.

What the authorship of the Mishnah heard and assumed others would hear were, of course, not only abstract relationships but also principles conveyed along with and through these relationships. For what was memorized was a fundamental notion, expressed in diverse examples but in recurrent rhetorical-syntactical patterns. Accordingly, what the readers of the Mishnah could and did hear was what lay far beneath the surface of the rule: both the unstated principle and the unsounded pattern. This means that their mode of thought was attuned to what lay beneath the surface, their minds and ears perceiving what was not said behind what was said, and how it was said. Social interrelationships within the community of Israel are left behind in the ritual speech of the Mishnah, just as within the laws natural realities are made to give form and expression to supernatural or metaphysical regularities. The Mishnah speaks of Israel, but the speakers are a group apart. The Mishnah talks of this-worldly things, but the things stand for and evoke another world entirely.

The language of the Mishnah and its grammatically formalized rhetoric, not to mention its logic requiring an active intellect to grasp what is implicit, create a world of discourse quite separate from the concrete realities of a given time, place, or society. The exceedingly limited repertoire of grammatical patterns by which all things on all matters are said gives symbolic expression to the notion that beneath the accidents of life are a few comprehensive relationships: Unchanging and enduring patterns lie deep in the inner structure of reality and impose structure upon the accidents of the world. Relying entirely on the traits of syntax and grammar that are before us, what can we say about the deepest convictions concerning reality characteristic of a people who spoke in the ways we have considered? There is a deep sense of balance, of complementarity, of the appropriateness of opposites in the completion of a whole thought. Many times do we hear: "If thus, then so, and if not thus, then not so." Mishnaic rhetoric demands (because the Mishnah's creators' sense of grammar requires) the completion of the positive by the negative and of the negative by the positive. The contrastive complex predicate is testimony to the datum that order consists in completion and wholeness. So, too, the many balanced declarative sentences before us reveal the same inner conviction that in the completion of a pattern, in the working out of its single potentiality through a sequence of diverse actualities, lies what besought order and wholeness. The fact that it is the intermediate division that constitutes the formulary context of the Mishnah needs no further specification. Accidents do require specification and repetition, yet the Mishnah is scarcely satisfied to give a single instance of a rule from which we may generalize. It strongly prefers to give us three or six or nine instances, on the basis of which we may then conclude that there is, indeed, an underlying rule.

For the framers of the document, it is the mind of the hearer that makes sense of the phrases and clauses of the subject and that perceives the relationship, endowing whole meaning upon the clauses of the subject required by the predicate. The mind of the hearer is central in the process by which apocopation attains meaning. The capacity for perceiving the rational and orderly sense of things exhibited by that mind is the unstated necessity of apocopation. Hearing discrete rules, applicable to cases related in theme and form, but not in detail and concrete actualities, the hearer puts together two things: first, the repetition of grammatical usages, and, second, the repetition of the same principle, the presence of which is implied by the repetition of syntactical patterns in diverse cases. These two—stable principle and disciplined grammar autonomous of meaning—are never stated explicitly but, invariably are implicitly present. The relationships revealed by deep grammatical consistencies internal to a sentence and the implicit regularities revealed by the congruence and cogency of specified cases rarely are stated but always are to be discerned. Accordingly, the one thing that the Mishnah invariably does not make explicit but that is always necessary to know is, I stress, the presence of the active intellect, the participant who is the hearer. It is the hearer who ultimately makes sense of, who perceives the sense in, the Mishnah.

This means that reality for the Mishnaic rhetoric consists in the grammar and syntax of language as well as in consistent and enduring patterns of relationship among diverse and changing concrete things or persons. What lasts is not the concrete thing but the abstract interplay governing any and all sorts of concrete things. There is, therefore, a congruence between rhetorical patterns of speech, on the one hand, and the framework of cogent discourse, the logic established by these same patterns, on the other. The Mishnah speaks openly about public matters, yet its deep substructure of syntax and grammatical forms shapes what is said into an essentially ritualistic language. It takes many

years to master the difficult argot, though only a few minutes to
memorize the simple patterns. That paradox reflects the very
particular situation of the creators of the Mishnah.

The extraordinary lack of a context of communication—specification of speaker or hearer—furthermore suggests that for
the Mishnah, language is a self-contained formal system used
more or less incidentally for communication. It is a system for
description of a reality, the reality of which is created and
contained by, and exhausted within, the description. The saying
of the words, whether heard meaningfully by another or not, is
the creation of the world. Speech is action and creation. The
speech-community represented by the Mishnah stands strongly
not only against nuance but also against change. The imposition
of conventional and highly patterned syntax is clearly meant to
preserve what is said without change (even though we know that
changes in the wording of traditions were effected for many
centuries thereafter). The language is meant to be unshakeable,
and its strict rules of rhetoric are meant not only to convey but
also to preserve equally strict rules of logic, or, more accurately,
equally permanent patterns of relationship.

What was at stake in this formation of language in the service of
permanence? Clearly, how things were said was intended to
secure eternal preservation of what was said. Change affects the
accidents and details. It cannot reshape enduring principles, and
language will be used to effect their very endurance. What is said,
moreover, is not to be subjected to pragmatic experimentation.
The unstated but carefully considered principles shape reality and
are not shaped and tested by and against reality. Use of pat
phrases and syntactical clichés divorced from different thoughts
to be said and different ways of thinking testifies to the prevailing
notion of an unstated, but secure and unchanging, reality behind
and beneath the accidents of context and circumstance.

The Mishnah derives its cogency not only from the order and
sequence of its sentences, whether episodic and miscellaneous or
sustained and protracted in proposition and discourse, but also
from the exposition of the topic at hand and from the
proposition concerning that topic that the framers of the
Mishnah wished to lay forth. The Mishnah's authorship
appealed to only a single logic of cogent discourse, and that was

the same logic that served for the presentation and demonstration of propositions: philosophical logic of a syllogistic character. The correspondence between the logic employed and the rhetoric that conveys that logic forms a powerful testimony to the cogency of the document as a whole. Finally, rhetoric joins to topic and logic in the expression of philosophy. The arcane and tedious detail of the Mishnah, as we shall see, comprises a set of statements on a program of philosophy and metaphysics, ethics and politics. When, in a later chapter, we ask about the system of the Mishnah, we shall understand why the framers of the Mishnah chose the forms of rhetoric and the modes of logic discourse that they did in order to convey the message that they wished to present through the construction of the system that they made.

I have now surveyed the traits of rhetorical forms and modes of logical cogency characteristic of a document. These have allowed us to see the Mishnah not as a random collection of this and that but as a well-crafted and carefully composed statement, one that can be read on its own terms and by rules that apply in particular to it. The systemic statement of the Mishnah, analyzed for a different purpose in chapter 10, shows us how carefully were chosen the rhetorical and logical conventions of the document. It suffices at this point to point out that analytical tools do permit us to demonstrate the autonomy of a document that, in the case of the Mishnah, exhibits cogent traits of aesthetics and intellect and shows itself to be a closed and coherent systemic statement. But the case at hand proves easy since the authorship of the Mishnah chose to set forth a topical account. What about the numerous writings of the canon of the dual Torah that are organized not along autonomous lines of topics and programs, but as commentary to another, prior writing? We turn to a sustained account of how the same methods used for the Mishnah sustain the argument that Midrash-compilations likewise form autonomous statements.

CHAPTER FOUR

Systemic Discourse as Scriptural Exegesis

The writings of the Judaism of the dual Torah derive from two documents, of which the Mishnah is the less well known. The better known one is, of course, the Hebrew Scriptures or Old Testament. An account of the kind of writing (rhetoric, logic of cogent discourse, topic) we find in Scripture, however, would provide no indicative data for the description of the documentary corpus of the Judaism of the dual Torah. The reason is that the modes of thought and composition in the Hebrew Scriptures, even in the Pentateuch, attracted no imitators or continuators in that particular Judaism. Authorships in other Judaisms treated Scripture as a model because what they wrote had to be set into relationship with the established, authoritative Scripture. Otherwise, in the setting of Israelite culture, the new writings could find no ready hearing. The fact was that from the formation of ancient Israelite Scripture into a holy book in Judaism, beginning with the aftermath of the return to Zion and the creation of the Torah-book in Ezra's time (ca. 450 B.C.E.), the established canon of revelation (whatever its contents) presented a considerable problem to coming generations.

Over the seven hundred years between the formation of the Pentateuch in ca. 500 B.C.E. to the appearance of the Mishnah in ca. 200 C.E., four conventional ways to accommodate new writings to the established canon of received Scripture came to

94

the fore. First and simplest, a writer would sign a famous name to his book, attributing his ideas to Enoch, Adam, Jacob's sons, Jeremiah, Baruch, and any number of others, down to Ezra. Second, he might also imitate the style of biblical Hebrew and so, obscuring the borders between Scripture and contemporary writings, try to creep into the canon by adopting the stylistic cloak of Scripture. Third, he would surely claim his work was inspired by God, a new revelation for an open canon. Fourth, at the very least, someone would link his opinions to biblical verses through the exegesis of the latter in line with the former, so that Scripture would validate his views. Most of the authors of the pseudepigraphic books of the Old Testament took the first route; the writers of the Dead Sea Psalms and other compositions, the second; the writers of some of the pseudepigraphs, the third; the school of Matthew, the fourth. From the time of Ezra to the Mishnah in the second century c.e., we have not got a single book, clearly claiming religious sanction and standing as a holy book and authority over Israel, the Jewish nation, that fails to conform to one or more of these conventions. In these ways the new found its place in the framework of the old. Accordingly, we may describe how Israelite culture over the period of six hundred years dealt with the intimidating authority and presence of Scripture. We find essentially two modes of accommodation: imitation and augmentation. The newcomers would either imitate the old or they would link the new to the established. But some authorships within the Judaism of the dual Torah addressed the problem of the written Torah in their own way.

First, the authorship of the Mishnah set forth a freestanding document, in its own language, within its own rhetoric, made cogent by a logic of sustained discourse that we can scarcely find in Scripture. That is not to suggest that authorships within the Judaism of the dual Torah proposed to ignore God's word to Moses at Sinai. Quite to the contrary. But they had to address the written Scriptures in a way that would suit their system-building program, and this fact presents no surprise whatsoever. They, too, undertook the composition of collections of biblical exegesis (midrashim). The analysis of the important compilations of scriptural exegeses (Midrash-compilations) shows us that through these compilations, too, authorships made original and important statements. Every compilation of Midrash-exegeses assigned to late antiquity except for one sets forth a systemic statement, built upon rhetoric and logic as autonomous of the Pentateuch's as of the Mishnah's. Analysis of the evidence of Midrash-compilations, as much as of the Mishnah and its documents of amplification and augmentation, provides insight into the move from writing to religion, in the case of the Judaism of the dual Torah. Here again, special reference to issues of rhetoric and logic permit us to see the documents that address Scripture as autonomous statements, each standing on its own and making its particular point in the manner its authorship found suitable.

In the context of systemic analysis, what we want to know about Midrash-compilations produced by the Judaism of the dual Torah, however, takes on its own definition. The questions that concern us run parallel to those that occupied us in our first encounter with the Mishnah. They are these: Is a Midrash-compilation an autonomous document, with its own distinctive message expressed through rhetoric and logic particular to its authorship? Or is such a document a composite of ready-made data as, for example, comments on verses of Scripture, viewed as the critical center of discourse? If the former is the case, then we may appeal to such writings in our search for the description of the religion, the Judaism of the dual Torah. The reason is that, in Midrash-compilations as much as in the Mishnah (and other writings), we may hope to find important components of the world view, significant accounts of the way of life, and consequential discourse on the "Israel" of the Judaism of the dual Torah. These compilations, therefore, will be seen to comprise components of the systemic statement, as much as does the Mishnah. But if such compilations present no sustained viewpoint, make no statement, address no "Israel," then they emerge as systemically inert. That is to say, they contain information but no viewpoint we can identify and spell out. They tell us what people were thinking about this and that, but they do not attest to the formation and composition of a Judaic system.

At stake in our reading of Midrash-compilations, just as in our encounter with the Mishnah, therefore, is the issue of whether or not we deal with writings that constitute documents of a religious system. We therefore have to employ the same methods that allowed us to reach the conclusion that the Mishnah forms a single, autonomous, freestanding statement, one that we may read as a cogent address to an "Israel" about an ineluctable question, one that supplies a self-evidently valid answer composed of a way of life, world view, and definition of an "Israel," that is, a Judaism in response to a critical issue. Admittedly, in the case of any Midrash-compilation, we may hardly claim that the document is freestanding, since all Midrash-compilations by definition repeatedly refer to and adduce in evidence verses of Scripture. But this obvious fact does not complicate our study. For if we can show that a document employs a sustained rhetoric of its own, a fixed set of forms, to make a sustained case of its own through resort to an appropriate logic of coherent discourse, then the utilization of Scripture by itself forms a merely adventitious fact of composition. That is to say, Scripture serves as part of the grammar and syntax of expression, perhaps even of thought. But just as grammar and syntax do not dictate what we think but only how we say what we think, and just as grammar and syntax permit an unlimited range of thought to come to full expression, so it is the case with Scripture. People could and did quote Scripture for every conceivable proposition and its opposite; Scripture then dictated not what they would say but only conventions of speech, that is to say, a syntax and grammar of a rather odd kind.

This brings us to ask how the method of documentary analysis deals with two Midrash-compilations, Sifra and Leviticus Rabbah, both of them dealing with the same book of the Pentateuch, namely, Leviticus. We ask of these documents precisely the same questions we addressed to the Mishnah, namely, whether they constitute written evidence that forms a statement of religion— one that, like the Mishnah, is coherent, systematic, systemic. In treating the rhetoric and logic of not one but two documents that appeal to the same biblical book, I am able to show that people said and did whatever they wanted to in their encounter with Scripture. In the case of one document, we find a sustained statement directed at systemic issues. In the case of the other, we find an equally sustained statement concerning theological issues. But whatever the respective authorships did, we have in hand methods to identify rhetorical and logical conventions, even where, in the respective Midrash-compilations, these conventions are entirely different from one another. I can also indicate the precise ways in which verses of Scripture found their place in the writing of the Judaism of the dual Torah—verses of Scripture as radically isolated components of speech but not as formative and definitive sentences. For, as we shall see, both documents appealed to the same piece of Scripture, but each authorship utilized verses of Scripture in whatever way it found interesting, never bound by the system, structure, and (not uncommonly) the sense of what they cited, except as it served the system, structure, and sense they proposed to set forth. In the present chapter we shall encounter Sifra, which makes a systemic statement profoundly shaped by the unfolding from the Mishnah of the Judaism of the dual Torah. There is no understanding of that writing without knowledge of the Mishnah. In the following chapter we shall deal with Leviticus Rabbah, a piece of writing that in the encounter with Leviticus makes a statement out of all relationship with the Mishnah, a statement that is not narrowly systemic but broadly theological in its focus and structure. In both cases we shall center on the same question, now fully exposed: Do we deal with a document of an autonomous character, one that makes its own statement in its own way, or do we have in hand a miscellany, a piece of writing that, from the viewpoint of systemic analysis of the documentary evidences of a religion, proves merely informative but in no way indicative?

Our survey of rhetoric and logic in Sifra will lead us to understand how a piece of writing functions within the framework of systemic discourse. We begin with the question of form-analysis. Can we identify the rhetorical patterning of language that predominates in the document, much as we found in the case of the Mishnah? A particular chapter of Sifra suffices to set on display the repertoire of forms on which our authorship has drawn. One peculiarity of the document requires clarification at the outset, or even the passage at hand will prove puzzling. It is that the authorship of Sifra acknowledges the existence of two prior writings, Scripture and the Mishnah. And, as we see in each of the 272 chapters of Sifra, the intent is to show the dependency of the Mishnah upon Scripture, a point that will occupy us later on. To point out the matter for later discussion, I put in boldface type citations of the Mishnah or the Tosefta occurring within any quotations below.

14. Parashat Vayyiqra Dibura Denedabah

Parashah 7

XIV:I.1. A. ["If his offering to the Lord is a burnt offering of birds, he shall choose [bring near] his offering from turtledoves or pigeons. The priest shall bring it to the altar, pinch off its head, and turn it into smoke on the altar; and its blood shall be drained out against the side of the altar. He shall remove its crop with its contents and cast it into the place of the ashes, at the east side of the altar. The priest shall tear it open by its wings, without severing it, and turn it into smoke on the altar, upon the wood that is on the fire. It is a burnt offering, an offering by fire, of pleasing odor to the Lord" (Lev. 1:14-17)]:

B. "[The priest] shall bring it [to the altar]:"

C. What is the sense of this statement?

D. Since it is said, "he shall choose [bring near] his offering from turtledoves or pigeons," one might have supposed that there can be no fewer than two sets of birds.

E. Accordingly, Scripture states, "[The priest] shall bring it [to the altar]" to indicate, [by reference to the "it,"] that even a single pair suffices.

Reduced to its simplest syntactic traits, the form consists of the citation of a clause of a verse, followed by secondary amplification of that clause. We may call this *commentary form*, in that the rhetorical requirement is citation plus amplification. Clearly, the form sustains a variety of expressions similar to the one at hand: "What is the sense of this statement . . . since it is said . . . accordingly Scripture states. . . . " But for our purposes there is no need to differentiate within the commentary form.

2. A. "The priest shall bring it to the altar, pinch off its head:"

B. Why does Scripture say, "The priest . . . pinch off . . . "?

C. This teaches that the act of pinching off the head should be done only by a priest.

D. But is the contrary to that proposition not a matter of logic:

E. if in the case of a beast of the flock, to which the act of slaughter at the north side of the altar is assigned, the participation of a priest in particular is not assigned, to the act of pinching the neck, to which the act of slaughter at the north side of the altar is not assigned, surely should not involve the participation of the priest in particular!

F. That is why it is necessary for Scripture to say, "The priest . . . pinch off . . . ,"

G. so as to teach that the act of pinching off the head should be done only by a priest.

3. A. Might one compose an argument to prove that one should pinch the neck by using a knife?

B. For lo, it is a matter of logic.

C. If to the act of slaughter [of a beast as a sacrifice], for which the participation of a priest is not required, the use of a correct utensil is required, for the act of pinching the neck, for which the participation of a priest indeed is required, surely should involve the requirement of using a correct implement!

D. That is why it is necessary for Scripture to say, "The priest . . . pinch off. . . . "

4. A. Said R. Aqiba, "Now would it really enter anyone's mind that a non-priest should present an offering on the altar?

B. "Then why is it said, 'The priest . . . pinch off . . . '?

C. "This teaches that the act of pinching the neck must be done by the priest using his own finger [and not a utensil]."

5. A. Might one suppose that the act of pinching may be done either at the head [up by the altar] or at the foot [on the pavement down below the altar]?

B. It is a matter of logic:

C. If in the case of an offering of a beast, which, when presented as a sin-offering is slaughtered above [at the altar itself] but when slaughtered as a burnt offering is killed below [at the pavement, below the altar], in the case of an offering of fowl, since when presented as a sin-offering it is slaughtered down below, surely in the case of a burnt offering it should be done down below as well!

D. That is why it was necessary for Scripture to make explicit [that it is killed up by the altar itself:] "The priest shall bring it to the altar, pinch off its head, and turn it into smoke on the altar."

E. The altar is explicitly noted with respect to turning the offering into smoke and also to pinching off the head.

F. Just as the offering is turned into smoke up above, at the altar itself, so the pinching off of the head is to be done up above, at the altar itself.

The form at hand is to be characterized as a dialectical exegetical argument, in which we move from point to point in a protracted, yet very tight, exposition of a proposition. The proposition is both implicit and explicit. The implicit proposition is that "logic" does not suffice, a matter vastly spelled out in my book, *Uniting the Dual Torah*. The explicit proposition concerns the subject matter at hand. We may identify the traits of this form very simply: citation of a verse or clause plus a proposition that interprets that phrase, then "it is a matter of logic," followed by the demonstration that logic is insufficient for the determination of taxa.

XIV:II.1. A. " . . . pinch off its head:"

B. The pinching off of the head is done at the shoulder.

C. Might one suppose that it may be done at any other location?

D. It is a matter of logic. Lo, I shall argue as follows:

E. Here an act of pinching off the neck is stated, and elsewhere we find the same [Lev. 5:8: "He shall bring them to the priest, who shall offer first the one for the sin offering, pinching its head at the nape without severing it"].

F. Just as pinching off at the neck in that passage is to be done at the nape of the neck, so pinching off at the neck in the present context is to be done at the nape of the neck.

G. Perhaps the analogy is to be drawn differently, specifically, just as the pinching stated in that other passage involves pinching the neck without dividing the bird [Lev. 5:8: "without severing it"], so the importance of the analogy is to yield the same rule here.

H. In that case, the priest would pinch the neck without severing it.

I. Accordingly, [the ambiguous analogy is such as to require] Scripture to state, " . . . pinch off its head."

Here we have an example of the dialectical exegesis of the limitations of logic for definition of taxa.

2. A. "[turn it into smoke on the altar;] and its blood shall be drained out:"

B. Can one describe matters in such a way?

C. Specifically, after the carcass is turned into smoke, can one drain out the blood?

D. But one pinches the neck in accord with the way in which one turns it into smoke:

E. Just as we find that the turning of the carcass into smoke is done up to the head by itself and then the body by itself, so in the act of pinching the neck, the head is by itself and the body is by itself.

3. A. And how do we know that in the case of turning a carcass into smoke, the head is done by itself?

B. When Scripture says, "The priest [shall tear it open by its wings, without severing it,] and turn it into smoke on the altar" (Lev. 1:17),

C. lo, the turning of the body into smoke is covered by that statement.

D. Lo, when Scripture states here, "pinch off its head, and turn it into smoke on the altar," it can only mean that the head is to be turned into smoke by itself.

E. Now, just as we find that the turning of the carcass into smoke is done up to the head by itself and then the body by itself, so in the act of pinching the neck, the héad is by itself and the body is by itself.

XIV:II.2 and 3 present in a rather developed statement the simple exegetical form. The formal requirement is not obscured, however, since all we have is the citation of a clause followed by secondary amplification. This version of commentary form obviously cannot be seen as identical to the other, but so far as the dictates of rhetoric are concerned, there is no material difference, since the variations affect only the secondary amplification of the basic proposition, and in both cases the basic proposition is set forth by the citation of the verse or clause followed by a sentence or two of amplification.

XIV:III.1. A. " . . . and its blood shall be drained out [against the side of the altar]:"

B. all of its blood: he takes hold of the head and the body and drains the blood out of both pieces.

This is commentary form.

2. A. " . . . against the side of the altar:"

B. not on the wall of the ramp up to the altar, and not on the wall of the foundation, nor on the wall of the courtyard.

3. A. It is to be on the upper half of the wall.

B. Might one suppose it may be on the lower half of the wall?

C. It is a matter of logic: in the case of the sacrifice of a beast, which, if done as a sin-offering, has its blood tossed on the upper part of the wall, and if done as a burnt offering, has its blood tossed on the lower part of the wall,

D. in the case of the sacrifice of a bird, since, if it is offered as a sin offering, the blood is tossed at the lower half of the wall, shall logic not dictate that if it is offered as a burnt offering, its blood shall be tossed on the lower part of the wall as well?

E. That is why it is necessary for Scripture to frame matters in this way:

F. "The priest shall bring it to the altar, pinch off its head, and turn it into smoke on the altar; and its blood shall be drained out against the side of the altar,"

G. the altar is noted with respect to turning the carcass into smoke and also with reference to the draining of the blood.

H. Just as the act of turning the carcass into smoke is done at the topside of the altar, so the draining of the blood is done at the topside of the altar.

This is the dialectical exegetical form. Now we come to a third usage.

4. A. How does the priest do it?

B. The priest went up on the ramp and went around the circuit. He came to the southeastern corner. He would wring off its head from its neck and divide the head from the body. And he drained off its blood onto the wall of the altar [M. Zeb. 6:5B-E].

C. If one did it from the place at which he was standing and downward by a cubit, it is valid. R. Simeon and R. Yohanan ben Beroqah say, "The entire deed was done only at the top of the altar" [T. Zeb. 7:9C-D].

What we have now is the verbatim citation of passages of the Mishnah and the Tosefta, joined to its setting in the exegetical framework of Sifra by some sort of joining formula. We shall call this formal convention *Mishnah-citation-form*. Its formal requirement is simply an appropriate link.

XIV:IV.1. A. "He shall remove its crop [with its contents and cast it into the place of the ashes, at the east side of the altar]:"

B. this refers to the bird's crop.

C. Might one suppose that one should extract the crop with a knife and remove it surgically?

D. Scripture says, " . . . with its contents."

E. He should remove it with its contents [including the innards, or, alternatively, the feathers].

F. Abba Yosé b. Hanan says, "He should remove the intestines with it."

As a variation on commentary form, we have secondary development at C, might one suppose? I am not inclined to think a sizable catalogue of variations on commentary form will materially advance our inquiry.

This one example allows us to identify the forms of Sifra. A simple formal program, consisting of three types of forms, served for every statement in the illustrative material surveyed above. An author of a pericope could make use of only one or more of these three forms: commentary, dialectical, and citation forms. The commentary form consists of a phrase of Scripture followed by some words of amplification; the dialectical, the largest and most distinctive category, involves a sustained argument; and the citation form provides for the verbatim citation of a passage of the Mishnah. To summarize results presented elsewhere, the following chart tells us the proportions of each form to the document as a whole:

Form	Number of Entries	Percentage of the Whole
Commentary	121	55%
Dialectical	57	26%
Citation	42	19%
Total	**220**	**100%**

It follows that in form, Sifra's authorship planned to—and did—produce a commentary to the book of Leviticus, and that that commentary would encompass two major, though not ubiquitous, concerns. On the basis merely of the formal characteristics of the document, we may say that these were, first, the demonstration that if we wish to classify things, we must follow the taxa dictated by Scripture rather than rely solely upon the traits of the things we wish to classify, and, second, the citation of passages of the Mishnah or the Tosefta in the setting of Scripture.

The forms of the document admirably expressed the polemical purpose of the authorship at hand: (1) it wished to prove that a taxonomy resting on the traits of things without reference to Scripture's classifications cannot serve; (2) it wished to restate the oral Torah in the setting of the written Torah; (3) it wished to accomplish the whole by rewriting the written Torah. The dialectical form accomplished the first purpose, the citation form the second, and the commentary form the third.

What about the logics? Counting each entry as a single item presents a gross and simple picture of the proportions of the types of logics we have catalogued. Since numerous entries in each of the catalogues encompass more than a single item, the understatement of the numbers of examples in any one catalogue will be balanced by understatements of the numbers of examples in the other catalogues. Overall, my count is as follows:

Type of Logic	Number of Entries	Percentage of the Whole
Philosophical	73	30.4%
Teleological	1	0.4%
Fixed Associative	43	17.9%
Methodical-Analytical	123	51.0%
Total	**240**	**99.7%**

The operative logics are mainly propositional (approximately 82 percent) inclusive of philosophical, teleological, and methodical-analytical compositions. That fact tells us our authorship has not set forth a commentary but rather has made use of Scripture in order to write its statement, and, as we shall see presently, that statement addresses an issue of profound consequence for the system of the Judaism of the dual Torah.

Despite the predominance of commentary form, in fact, we deal in Sifra with something other than an episodic commentary governed by the amplificatory task of rereading Scripture. Quite to the contrary, in Sifra an authorship has chosen to write with Scripture. What makes me take this position? The indicative consideration is simple and appeals to negative validation. An authorship intending what we now call a commentary will have found paramount use for the logic of fixed association, yet that logic clearly served only a modest purpose in the context of the document as a whole. Our authorship by contrast developed a tripartite rhetorical-logical program. First, it wished to demonstrate the limitations of the logic of hierarchical classification, such as predominates in the Mishnah, which forms a constant theme of the methodical-analytical logic. It proposed, second, to restate the Mishnah within the context of Scripture, that is, to rewrite the written Torah to make a place for the oral Torah. This is worked out in the logic of propositional discourse. And, finally, it wished in this process of rewriting to re-present the whole Torah as a cogent and unified document, and through the logic of fixed association they did in fact re-present the Torah. The three logics correspond, in their setting within the inner structure of cogent discourse, to the three paramount purposes to which our authorship devoted Sifra. This result corresponds to the one for form-analysis as well.

Let me now expand upon the argumentative and propositional character of the logic of cogent discourse. The logics of cogent discourse in Sifra prove familiar to us. But one stands out, the one of methodical analysis, which repeatedly asks a single question of a vast range of diverse material. The net effect is to impart to a diverse text, covering many topics, a coherent character. Asking the same question of many things and producing answers of the same sort, utilizing rhetoric of a single pattern, thus turns discrete sentences into a cogent whole, even while not appealing to a common sense or a common proposition for that purpose. There are two paramount, recurrent models of methodical analysis. The first I call *inclusionary/exclusionary*, in that we repeatedly ask whether the law encompasses case X, and if so, does it also encompass case Y? (Or, the language of the case at hand excludes case X and also case Y.) What is at stake in this methodical analysis is the transformation of a case into an encompassing rule, and that is accomplished by generalizing on the case and so discovering, on the basis of the language of Scripture, both its extent and also its limits. The second is the demonstration that the taxonomic system of the Mishnah, which appeals solely to the indicative traits of things and not to Scripture's classification, is insufficient to establish rules.

Let me give a single instance from Sifra of the first methodical-analytical pattern, the inclusionary/exclusionary exercise, and the second, the insufficiency of logic unaffected by scriptural principles of category-formation or taxonomy, and the reader will in other examples given elsewhere in this book find counterparts—sometimes formally, always intellectually and logically. The operative rhetoric here is "I know only this . . . how about that. . . . ?"

> **CLXIV:I.1.** A. "And whoever sits on anything on which he who has the discharge has sat will be unclean [shall wash his clothes and bathe himself in water and be unclean until the evening]" (Lev. 15:6).
>
> B. I know only that this is the case if he sits on it and [actually] touches it. [That is to say, if the Zab, the one unclean by a flux, is in direct contact with the chair, then he imparts uncleanness to it.]
>
> C. How do I know that [if the Zab sits on] ten chairs, one on the other, and even [if he sits on] top of a heavy stone, [what is underneath is clean]? [If the chair bears the weight of the Zab, even though the Zab is not touching the chair, being separated by a stone, for instance, the chair is made unclean.]
>
> D. Scripture says, "And he who sits on the utensil on which the Zab has sat will be unclean"
>
> E. In any place in which the Zab sits and imparts uncleanness, the clean person sits and becomes unclean.
>
> F. I know only that when the Zab sits on it, and the Zab is there [that it is unclean]. How do I know that I should treat the empty as the full one?
>
> G. Scripture says, "Utensil"—to treat the empty like the full.
>
> H. I know only that this [rule concerning transmission of the Zab's uncleanness merely through applying the burden of his weight, even without his actually being in contact with the object] applies to the chair. How do I know that it applies to the saddle?

Now we shift to the critique of classification based on the hierarchical logic of taxonomy as it is evidenced in the Mishnah:

I. And it is logical:

J. If we have found that Scripture does not distinguish between the one who carries and the one who is carried in respect to sitting, so we should not distinguish between the one who is carried and the one who carries with respect to the saddle.

K. But what difference does it make to me that Scripture did not distinguish between carrying and being carried in respect to the chair?

L. For it did not distinguish touching it and carrying it.

M. Should we not distinguish between carrying and being carried with reference to the saddle,

N. for lo, it has indeed distinguished touching it from carrying it?

O. Scripture [accordingly is required] to state, "A utensil"— to encompass even the saddle.

Here is a fine example of a mode of logic that establishes its fixed and formal character through repetition. When we see enough cases of what we have in hand, we realize that the logic of methodical analysis, of asking the same question many times, does serve in Sifra to establish a profound sense of cogency and coherence among topically diverse discourses. The inclusionary method will utilize diverse rhetoric, but it always is characterized by the intent to encompass within a single law a variety of cases.

The intent is, therefore, the same as that of the Mishnah, namely, to show the rule governing diverse cases. The contrary exercise, the one that excludes examples from a rule, is to be stipulated. That, of course, is also what the framers of the Mishnah propose through their making of lists of like and unlike things and their determining of the rule that governs them all. So when the framers of the Mishnah appeal to the making of lists, they do no more, and no less, than is accomplished by our authorship in its exegetical exercises of exclusion and inclusion. Here, therefore, our authorship demonstrates through rewriting the written Torah the possibility of doing precisely what the oral Torah is meant to do. The judgment on modes of cogent discourse operative in the Mishnah is tacitly negative; we do things this way because this is the way to do them, that is to say, through appeal to and amplification of the written Torah—not through appeal to and ordering of traits of things sorted out independently of the written Torah.

Now that we have briefly examined the way in which an analysis of the rhetoric and logic of the document coheres and shown that in Sifra a highly restricted repetoire of formalization of language and thought dictated how people would make their statement, we have to turn to the statement that our authorship has made. For we should miss the exemplary value of the present exercise as a mode of reading writing for the study of religion if we did not allow the systemic statement to make its appearance. We should be left with a merely formal exercise, identifying recurrent traits of expression and thought but ignoring the systemic meaning and weight of those traits.

What we find in Sifra is nothing less than a solution to a longstanding problem in the theology, literature, and law of the Judaism of the dual Torah. The problem was posed by the character and standing of the Mishnah. From the moment of its promulgation as the basis for the law of Judaism, the Mishnah was represented as authoritative and, therefore, in the context of Israel's life, as enjoying the standing of *torah,* divine revelation, yet clearly not like The Torah revealed by God to Moses at Sinai. There were two solutions to that problem: the one of the succeeding documents that undertook the exegesis, amplification, and application of the Mishnah; the other presented by the authorship of Sifra. The solution to that problem worked out by the authorities succeeding the Mishnah, namely, the authorships of the Tosefta, ca. 300 c.e., the Talmud of the Land of Israel or Yerushalmi, ca. 400 c.e., and the Talmud of Babylonia or Bavli, ca. 600 c.e., was to treat the word or conception *torah* as a common noun signifying, among other things, process, status, or classification. Then the Mishnah found ample place for itself within the capacious classification *torah.*

The solution to that problem worked out by the authorship of Sifra was to treat the word *torah* as solely a proper noun, The Torah, but *also* to insist that the Mishnah found a fully legitimate position within The Torah. That solution required the authorship of the Mishnah to undertake a profound and thoroughgoing critique of the logic of the Mishnah, both as that logic dictated the correct joining of two or more sentences into a cogent thought and as that logic governed the formation of propositions for analysis. In fact, the authorship of Sifra set

forth a systematic critique of the Mishnah in its principal
definitive traits: its topical program and arrangement, its
principles of cogent discourse, and its logic of critical analysis
and probative demonstration of propositions. It furthermore set
forth a sizable portion of the Mishnah's contents, as these
pertained to the book of Leviticus, within its own definition of
the correct topical program and arrangement, its own principles
of cogent discourse, and its own logic of critical analysis and
proof. These two solutions came to full expression, one
paramount in the several works of exegesis and amplification
that adopted the Mishnah, the oral Torah, as the basic text, the
other paramount in Sifra. Sifra's authorship explored profound
issues of the fundamental and generative structure of right
thought, yielding, as a matter of fact, both Scripture and the
Mishnah. This approach insisted that *torah* always was a proper
noun. There was, and is, only The Torah. But The Torah
demanded expansion and vast amplification. When we know the
principles of logical structure and especially those of hierarchical classification that animate The Torah, we can undertake part
of the task of expansion and amplification, that is, join in the
processes of thought that, in the mind of God, yielded The
Torah. For when we know how God thought in giving The
Torah to Moses at Sinai and so can account for the classifications
and their ordering in the very creation of the world, we can
ourselves enter into The Torah and participate in its processes.

Sifra's authorship conducts a sustained polemic against the
failure of the Mishnah to cite Scripture in that it systematically
links its ideas to Scripture through the medium of formal
demonstration by exegesis. Sifra's rhetorical exegesis, as we
noted in treating Sifra's forms, follows a standard redactional
form: Scripture will be cited, then a statement will be made about
its meaning or a statement of law correlative to that Scripture will
be given; that statement sometimes cites the Mishnah, often
verbatim. Finally, the authors of Sifra invariably state, "Now is
that not (merely) logical?" And the point of that statement will
be, "Can this position not be gained through the working of
mere logic, based upon facts supplied (to be sure) by Scripture?"
The polemical power of Sifra lies in its repetitive demonstration
that the stated position, citation of a Mishnah-pericope, is not
only not the product of logic, but is, and only can be, the product

of exegesis of Scripture. Sifra's writers carried to a much more profound level of thought the critique of the Mishnah. They did so by rethinking the logical foundations of the entire Torah.

To understand how they accomplished that intellectual feat, let us briefly review what we have already established concerning the Mishnah's logic of cogent discourse, which establishes propositions that rest upon philosophical bases, for example, through the proposal of a thesis and the composition of a list of facts that prove the thesis. This, to us entirely familiar, Western mode of scientific expression through the classification of data that earlier I have called the science of making lists (*Listenwis-senschaft*) is exemplified by the Mishnah. The issue at hand is one of connection, that is, not of fact (such as is conveyed by the statement of the meaning of a verse or a clause of a verse) but of the relationship between one fact and another. This relationship or connection is shown in a conclusion, different from the established facts of two or more sentences, that we propose to draw when we set up as a sequence two or more facts and claim out of that sequence to propose a proposition different from, and transcending, the facts at hand.

If we ask ourselves what is at stake in the internal debate before us, we have to revert to the issue of the source and authority of the oral Torah, to which I referred at the outset. Not only does the authorship of the Mishnah not cite Scripture; it also imposes its own taxonomic scheme on the facts of Scripture, defining and working out its own conception of the classification of things. Along these lines, for instance, Mishnah-tractate Avot, 250 C.E., represents the authority of the sages cited in Avot as autonomous of Scripture. These authorities in Avot do not cite verses of Scripture, but what they themselves say constitutes a statement of the Torah. There can be no clearer way of saying that what these authorities present in and of itself falls into the classification of the Torah. This fact then defines what is at stake in the dispute between the authorship of the Mishnah and the later authorship of Sifra. It concerns the teaching of the authorities of the oral Torah derived from authorities who stand in a direct line to Sinai. The Mishnah's authorities maintain that they—and with them the oral Torah—enjoy the standing and authority of God's revelation to Moses at Sinai and form part of the Torah of Sinai. The authorship of Sifra shows not only that

that is not possible but also that the center and soul of the
Mishnah's processes of thought, the work of correct classification (ensuring that the right rule applies to the right object,
person, action, and circumstance), derive from Scripture's
classifications, not from those made up and treated as
self-evident by the Mishnah's philosophers.

The solution to the problem of the authority of the Mishnah,
that is to say, its relationship to Scripture, was worked out in the
period after the closure of the Mishnah. Since no one now could
credibly claim to sign the name of Ezra or Adam to a book of this
kind, and since biblical Hebrew had provided no apologetic
aesthetics whatsoever, the only two options lay elsewhere. They
were, first, to provide a story of the origin of the contents of the
oral Torah, beginning with the Mishnah, and, second, to link
each allegation of the oral Torah, again starting with the
Mishnah, through processes of biblical (not Mishnaic) exegesis,
to verses of the Scriptures. Sifra's authorship chose the second
way, and that defines the stake in their debate with the Mishnah's
writers. In this way the authorship would establish for the
Mishnah the standing that the uses to which the document was to
be put demanded for it: a place in the canon of Israel, a
legitimate relationship to the Torah of Moses. And with the
notion that the Mishnah and later writings that amplified its law
formed a component of the oral Torah, the writing down of the
oral Torah began. Let me now explain how the Sifra's
authorship accomplished its purposes.

To grasp Sifra's authorship's critique of the Mishnah, we have
now to review the Mishnah's fundamental trait of intellect. The
system of philosophy expressed through concrete and detailed
law presented by the Mishnah consists of a coherent logic and
topic, a cogent world view and comprehensive way of living. It is
a world view that speaks of transcendent things, a way of life in
response to the supernatural meaning of what is done, a
heightened and deepened perception of the sanctification of
Israel in deed and in deliberation. That paramount concern
accounts for the centrality of classification, the appeal of the
logic of hierarchical classification in the demonstration of
comparisons and contrasts, in the formation of the thought of
the document. For sanctification in the Mishnah's system means
establishing the stability, order, regularity, predictability, and

reliability of Israel in the world of nature and supernature, in particular at moments and in contexts of danger. And it is through assigning to all things their rightful name, through setting all things in their proper positions, that we discover the laws of stability, order, regularity, and predictability. Danger means instability, disorder, irregularity, uncertainty, and betrayal. Each topic of the system as a whole takes up a critical and indispensable moment or context of social being. Through what is said in regard to each of the Mishnah's principal topics, what the system as a whole wishes to declare is fully expressed. Yet if the parts severally and jointly give the message of the whole, the whole cannot exist without all of the parts, so well joined and carefully crafted are they all.

At issue between the framers of the Mishnah and the authorship of Sifra are the correct sources of classification. The framers of the Mishnah effect their taxonomy through the traits of things. The authorship of Sifra insists that the source of classification is Scripture. Sifra's authorship time and again demonstrates that classification cannot be carried out without Scripture's data, and that, it must follow, hierarchical arguments based on extrascriptural taxa always fail.

Let me present a single sustained example of how Sifra's authorship rejects the principles of the logic of hierarchical classification *as these are worked out by the framers of the Mishnah.* I emphasize that the critique applies to the way in which a shared logic is worked out by the other authorship. For it is not the principle that like things follow the same rule, unlike things, the opposite rule, that is at stake. Nor is the principle of hierarchical classification embodied in the argument *a fortiori* at issue. What our authorship disputes is that we can classify things on our own by appealing to their traits or indicative characteristics, that is, utterly without reference to Scripture. The argument is simple. On our own, we cannot classify species into genera. Everything is different from everything else in some way. But Scripture tells us what things are like what other things for what purposes; hence, Scripture imposes on things the definitive classifications—that and not traits we discern in the things themselves. When we see the nature of the critique, we shall have a clear picture of what is at stake when we examine, in some detail, precisely how the Mishnah's logic does its work. That is why at the outset I present a complete composition in which Sifra's authorship tests the modes of classification characteristic of the Mishnah, resting as they do on the traits of things viewed out of the context of Scripture's categories of things.

5. Parashat Vayyiqra Dibura Denedabah Parashah 3
V:I.1. A. "[If his offering is] a burnt offering [from the herd, he shall offer a male without blemish; he shall offer it at the door of the tent of meeting, that he may be accepted before the Lord; he shall lay his hand upon the head of the burnt offering, and it shall be accepted for him to make atonement for him]" (Lev. 1:2):

B. Why does Scripture refer to a burnt offering in particular?

C. For one might have taken the view that all of the specified grounds for the invalidation of an offering should apply only to the burnt offering that is brought as a free will offering.

D. But how should we know that the same grounds for invalidation apply also to a burnt offering that is brought in fulfillment of an obligation [for instance, the burnt offering that is brought for a leper who is going through a rite of purification, or the bird brought by a woman who has given birth as part of her purification rite, Lev. 14, 12, respectively]?

E. It is a matter of logic.

F. Bringing a burnt offering as a free will offering and bringing a burnt offering in fulfillment of an obligation [are parallel to one another and fall into the same classification].

G. Just as a burnt offering that is brought as a free will offering is subject to all of the specified grounds for invalidation, so to a burnt offering brought in fulfillment of an obligation, all the same grounds for invalidation should apply.

H. No, [that reasoning is not compelling. For the two species of the genus, burnt offering, are not wholly identical and can be distinguished, on which basis we may also maintain that the grounds for invalidation that pertain to the one do not necessarily apply to the other. Specifically:] if you have taken that position with respect to the burnt offering brought as a free will offering, for which there is no equivalent, will you take the same position with regard to the burnt offering brought in fulfillment of an obligation, for which there is an equivalent? [For if one is obligated to bring a burnt offering by reason of obligation and cannot afford a beast, one may bring birds, as at Lev. 14:22, but if one is bringing a free will offering, a less expensive form of the offering may not serve.]

I. Accordingly, since there is the possibility in the case of the burnt offering brought in fulfillment of an obligation, in which case there is an acceptable equivalent [to the more expensive beast, through the less expensive birds], all of the specified grounds for invalidation [which apply to the in any case more expensive burnt offering brought as a free will offering] should not apply at all.

J. That is why in the present passage, Scripture refers simply to "burnt offering," [and without further specification, the meaning is then simple:] all the same are the burnt offering brought in fulfillment of an obligation and a burnt offering brought as a free will offering in that all of the same grounds for invalidation of the beast that pertain to the one pertain also to the other.

2. A. And how do we know that the same rules of invalidation of a blemished beast apply also in the case of a beast that is designated in substitution of a beast sanctified for an offering [in line with Lev. 27:10, so that, if one states that a given, unconsecrated beast is to take the place of a beast that has already been consecrated, the already-consecrated beast remains in its holy status, and the beast to which reference is made also becomes consecrated]?

B. The matter of bringing a burnt offering and the matter of bringing a substituted beast fall into the same classification [since both are offerings that in the present instance will be consumed upon the altar, and, consequently, they fall under the same rule as to invalidating blemishes].

C. Just as the entire protocol of blemishes apply to the one, so in the case of the beast that is designated as a substitute, the same invalidating blemishes pertain.

D. No, if you have invoked that rule in the case of the burnt offering, in which case no status of sanctification applies should the beast that is designated as a burnt offering be blemished in some permanent way, will you make the same statement in the case of a beast that is designated as a substitute? For in the case of a substituted beast, the status of sanctification applies even though the beast bears a permanent blemish! [So the two do not fall into the same classification after all, since to begin with one cannot sanctify a permanently blemished beast, which beast can never enter the status of sanctification, but through an act of substitution, a permanently blemished beast can be placed into the status of sanctification.]

E. Since the status of sanctification applies [to a substituted beast] even though the beast bears a permanent blemish, all of the specified grounds for invalidation as a matter of logic should not apply to it.

F. That is why in the present passage, Scripture refers simply to "burnt offering," [and without further specification, the meaning is then simple:] all the same are the burnt offering brought in fulfillment of an obligation and a burnt offering brought as a substitute for an animal designated as holy, in that all of the same grounds for invalidation of the beast that pertain to the one pertain also to the other.

3. A. And how do we know [that the protocol of blemishes that apply to the burnt offering brought as a free will offering apply also to] animals that are subject to the rule of a sacrifice as a peace offering?

B. It is a matter of logic. The matter of bringing a burnt offering and the matter of bringing animals that are subject to the rule of a sacrifice as a peace offering fall into the same classification [since both are offerings and, consequently under the same rule as to invalidating blemishes].

C. Just as the entire protocol of blemishes apply to the one, so in the case of animals that are subject to the rule of a sacrifice as a peace offering, the same invalidating blemishes pertain.

D. And it is furthermore a matter of an argument *a fortiori*, as follows:

E. If to a burnt offering which is valid when in the form of a bird, [which is inexpensive], the protocol of invalidating blemishes apply, to peace offerings, which are not valid when brought in the form of a bird, surely the same protocol of invalidating blemishes should also apply!

F. No, if you have applied that rule to a burnt offering, in which case females are not valid for the offering as male beasts are, will you say the same of peace offerings? For female beasts as much as male beasts may be brought for sacrifice in the status of the peace offering. [The two species may be distinguished from one another].

G. Since it is the case that female beasts as much as male beasts may be brought for sacrifice in the status of the peace offering, the protocol of invalidating blemishes should not apply to a beast designated for use as peace offerings.

H. That is why in the present passage, Scripture refers simply to "burnt offering," [and without further specification, the meaning is then simple:] all the same are the burnt offering brought in fulfillment of an obligation and an animal designated under the rule of peace offerings, in that all of the same grounds for invalidation of the beast that pertain to the one pertain also to the other.

The systematic exercise proves that the same rules of invalidation apply throughout for beasts that serve in three classifications of offerings—burnt offerings, substitutes, and peace offerings. The comparison of the two kinds of burnt offerings, voluntary and obligatory, shows that they are sufficiently different from each other that, as a matter of logic, what pertains to the one need not apply to the other. Then come the differences between an animal that is consecrated and one that is designated as a substitute for one that is consecrated. Finally, we distinguish between the applicable rules of the sacrifice; a burnt offering yields no meat for the person in behalf of whom the offering is made, while one sacrificed under the rule of peace offerings does. What is satisfying, therefore, is that we run the changes on three fundamental differences and show that in each case, the differences between like things are greater than the similarities. I cannot imagine a more perfect exercise in the applied and practical logic of comparison and contrast.

We may now state very simply the systemic position set forth by Sifra. The authorship of Sifra concurs in the fundamental principle that sanctification consists in calling things by their rightful name, or, in philosophical language, discovering the classification of things and determining the rule that governs diverse things. The authorship differs from the view of the Mishnah's concerns in *the origins of taxa:* How do we know what diverse things form a single classification of things? Taxa originate in scripture. Accordingly, at stake in the critique of the Mishnah are not the principles of logic necessary for under-standing the construction and inner structure of creation. All parties among sages concurred that the inner structure set forth by a logic of classification alone could sustain the system of ordering all things in proper place and under the proper rule. The like belongs with the like and conforms to the rule governing the like; the unlike goes over to the opposite and conforms to the opposite rule. When we make lists of the like, we know the rule governing all the items on those lists, respectively, as well as the opposite rule governing all items sufficiently unlike to be placed on other lists. That rigorously philosophical logic of analysis, comparison, and contrast served because it was the only logic that could serve a system that proposed to make the statement concerning order and right array.

We may state the upshot of Sifra's authorship's systemic discourse in a very simple way. Time and again Sifra's authorship demonstrates that the formation of classifications based on monothetic taxonomy, that is to say, traits that are not only common to both items but that are shared throughout both items subject to comparison and contrast, simply will not serve. For at every point at which someone alleges uniform, that is to say, monothetic likeness, Sifra's authorship will demonstrate difference. Then how to proceed? By appeal to some shared traits as a basis for classification: this is not like that, and that is not like this, but the indicative trait that both exhibit is such and so—which is polythetic taxonomy. The self-evident problem in accepting differences among things and in insisting, nonetheless, on their monomorphic character for purposes of comparison and contrast cannot be set aside. If I can adduce in evidence for a shared classification of things only a few traits among many characteristic of each thing, then what stops me from treating all things alike?

Polythetic taxonomy opens the way to an unlimited excercise in finding what diverse things have in common and in imposing, for that reason, one rule on everything. Then the very working of *Listenwissenschaft* as a tool of analysis, differentiation, comparison, contrast and the descriptive determination of rules yields the opposite of what is desired: chaos, not order; a mass of exceptions, not rules; a world of examples, each subject to its own regulation, not a world of order and proportion, composition, and stability. That furthermore explains the appeal to Scripture and, in our case, to Leviticus. God made the world. God through Adam called all things by their rightful names, placing each in its correct place in relationship to all others. We have the power to place all things into relationship with all others of the same genus because Scripture has endowed us with that power. The foundations of all scientific knowledge, achieved through the analytical processes of comparison and contrast, classification and differentiation, yielding the rule for the like, the opposite rule for the unlike, rest upon Scripture. That is why, quite by the way, the Mishnah cannot make its statement independent of Scripture, but only within the framework of Scripture.

We now see how, through the reform of practical reason, our authorship united the dual Torah and uncovered the single, uniform foundations for the multiform and polythetic realm of creation, inclusive of the celebration of creation in the cult that the book of Leviticus sets forth. Having said that, I may conclude with the obvious fact that only through attending to the book of Leviticus, read as the priestly authorship of the Priestly Code wanted it read in relationship with Genesis 1:1–2:4, and no other book of the Pentateuch, can our authorship have made the point that it wished to make. It was, in an odd way, a generalization particular to its example. But the example encompassed the very structure of creation and the foundation of all nature—and supernature.

The methods illustrated in the analysis of Sifra should not be obscured by these results. We wanted to know whether our document resorts to a limited repertoire of forms and patterns of language, on which basis we may claim that our authorship has made clear-cut choices as to how it proposes to compose its document. We indeed have identified a restricted formal program. We need hardly observe that this program in no way served the plan of the authorship of the Mishnah, which found useful not a single one of the forms paramount in Sifra. We further wanted to find out whether a single paramount logic of cogent discourse served the authorship of this "commentary" to Leviticus, and, as we recall, we discovered precisely that, namely, the one of methodical analysis. Accordingly, we have shown that this document stands on its own and differs from the Mishnah in rhetoric and logic. On that basis, we may fairly claim to have shown methods that demonstrate the autonomy of the Midrash-compilation just now surveyed. We can also state with some precision the message that this authorship proposes to deliver. And a clear statement of what is at stake allows us entry into the religious world view that is represented and invoked by Sifra's writers. The authorship of Sifra never called into

question the self-evident validity of taxonomic logic. Its critique
is addressed only to how the Mishnah's framers delineate and
identify the origins of taxa. But that critique proves fundamental to the case that the authorship proposed to make.

For, intending to demonstrate that The Torah was a proper
noun, and that everything that was valid came to expression in
the single, cogent statement of The Torah, the authorship at
hand identified the fundamental issue. It is the debate over the
way we know things. In insisting, in agreement with the framers
of the Mishnah, that there are not only cases but also rules, not
only species but also genera, the authorship of Sifra also made its
case in behalf of the case for The Torah as a proper noun. This
carries us to the theological foundation for Sifra's authorship's
sustained critique of applied reason.

In appealing to the principle, for taxonomy, of *sola Scriptura,* I
mean to set forth what I conceive really to be at stake. It is the
character of The Torah and what it is in The Torah that we wish
to discern. The answer to that question requires theological, not
merely literary and philosophical, reflection on our part. For I
maintain that in their delineation of correct hierarchical logic,
our authorship uncovered within The Torah (and hence, by
definition, the written and oral components of The Torah alike)
an adumbration of the working of the mind of God. This can be
said because the premise of all discourse is that The Torah was
written by God, that is, dictated by God to Moses at Sinai. And
that will in the end explain why our authorship for its part have
entered into The Torah long passages not merely of clarification
but of active intrusion, making itself a component of the
interlocutorial process. By returning to Scripture as the source
for taxa, by appealing to Scripture and Scripture alone as the
criterion for like and unlike, and by then restating the whole of
Scripture, for the book of Leviticus, to encompass words not in
the original, written Torah but only in the other, oral Torah,
that authorship accomplished its purposes.

Two solutions to the problem of the Mishnah competed, at
least in logic and intellect. A brief review at the end places into
context the conclusion of the study as a whole. The one
transformed the word "torah" into a common noun, denoting
many things, above all, status and classification. Hence a sage
taught Torah, as we noted above. That meant a teaching, book,

or person might enter the status of torah or the classification of torah. That left ample space for actions, persons, books, and a broad range of categories of entities, so that torah might serve as an adjective as well as a common noun: a Torah-teaching, a Torah-community, and the like. While, therefore, the Torah remained the scroll that contained the Pentateuch, a variety of other meanings broadened the sense of "torah." In consequence, from the Mishnah onward the canon of Judaism called torah or the Torah found ample space for endless candidates for inclusion.

The other solution—the one set forth in Sifra—preserved the limited sence of the word "torah", referring always and only to The Torah, that is to say, the Pentateuch. But then this other approach reread The Torah, the written Torah, and found space for a variety of fresh candidates for inclusion. This was accomplished through a vast restatement of The Torah, a new and extraordinarily widened statement of what was encompassed within the Torah. A brief reprise of the meanings associated with the word "torah" will show us how our authorship implicitly restricted matters. In other writings than Sifra, for instance, the Talmuds, of the Land of Israel and of Babylonia, "torah" has these meanings:

1. When the Torah refers to a particular thing, it is to a scroll containing divinely revealed words.
2. The Torah may further refer to revelation, not as an object but as a corpus of doctrine.
3. When one "does Torah," the disciple studies or learns, and the master teaches or exemplifies Torah. Hence while the word "torah" never appears as a verb, it does refer to an act.
4. The word also bears a quite separate, generic sense, as cateogry or classification or corpus of rules; for example, "the torah of driving a car" is a usage entirely acceptable to some documents.
5. The word "torah" very commonly refers to a status, distinct from and above another status, as in teachings of Torah against teachings of scribes.
6. Obviously, no account of the meaning of the word "torah" can ignore the distinction between the two Torahs, written and oral.

7. Finally, as I have already explained, the word "torah" refers to a source of salvation, often fully worked out in stories about how the individual and the nation will be saved through Torah.

If I had to summarize all possible usages, as common noun and even as adjective, that the word "torah" sustains outside of Sifra, I should state things in a simple way: for the two Talmuds, "torah" refers to a process, not only to a particular document. "Torah" as status or as process can characterize persons, gestures, many kinds of objects, and actions.

Sifra's authorship took the route of penetrating into the deep structures of thought; it proposed to rewrite the written Torah by restating within its lines many of the pertinent rules of the oral Torah. If Sifra had taken first place in the curriculum of Judaism, its representation of the written Torah and the oral Torah all together and all at once would have opened a different path altogether. For it is one thing to absorb the Torah, oral and written, and it is quite another to join in the processes of thought, the right way of thinking, that sustain the Torah. The authorship of Sifra proposed to regain access to the modes of thought that guided the formation of the Torah, oral and written alike: comparison and contrast in this way, not in that; identification of categories in one manner, not in another. Since those were the modes of thought that, in our authorship's conception, dictated the structure of intellect upon which the united Torah rested, a simple conclusion is the sole possible one.

Now to answer the question of the basis on which our authorship represented itself as participants in The Torah, such that it was prepared to re-present, that is to say, simply rewrite (and therefore, themselves write) The Torah. In its analysis of the deepest structures of intellect of the Torah, the authorship of Sifra supposed to enter into the mind of God, showing how God's mind worked when God formed the Torah, written and oral alike. And there, in the intellect of God, in the authorship's judgment humanity gained access to the only means of uniting the Torah, because that is where the Torah originated. But in discerning how God's mind worked, the intellectuals who created Sifra claimed for themselves a place in that very process of thought that had given birth to The Torah. Our authorship could rewrite the Torah because, knowing how The Torah originally was written, it too could write (though not reveal) The Torah. Such were the stakes—considerable indeed. And such was the basic structure of the Judaism that Sifra's authorship had in mind.

The message of the authorship of Sifra is so narrowly focused on systemic interests, however, that the reader may wonder whether a more wide-ranging Midrash-compilation also can be shown by the methods under discussion here to form an autonomous piece of writing and to set forth a cogent statement. Taking theological, as distinct from systemic, interests as our criterion, we turn to another treatment of the book of Leviticus, Leviticus Rabbah, to show that the same methods used here serve in that document to demonstrate the autonomy and cogency of discourse of yet another Midrash-compilation.

CHAPTER FIVE

Theological Discourse as
Scriptural Exegesis

System framers within the Judaism of the dual Torah utilized the literary and rhetorical forms of scriptural exegesis and commentary not only for argument about issues vital within their circles but also for discourse on topics of broad and general concern. Theological discourse, requiring proposition, evidence, and argument, presented special problems for those who proposed to deliver their theological judgments through Scripture. Facing inward discourse, the authorship of Sifra found no doctrines but only examples of the correct classification of things. But what if an authorship turned to the book of Leviticus not only for evidence about the proper ordering of things but also for proof of theological propositions of public consequence? And what if that authorship sought within Scripture not natural philosophy but theological truth and solace? Then Scripture's very character, as a highly propositional writing with its own rhetoric, logic, and topical and propositional program, intervened. When, therefore, we see a second piece of writing a theological exercise tied to a book of Scripture as a kind of commentary, we find out how an authorship made a statement we can readily identify as religious, not merely philosophical and of inward, systemic concern. The fact that there are two distinct readings of the writing of the book of Leviticus in the canon of the Judaism of the dual Torah furthermore allows us to see how two distinct authorships made use of Scripture for highly contemporary and vivid discourse of a most argumentative and acutely relevant character.

Leviticus Rabbah falls into the classification of a cogent composition, put together with purpose and intended as a whole to bear a meaning and state a message. Like Sifra, it is the opposite of an anthology or miscellany. The pertinence to the study of the form-analysis of writings and the inquiry into their autonomy is clear as well. Like the writers of the Mishnah and of Sifra, the authorship of Leviticus Rabbah made use of a limited repertoire of forms, producing literary structures that adhered to fixed conventions of expression, organization, and proportion, extrinsic to the message of the authorship. In the work of redaction, this authorship, like others, found itself restricted to an equally circumscribed set of alternatives about how to arrange received materials. When we divide up the document's undifferentiated columns of words and sentences and point to the boundaries that separate one completed unit of thought or discourse from the next such completed composition, we produce rather sizable statements conforming to a single set of patterns. While in the Mishnah we can distinguish a few sentences as a paragraph, and a few paragraphs as a concluded statement (a completed unit of discourse), in Leviticus Rabbah we cannot. Rather, our divisions encompass many more sentences and a great many more words than is the case in the Mishnah. When we divide a given *parashah*, or chapter, of Leviticus Rabbah into its subdivisions, we find these subdivisions sustained and on occasion protracted, but also stylistically cogent and well composed.

In showing how I propose to translate writing into religion, as before, I turn first to the analysis of the formal traits of language, then to the logic of coherent discourse. In Leviticus Rabbah the repeated patterns follow protracted orbits, covering a sizable volume of material. The patterns are large in scale. They are not comparable to the small-scale syntactic formalizations that the Mishnah's authors use to good effect, for example, three or five sentences made up of parts of the speech arranged in exactly the same way. Where the authorship of Leviticus Rabbah excels is at holding in balance a rather substantial composite of seemingly diverse materials, systematically and patiently working its way from one to the next, apparently miscellaneous, observation and only at the end drawing the whole to an elegant and satisfying conclusion. So we look for large-scale patterns and point to such unusually sizable compositions as characteristic because they recur and define discourse. How shall we proceed to identify the structures that define the document before us? It seems to me we had best move first to the analysis of a single *parashah*. We seek, within that *parashah,* to identify what holds the whole together.

As we shall see in the major disquisitions marked with Roman numerals I–III, the propositional purpose here is to emphasize the equality of the anointed priest and ordinary Israelites. The expiation demanded of the one is no greater than that of the other. Considering the importance of the anointed priest, the ceremony by which he attains office, the sanctity attached to his labor, we cannot miss the polemic. What the anointed priest does unwittingly will usually involve some aspect of the cult. When the community commits a sin unwittingly, it will not involve the cult but some aspect of the collective life of the people. The one is no more consequential than the other; the same penalty pertains to both. So the people and the priest stand on the same plane before God. And the further meaning of the verse of Job then cannot be missed. When God hides his face, in consequence of which the people suffer, it is for a just cause. No one can complain; he is long-suffering but in the end exacts his penalties. And these will cover not unwitting sin, such as Leviticus knows, but deliberate sin, as with the generation of the Flood, Sodom, and the ten tribes. There would then appear to be several layers of meaning in the exegetical construction, which we must regard as a sustained and unified one, a truly amazing achievement.

Leviticus Rabbah Parashah 5

V:I.1.   A. "If it is the anointed priest who sins, [thus bringing guilt on the people, then let him offer to the Lord for the sin which he has committed a young bull without blemish]" (Lev. 4:3).

B. "When he is quiet, who can condemn? When he hides his face, who can set him right [Revised Standard Version: behold him] [whether it be a nation or a man? that a godless man should not reign, that he should not ensnare the people]" (Job 34:29-30).

C. R. Meir interpreted [the matter in this way:] "'When he is quiet'—in his world, 'when he hides his face'—in his world.

D. "The matter may be compared to the case of a judge who draws a veil inside and so does not see what goes on outside.

E. "So the people of the generation of the flood thought: 'The thick clouds cover him, so he will not see [what we do]' (Job 22:14)."

F. They said to him, "That's enough from you, Meir."

2. A. Another interpretation: "When he is quiet, who can condemn? When he hides his face, who can set him right?" (Job 34:29)

B. When he gave tranquility to the generation of the flood, who could come and condemn them?

C. What sort of tranquility did he give them? "Their children are established in their presence, and their offspring before their eyes. [Their houses are safe from fear, and no rod of God is upon them]" (Job 21:8).

D. R. Levi and rabbis:

E. R. Levi said, "A woman would get pregnant and give birth in three days. [How do we know it?] Here, the word, 'established,' is used, and elsewhere: 'Be established in three days' (Ex. 19:15). Just as the word, 'established,' used there involves a span of three days, so the word, 'established,' used here means three days."

F. Rabbis say, "In a single day a woman would get pregnant and give birth.

G. "Here, the word, 'established,' is used, and elsewhere: 'And be established in the morning' (Ex. 34:2). Just as the word 'established' stated there involves a single day, so the word 'established' used here involves a single day."

3. A. "And their offspring before their eyes"—for they saw children and grandchildren.

B. "They send forth their little ones like a flock, [and their children dance]" (Job 21:11).

C. [The word for "children" means] "their young."

D. Said R. Levi, "In Arabia for children they use the word 'the young.'"

4. A. "And their children dance" (Job 21:11)—

B. ["they dance"] like devils.

C. That is in line with the following verse of Scripture: "And satyrs will dance there" (Is. 13:21).

5. A. They say: When one of them would give birth by day, she would say to her son, "Go and bring me a flint, so I can cut your umbiblical cord."

B. If she gave birth by night, she would say to her son, "Go and light a lamp for me, so I can cut your umbilical cord."

C. There was the following case: A woman gave birth by night and said to her son, "Go and light a lamp for me, so I can cut your umbilical cord."

D. [In Aramaic:] When he went out to fetch it, a devil, Ashmadon [Asmodeus], head of the spirits, met him. While the two were wrestling with one another, the cock crowed. [Ashmadon] said to him, "Go, boast to your mother that my time has run out, for if my time had not run out, I could have killed you."

E. He said to him, "Go, boast to your mother's mother that my mother had not cut my umbilical cord, for if my mother had cut my umbilical cord, I would have beaten you."

F. This illustrates that which is said: "Their houses are safe from fear" (Job 21:9)—from destroying spirits.

6. A. "And no rod of God is upon them"—[for their houses are free from suffering.

B. [And this further] illustrates that which is said: "[When he is quiet, who can condemn,] when he hides his face, who can put him right" (Job 34:30).

C. When [God] hides his face from them, who can come and say to him, "You have not done right."

D. And how, indeed, did he hide his face from them? When he brought the flood on them.

E. That is in line with the following verse of Scripture: "And he blotted out every living substance which was upon the face of the earth" (Gen. 7:23).

7. A. "Whether it be to a nation [or a man together]" (Job 34:29)—this refers to the generation of the flood.

B. "Or to a man"—this refers to Noah.

C. "Together"—he had to rebuild his world from one man, he had to rebuild his world from one nation.

On the surface, the sole point of contact between the base-verse and the intersecting verse, Leviticus 4:3 and Job 34:29-30, is in the uncited part of the passage of Job, "that he should not ensnare the people." The anointed priest has sinned and in so doing has brought guilt on the entire people. If, however, that is why the entire assembly of exegeses of Job has been inserted here, that theme plays no role in making the collection of materials on Job. For at no point in the present unit (or in the next one) does the important segment of the passage of Job come under discussion. The interpretation of Job 34:29 in light of the story of the Flood predominates here. V:I.1 has Meir's view that the entire passage refers to God's failure to intervene, with special reference to the Flood. V:I.2 pursues the same line of thought. V:I.3 illustrates the notion that their children "are established in their presence," and V:I.3-4 continues to spell out the phrase-by-phrase exegesis of the same verse. V:I.5 pursues the same line of thought. V:I.6 shifts the ground of interpretation. Now God is "quiet," but later, in "hiding his face," he brings punishment on them. V:I.7 completes the exegesis of the cited passage of Job in line with the view that Job was a contemporary of Noah and spoke of his ties. Noah might then serve as the counterpart and opposite of the priest who brings guilt on the people. But that is by no means the clear intent of the passage at hand.

V:II.1. A. Another interpretation: "When he is quiet, who can condemn" (Job 34:29).

B. When he gave tranquility to the Sodomites, who could come and condemn them?

C. What sort of tranquility did he give them?

D. "As for the earth, out of it comes bread, but underneath it is turned up as by fire. Its stones are the place of sapphires, and it has dust of gold" (Job 28:5-6).

2. A. "That path no bird of prey knows, and the falcon's eye has not seen it" (Job 28:7).

B. R. Levi in the name of R. Yohanan bar Shahina: "The falcon [bar hadayya-bird] spots its prey at a distance of eighteen miles."

C. And how much is its portion [of food]?

D. R. Meir said, "[A mere] two handbreadths."

E. R. Judah said, "One handbreadth."

F. R. Yose said, "Two or three fingerbreadths."

G. [In Aramaic:] And when it stood on the trees of Sodom, it could not see the ground because of the density of [the foliage of] the trees.

3. A. "When he hides his face, who can put him right?"—

B. When he hid his face from them, who comes to say to him, "You did not do rightly"?

C. And when did he hide his face from them?

D. When he made brimstone and fire rain down on them.

E. That is in line with the following verse of Scripture: "Then the Lord made brimstone and fire rain on Sodom and Gomorrah" (Gen. 19:24).

The second unit simply carries forward the exercise of reading Job 28:5ff., now in line with the story of Sodom and Gomorrah, rather than the generation of the Flood. The message is being delivered through examples. But we are not in doubt as to the proposition.

V:III.1. A. Another interpretation of "When he is quiet, who can condemn? When he hides his face, who can set him right?" (Job 34:29).

B. When he gave tranquility to the ten tribes, who could come and condemn them?

C. What sort of tranquility did he give them? "Woe to those who are at ease in Zion, and to those who feel secure on the mountain of Samaria, the notable men of the first of the nations, to whom the house of Israel to come" (Amos 6:1).

2. A. "Woe to those who are at ease in Zion" refers to the tribe of Judah and Benjamin.

B. "Those who feel secure on the mountain of Samaria" refers to the ten tribes.

C. "The notable men of the first of the nations" who derive from the two noteworthy names, Shem and Eber.

D. When the nations of the world eat and drink, they pass the time in nonsense-talk, saying, "Who is a sage, like Balaam! Who is a hero, like Goliath! Who is rich, like Haman!"

E. And the Israelites come after them and say to them, "Was not Ahitophel a sage, Samson a hero, Korah rich?"

3. A. "Pass over to Calneh and see, [and thence go to Hamath the great, then go down to Gath of the Philistines. Are they better than these kingdoms? Or is their territory greater than your territory?]" (Amos 6:2).

B. [Calneh] refers to Ctesiphon.

C. "Hamath the great" refers to Hamath of Antioch.

D. "And go down to Gath of the Philistines" refers to the mounds of the Philistines.

E. "Are they better than these kingdoms? Or is their territory greater than your territory?"

F. "O you who put far away the evil day" (Amos 6:3) [refers to] the day on which they would go into exile.

4. A. "And bring near the seat of violence?" (Amos 6:3). This refers to Esau.

B. "Did you bring yourselves near to sit next to violence"— this refers to Esau.

C. That is in line with the following verse of Scripture: "For the violence done to your brother Jacob, [shame shall cover you]" (Obad. 1:40).

5. A. "[Woe to] those who lie upon beds of ivory" (Amos 6:4)—on beds made of the elephant's tusk.

B. "And stink on their couches" (Amos 6:4)—who do stinking transgressions on their beds.

C. "Who eat lambs from the flock [and calves from the midst of the stall]" (Amos 6:4).

D. They say: When one of them wanted to eat a kid of the flock, he would have the whole flock brought before them, and he would stand over it and slaughter it.

E. When he wanted to eat a calf, he would bring the entire herd of calves before him and stand over it and slaughter it.

6. A. "Who sing idle songs to the sound of the harp [and like David invent for themselves instruments of music]" (Amos 6:5).

B. [They would say that] David provided them with musical instruments.

7. A. "Who drink wine in bowls" (Amos 6:6).

B. Rab, R. Yohanan, and rabbis:

C. Rab said, "It is a very large bowl" [using the Greek].

D. R. Yohanan said, "It was in small cups."

E. Rabbis say, "It was in cups with saucers attached."

F. Whence did the wine they drink come?

G. R. Aibu in the name of R. Hanina said, "It was wine from Pelugta, for the wine would entice (PTH) the body."

H. And rabbis in the name of R. Hanina said, "It was from Pelugta [separation], since, because of their wine-drinking, the ten tribes were enticed [from God] and consequently sent into exile."

8. A. "And anoint themselves with the finest oils" (Amos 6:6).

B. R. Judah b. R. Ezekiel said, "This refers to oil of unripe olives, which removes hair and smooths the body."

C. R. Haninah said, "This refers to oil of myrrh and cinnamon."

9. A. And [in spite of] all this glory: "They are not grieved over the ruin of Joseph" (Amos 6:6).

B. "Therefore they shall now be the first of those to go into exile, [and the revelry of those who stretch themselves shall pass away]" (Amos 6:7).

C. What is the meaning of "the revelry of those who stretch themselves"?

D. Said R. Aibu, "They had thirteen public baths, one for each of the tribes, and one additional one for all of them together.

E. "And all of them were destroyed, and only this one [that had served all of them] survived.

F. "This shows how much lewdness was done with them."

10. A. "When he hides his face, who can set him right?" (Job 34:29).

B. When he hid his face from them, who then could come and say to him, "You did not do right"?

C. How did he hide his face from them? By bringing against them Sennacherib, the king of Assyria.

D. That is in line with the following verse of Scripture: "In the fourteenth year of King Hezekiah, Sennacherib, king of Assyria, came up [against all the fortified cities of Judah and took them]" (Is. 36:1).

11. A. What is the meaning of, "and took them"?

B. Said R. Abba b. R. Kahana, "Three divine decrees were sealed on that day.

C. "The decree against the ten tribes was sealed, for them to fall into the hand of Sennacherib; the decree against Sennacherib was sealed, for him to fall into the hand of Hezekiah; and the decree of Shebna was sealed, to be smitten with leprosy.

12. A. "Whether it be a nation [or a man]" (Job 34:29)—this refers to Sennacherib, as it is said, "For a nation has come up upon my land" (Joel 1:6).

B. ". . . or a man" (Job 34:29)—this refers to Israel: "For you, my sheep, the sheep of my pasture, are a man" (Ez. 34:31).

C. "Together" (Job 34:29)—this refers to King Uzziah, who was smitten with leprosy.

D. That is in line with the following verse of Scripture: "And

Uzziah the King was a leper until the day he died" (2 Chr. 26:21).

13. A. [Margulies: What follows treats ". . . whether it be a nation or a man together" (Job 34:29):] Now the justice of the Holy One, blessed be he, is not like man's justice.

B. A mortal judge may show favor to a community, but he will never show favor to an individual.

C. But the Holy One, blessed be he, is not so. Rather: "If it is the anointed priest who sins, [thus bringing guilt on the people,] then let him offer [for the sin which he has committed] a young bull [without blemish to the Lord as a sin-offering]" (Lev. 4:3-4).

D. "[If the whole congregation of Israel commits a sin unwittingly, and the thing is hidden from the eyes of the assembly, and they do any one of the things which the Lord has commanded not to be done and are guilty, when the sin which they have committed becomes known,] the assembly shall offer a young bull for a sin-offering" (Lev. 4:13-14). [God exacts the same penalty from an individual and from the community and does not distinguish the one from the other. The anointed priest and the community both become subject to liability for the same offering, a young bull.]

Finally, at V:III.13, we come to the verse with which we began. And we find a clear point of contact between the base-verse and the intersecting one, Job 34:29, as Margulies, editor of the Hebrew text, explains. Still, there is no clear reason for including a sustained exegesis of Amos 6:1ff. V:III.1 completes the original exegesis by applying the cited verse to the ten tribes, first tranquil, then punished, as at V:I, II.V:III.1.C then links Amos 6:1 to the present context. Once Amos 6:1 makes its appearance, we work through the elements of Amos 6:1-7. That massive interpolation encompasses V:III.2-9. V:III.10 resumes where V:III.1 left off. V:III.11 is tacked on to V:III.10.D, and then V:III.12-13 continue the exegesis in terms of Israelite history of Job 34:29. Then, as I said, V:III.13 stands completely separate from all that has gone before in V:I.1–III.12. What, then, is the primary intent of the exegete? It is to emphasize the equality of anointed priest and ordinary Israelites. Everyone is equally responsible before God. Now we proceed to a secondary expansion of the established proposition.

V:IV.1.   A.   Said R. Abbahu, "It is written, 'Take heed that you do not forsake the Levite [as long as you live in your land]' (Deut. 12:19). What follows thereafter? 'When the Lord your God enlarges your territory [as he has promised you]' (Deut. 12:20).

B.   "What has one thing got to do with the other?

C.   "Said the Holy One, blessed be he, 'In accord with your gifts will they enlarge your [place].'"

D.   R. Huna in the name of R. Aha, "If a slave brings as his offering a young bull, while his master brings a lamb, the slave takes precedence over his master.

E.   "This is in accord with what we have learned in the Mishnah: 'If the young bull of the anointed priest and the young bull of the community are waiting [sacrifice], the young bull of the anointed priest takes precedence over the young bull of the community in all aspects of the sacrificial rite' (M. Hor. 3:6)."

2.   A.   "A man's gift makes room for him and brings him before great men" (Prov. 18:16).

B.   There was the following case, R. Eliezer, R. Joshua, and R. Aqiba went to the harborside of Antioch to collect funds for the support of sages.

C.   [In Aramaic:] A certain Abba Yudan lived there.

D.   He wold carry out his religious duty [of philanthropy] in a liberal spirit, but had lost his money. When he saw our masters, he went home with a sad face. His wife said to him, "What's wrong with you, that you look so sad?"

E.   He repeated the tale to her: "Our masters are here, and I don't know what I shall be able to do for them."

F.   His wife, who was a truly philanthropic woman—what did she say to him? "You only have one field left. Go, sell half of it and give them the proceeds."

G.   He went and did just that. When he was giving them the money, they said to him, "May the Omnipresent make up all your losses."

H.   Our masters went their way.

I.   He went out to plough. While he was ploughing the half of the field that he had left, the Holy One, blessed be he, opened his eyes. The earth broke open before him, and his cow fell in and broke her leg. He went down to raise her up, and found a treasure beneath her. He said, "It was for my gain that my cow broke her leg."

J.   When our masters came back, [in Aramaic:] they asked

about a certain Abba Yudan and how he was doing. They said, "Who can gaze on the face of Abba Yudan [which glows with prosperity]—Abba Yudan, the owner of flocks of goats, Abba Yudan, the owner of herds of asses, Abba Yudan, the owner of herds of camels."

K. He came to them and said to them, "Your prayer in my favor has produced returns and returns on the returns."

L. They said to him, "Even though someone else gave more than you did, we wrote your name at the head of the list."

M. Then they took him and sat him next to themselves and recited in his regard the following verse of Scripture: "A man's gift makes room for him and brings him before great men" (Prov. 18:16).

3. A. R. Hiyya bar Abba called for charity contributions in support of a school in Tiberias. A member of the household of Siloni got up and pledged a litra of gold.

B. R. Hiyya bar Abba took him and sat him next to himself and recited in his regard the following verse of Scripture: "A man's gift makes room for him and brings him before great men" (Prov. 18:16).

4. A. [In Aramaic:] R. Simeon b. Laqish went to Bosrah. A certain Abba [Lieberman deletes: Yudan], "the Deceiver," lived there. It was not—Heaven forfend—that he really was a deceiver. Rather, he would practice [holy] deception in doing the religious duty [of philanthropy].

B. [In Aramaic:] He would see what the rest of the community would pledge, and he would then pledge to take upon himself [a gift equivalent to that of the rest of the] community.

C. R. Simeon b. Laqish took him and sat him next to himself and received in his regard the following verse of Scripture: "A man's gift makes room for him and brings him before great men" (Prov. 18:16).

We find neither a base-verse nor an intersecting one, such as characterized V:I–III. Rather, what will be the secondary verse—Proverbs 18:16—comes in the distant wake of a problem presented by the information of Leviticus 4. Specifically, we find reference to the sacrifice of the young bulls of the high priest, of the community, and of the ruler. The issue then naturally arises, which one comes first? The Mishnah answers this question, at M.

Horayot 3:6. Reflection upon that answer generates the
observation that the anointed priest comes first, as in Scripture's
order, in particular when the offerings are of the same value.
But if one offering is more valuable than the other, the more
valuable offering takes precedence. Then comes secondary
reflection on the fact that a person's gift establishes his rank even
if it is on other grounds lower than what he otherwise would
attain. V:IV.1 does not pursue that secondary reflection, but
invites it at 1.C. The invocation of Proverbs 18:16 then is not on
account of Leviticus 4 at all. It must follow that V:IV.2-4 would
better serve a compilation of materials on Deuteronomy
12:19-20 than the present passage. What follows V:IV.1 serves a
purpose in no way closely connected either to the sense or to the
syntax of our passage. The entire complex, V:VI.2-4, occurs at
Y. Horayot 3:4. It is lifted whole, attached because of the obvious
relevance to V:VI.1. We find no pretense, then, that these stories
relate in any way to Leviticus 4. For the storyteller at V:VI.2, the
climax comes at L–M, the sages' recognition that their placing of
Abba Yudan at the head of the list had made possible the
serendipitous accident. V:VI.3 and 4 omit the miraculous aspect
entirely.

V:V.1.   A. Reverting to the base-text: "If it is the anointed priest
who sins" (Lev. 4:3).

B. This refers to Shebna.

2.   A. "[Thus says the Lord, God of hosts,] 'Come, go to this
steward (SKN), to Shebna, who is over the household, [and say to
him, 'What have you to do here and whom have you here, that
you have hewn here a tomb for yourself, you who hew a tomb on
the height and carve a habitation for yourself in the rock? Behold,
the Lord will hurl you away violently, O you strong young man!
He will seize firm hold on you, and whirl you round and round
and throw you like a ball into a wide land; there you shall die, and
there shall be your splendid chariots, you shame of your master's
house. I will thrust you from your office and you will be cast down
from your station]" (Is. 22:15-19).

B. R. Eliezer said, "He was a high priest."

C. R. Judah b. Rabbi said, "He was steward."

D. In the view of R. Eliezer, who said he was a high priest, [we
may bring evidence from Scripture,] for it is written, "And I will

clothe him with your robe [and will bind your girdle on him and will commit your authority into his hand]" (Is. 22:21).

E. In the view of R. Judah b. Rabbi, who said he was steward, [we may bring evidence from Scripture,] for it is written, "And I will commit your authority to his hand" (Is. 22:21).

F. R. Berekiah said, "What is a 'steward'? It is one who comes from Sikhni."

3. A. And he went up and was appointed *komes opsarion* [the Greek for chief cook] in Jerusalem.

B. That is in line with the prophet's condemnation, saying to him, "What have you to do here, and whom have you here" (Is. 22:16).

C. "You exile, son of an exile! What wall have you built here, what pillar have you put up here, and what nail have you hammered in here?!"

D. R. Eleazar said, "A person has to have a nail or a peg firmly set in a synagogue so as to have the right to be buried in that place [in which he is living]."

E. "And have you hewn here a tomb for yourself?" (Is. 22:16). He made himself a kind of a dovecot and put his tomb on top of it.

F. "You who hew a tomb on the height" (Is. 22:16)—

G. R. Ishmael in the name of Mar Uqba, "On the height the decree was hewn out concerning him, indicating that he should not have a burial place in the land of Israel."

H. "You who carve a habitation for yourself in the rock" (Is. 22:16)—a stone coffin.

I. "Behold, the Lord will hurl you away violently" (Is. 22:17)—one rejection after another.

J. ". . . hurl away violently (GBR)"—[since the word GBR also means cock:] said R. Samuel b. R. Nahman, "[In Aramaic:] it may be compared to a cock which is driven and goes from place to place."

K. "He will seize a firm hold on you" (Is. 22:17), [since the words for "firm hold" may also be translated, "wrap around," thus: "And he will wrap you around"] the meaning is that he was smitten with *saraat* ["leprosy"] in line with that which you find in Scripture, "And he will wrap his lip around" (Lev. 13:45).

L. "And whirl you round and round [and throw you like a ball]" (Is. 22:18)—exile after exile.

M. "Like a ball"—just as a ball is caught from hand to

hand and does not fall to the ground, so [will it be for him].

N. "Into a wide land"—this means Casiphia (Ezra 8:17).

O. "There you shall die and there shall be your splendid chariots" (Is. 22:18)—

4. A. In accord with the position of R. Eliezer, who said that Shebna had been a high priest, [the reference to the splendid chariots implies] that he had been deriving personal benefit from the offerings.

B. In accord with the view of R. Judah b. Rabbi, who said that he had been steward, [the reference to the splendid chariots implies] that he had derived personal benefit from things that had been consecrated for use in the upkeep of the sanctuary.

C. "You shame of your master's house" (Is. 22:18).

D. In accord with the position of R. Eliezer, who said that Shebna had been a high priest, [the shame was] that he had treated the offerings in a disgraceful way.

E. In accord with the view of R. Judah b. Rabbi, who said that he had been steward, [the shame was] that he had treated both of his masters disgracefully, that is Hezekiah, on the one side, Isaiah on the other.

5. A. R. Berekhiah in the name of R. Abba b. R. Kahana: "What did Shebna and Joahaz [2 Kngs. 18:18] do? They wrote a message and attached it to an arrow and shot it to Sennacherib through the window. In the message was written the following: "We and everyone in Jerusalem want you, but Hezekiah and Isaiah don't want you."

B. Now this is just what David had said [would happen]: "For lo, the wicked bend the bow, they have fitted their arrow to the string" (Ps. 11:2).

C. "For lo, the wicked bend the bow"—this refers to Shebna and Joahaz.

D. "They have fitted their arrow to the string"—on the bowstring.

E. "To shoot in the dark at the upright in heart" (Ps. 11:2)—at two upright in heart, Hezekiah and Isaiah.

What the exegete contributes to the explanation of Leviticus 4:3 is simply the example of how an anointed priest may sin. The rest of the passage is a systematic exposition of the verses about Shebna. But the entire matter of Shebna belongs here only within Eliezer's opinion that he was a high priest. That is a rather remote connection to the present passage of Leviticus. So because of the allegation that Shebna was high priest, the entire passage—fully worked out on its own—was inserted here. The redactor then appeals to the theme, not to the content, in drawing together the cited verses of Leviticus and Isaiah. V:V.2, 4 are continuous with each other. V:V.3 inserts a systematic, phrase-by-phrase exegesis of Isaiah 22:15ff. V:V.5 then complements the foregoing with yet further relevant material. So the construction is cogent and well conceived, apart from No. 1, in which linkage to Leviticus 4:3 is farfetched.

V.VI.1.   A. "If it is the anointed priest who sins" (Lev. 4:3).

B. [What follows occurs at T. Hor. 2:4, explaining M. Hor. 3:4, cited above at V:IV.1.E:] [If] the anointed high priest must atone [for a sin] and the community must be atoned for [in line with Lev. 4:13], it is better that the one who [has the power to] make atonement take precedence over the one for whom atonement is made,

C. as it is written, "And he will atone for himself and for his house" (Lev. 16:17).

D. ["His house"] refers to his wife.

2.   A. "If it is the anointed priest who sins" (Lev. 4:3)—

B. Will an anointed priest commit a sin!

C. Said R. Levi, "Pity the town whose physician has gout [and cannot walk to visit the sick], whose governor has one eye, and whose public defender plays the prosecutor in capital cases."

3.   A. "[If it is the anointed priest who sins,] thus bringing guilt [on the people, then let him offer for the sin which he has committed a young bull . . .]" (Lev. 4:3).

B. Said R. Isaac, "It is a case of death by burning [inflicted on one who commits sacrilege by consuming offerings from the altar]."

C. "The matter may be compared to the keeper of a bear, who ate up the rations of the bear. The king said, 'Since he went and ate up the bear's rations, let the bear eat him.'

D. "So does the Holy One, blessed be he, say, 'Since Shebna enjoyed benefit from things that had been consecrated to the altar [for burning], let fire consume him.'"

4.   A. Said R. Aibu, "Once there was a butcher in Sepphoris, who fed Israelites carrion and torn-meat. On the eve of the Day of

Atonement he went out drinking and got drunk. He climbed up
to the roof of his house and fell off and died. The dogs began to
lick him.

B. "[In Aramaic:] They came and asked R. Hanina the law
about moving his corpse away from the dogs [on the Day of
Atonement].

C. "He said to him, "You will be holy people to me, therefore
you shall not eat any meat that is torn of beasts in the field, you
shall cast it to the dogs" (Ex. 22:30).

D. "'This man robbed from the dogs and fed carrion and
torn-meat to Israelites. Leave him to them. They are eating what
belongs to them.'"

5. A. "He shall bring the bull to the door of the tent of meeting
before the Lord, [and lay his hand on the head of the bull and kill
the bull before the Lord]" (Lev. 4:4).

B. Said R. Isaac, "The matter may be compared to the case of
a king, one of whose admirers paid him honor by giving him a
handsome gift and by offering him lovely words of praise. The
king then said, 'Set this gift at the gate of the palace, so that
everyone who comes and goes may see [and admire] it,'

C. "as it is said, 'And he shall bring the bull [to the door of the
tent of meeting].'"

The opening units, V:VI.1-4, form a kind of appendix of
miscellanies to what has gone before. V:VI.1 reaches back to
V:IV, explaining the passage of the Mishnah cited there. V:VI.2
is joined to V:VI.3, which relates to the cited passage to Shebna.
So V:VI.2-3 complete the discussion of V:V. It seems to me that
V:VI.4 is attached to V:VI.3 as an illustration of the case of a
public official who abuses his responsibility. V:VI.5 provides a
fresh point, moving on to a new verse. There is no intersecting
verse; the exegesis is accomplished solely through a parable.

V:VII.1. A. "[If the whole congregation of Israel commits a sin
unwittingly and the thing is hidden from the eyes of the assembly,
and they do any one of the things which the Lord has
commanded not to be done and are guilty, when the sin which
they have committed becomes known, the assembly shall offer a
young bull for a sin-offering and bring it before the tent of
meeting;] and the elders of the congregation shall lay their hands

[upon the head of the bull before the Lord]" (Lev. 4:13-15).

B. [Since, in laying their hands (SMK) on the head of the bull, the elders sustain (SMK) the community by adding to it the merit they enjoy,] said R. Isaac, "The nations of the world have none to sustain them, for it is written, 'And those who sustain Egypt will fall" (Ez. 30:6).

C. "But Israel has those who sustain it, as it is written: 'And the elders of the congregation shall lay their hands [and so sustain Israel] (Lev. 4:15).'"

2. A. Said R. Eleazar, "The nations of the world are called a congregation, and Israel is called a congregation.

B. "The nations of the world are called a congregation: 'For the congregation of the godless shall be desolate' (Job 15:34).

C. "And Israel is called a congregation: 'And the elders of the congregation shall lay their hands' (Lev. 4:15).

D. "The nations of the world are called sturdy bulls and Israel is called sturdy bulls.

E. "The nations of the world are called sturdy bulls: 'The congregation of [sturdy] bulls with the calves of the peoples' (Ps. 68:31).

F. "Israel is called sturdy bulls, as it is said, 'Listen to me, you sturdy [bullish] of heart' (Is. 46:13).

G. "The nations of the world are called excellent, and Israel is called excellent.

H. "The nations of the world are called excellent: 'You and the daughters of excellent nations' (Ex. 32:18).

I. "Israel is called excellent: 'They are the excellent, in whom is all my delight' (Ps. 16:4).

J. "The nations of the world are called sages, and Israel is called sages.

K. "The nations of the world are called sages: 'And I shall wipe out sages from Edom' (Ob. 1:8).

L. "And Israel is called sages: 'Sages store up knowledge' (Prov. 10:14).

M. "The nations of the world are called unblemished, and Israel is called unblemished.

N. "The nations of the world are called unblemished: 'Unblemished as are those that go down to the pit' (Prov. 1:12).

O. "And Israel is called unblemished: "The unblemished will inherit goodness' (Prov. 28:10).

P. "The nations of the world are called men, and Israel is called men.

Q. "The nations of the world are called men: 'And you men who work iniquity' (Ps. 141:4).

R. "And Israel is called men: 'To you who are men I call' (Prov. 8:4).

S. "The nations of the world are called righteous, and Israel is called righteous.

T. "The nations of the world are called righteous: 'And righteous men shall judge them' (Ez. 23:45).

U. "And Israel is called righteous: 'And your people—all of them are righteous' (Is. 60:21).

V. "The nations of the world are called mighty, and Israel is called mighty.

W. "The nations of the world are called mighty: 'Why do you boast of evil, O mighty man' (Ps. 52:3).

X. "And Israel is called mighty: 'Mighty in power, those who do his word' (Ps. 103:20).

We see two distinct types of exegeses, one to which the base-passage is central, the other to which it is peripheral. Yet the two passages belong together, and we have every reason to suppose that they were made up as a single cogent statement. V:VII.1 focuses upon the double meaning of the word SMK, "lay hands" and "sustain", drawing the contrast stated by Isaac. Once such a contrast is drawn, a catalogue of eight further contrasts will be laid out. Since the opening set, V:VII.2.A-B, depends upon the passage at hand, we must accept the possibility that Eleazar's statement has been constructed to work its way through the contrast established by Isaac, for both authorities make the same point. Even though the nations of the world are subject to the same language as is applied to Israel, they still do not fall into the same classification, for language is dual. When a word applies to Israel, it serves to praise, and when the same word applies to the nations, it underlines their negative character. Both are called a congregation, but the nations' congregation is desolate, and so throughout, as the context of the passage cited concerning the nations repeatedly indicates. The nations' sages are wiped out; the unblemished nations go down to the pit; the nations, called men, only work iniquity. Now that is precisely the contrast drawn in Isaac's saying, so, as I said, the whole should be deemed a masterpiece of unitary composition. Then the two types of exegesis—direct and peripheral—turn out to complement one another, each making its own point. That emerges from the substance of the exegesis as much as from the form, though I have underlined the form.

For at this point in our move from writing to religion, we are scarcely ready to address propositions of documents. There are two kinds of propositions, those on the surface, and those underneath. And it is at the foundations of documents, the implicit propositions, the self-evident facts, that the authorships make their most consequential statements. Time and again, details prove systemically inert, interesting but not indicative. But the main thing, that which lies at the bottom of things, proves to form the document's principal and systemically active religious message. That is why at this point we analyze form, aiming at defining the correct point at which we may turn to the contents of writings.

V:VIII.1. A. R. Simeon b. Yohai taught, "How masterful are the Israelites, for they know how to find favor with their creator."

B. Said R. Yudan, [in Aramaic:], "It is like the case of Samaritan [beggars]. The Samaritan [beggars] are clever at begging. One of them goes to a housewife, saying to her, 'Do you have an onion? Give it to me.' After she gives it to him, he says to her, 'Is there such a thing as an onion without bread?' After she gives him [bread], he says to her, 'Is there such a thing as food without drink?' So, all in all, he gets to eat and drink."

C. Said R. Aha [in Aramaic:], "There is a woman who knows how to borrow things, and there is a woman who does not. The one who knows how to borrow goes over to her neighbor. The door is open, but she knocks [anyhow]. Then she says to her neighbor, 'Greetings, good neighbor. How're you doing? How's your husband doing? How're your kids doing? Can I come in? [By the way], would you have such-and-such a utensil? Would you lend it to me? [The neighboring housewife] says to her, 'Yes, of course.'

D. "But the one who does not know how to borrow goes over to her neighbor. The door is closed, so she just opens it. She says [to the neighboring housewife], 'Do you have such-and-such a utensil? Would you lend it to me?' [The neighboring housewife] says to her, 'No.'"

E. Said R. Hunia [in Aramaic:], "There is a tenant-farmer who knows how to borrow things, and there is a tenant-farmer who does not know how to borrow. The one who knows how to borrow combs his hair, brushes off his clothes, puts on a good face, and then goes over to the overseer of his work to borrow from him. [The overseer] says to him, 'How's the land doing?' He says to him, 'May you have the merit of being fully satisfied with its [wonderful] produce.' 'How are the oxen doing?' He says to him, 'May you have the merit of being fully satisfied with their fat.' 'How are the goats doing?' 'May you have the merit of being fully satisfied with their young.' 'And what would you like?' Then he says, 'Now if you might have an extra ten denars, would you give them to me?' The overseer replies, 'If you want, take twenty.'

F. "But the one who does not know how to borrow leaves his hair a mess, his clothes filthy, his face gloomy. He too goes over to the overseer to borrow from him. The overseer says to him, 'How's the land doing?' He replies, 'I hope it will produce at least what [in seed] we put into it.' 'How are the oxen doing?' They're scrawny.' 'How are the goats doing?' 'They're scrawny too.' 'And what do you want?' 'Now if you might have an extra ten denars, would you give them to me?' The overseer replies, 'Go, pay me back what you already owe me!' "

G. Said R. Hunia, "David was one of the good tenant-farmers. To begin with, he starts a psalm with praise [of God], saying, 'The heavens declare the glory of God, and the firmament shows his handiwork' (Ps. 19:2). The Heaven says to him, 'Perhaps you need something?' 'The firmament shows his handiwork.' The firmament says to him, 'Perhaps you need something?'

H. "And so he would continue to sing: 'Day unto day utters speech, and night to night reveals knowledge' (Ps. 19:3).

I. "Said to him the Holy One, blessed be he, 'What do you want?'

J. "He said before him, 'Who can discern errors?' (Ps. 19:13).

K. "What sort of unwitting sin have I done before you?'

L. "[God] said to him, 'Lo, this one is remitted, and that one is forgiven you.'

M. "'And cleanse me of hidden sins' (Ps. 19:13). '. . . from the secret sins that I have done before you.'

N. "He said to him, 'Lo, this one is remitted, and that one is forgiven to you.'

O. "'Keep back your servant also from deliberate ones.' This refers to transgressions done in full knowledge.

P. "'That they may not have dominion over me. Then I shall be faultless' (Ps. 19:14). This refers to the most powerful of transgressions.

Q. "'And I shall be clear of great transgression' (Ps. 19:14)."

R. Said R. Levi, "David said before the Holy One, blessed be he, 'Lord of the age[s], you are a great God, and, as for me, my sins are great too. It will take a great God to remit and forgive great sins: "For your name's sake, O Lord, pardon my sin, for [your name] is great" (Ps. 25:11).' "

Once more, the construction appears from beginning to end to aim at a single goal. The opening statement, V:VIII.1.A, makes the point, and the closing construction, Gff., illustrates it. In the middle come three apt narratives serving as similes, all told in Aramaic and all following exactly the same pattern. Then the systematic account of a passage of Scripture is provided to make exactly the same point. I cannot state the exact sense of the passage on the heaven and the firmament, G, but from that point, the discourse is pellucid. Q-R should be separated from G-P, since what Levi's statement does is simply augment the primary passage. The unity of theme and conception accounts for the drawing together of the entire lot. To be sure, B-F can serve other purposes. But since Hunia's statement, E-F, introduces his exegesis of Psalm 19, the greater likelihood is that a single hand has produced the entire matter (possibly excluding Q-R) to make a single point. Why has the redactor thought the passage appropriate here? The offering for unwitting sin of Leviticus 4, to which K makes reference in the progression through the types of sins from minor to major for which David seeks forgiveness, certainly accounts for the inclusion of the whole. Then whoever made up the passage did not find the stimulus in Leviticus 4, for the rather general observation of V:VIII.1.A states the framer's message. That message pertains to diverse contexts, as the exposition of Psalm 19 makes clear; nothing would compel someone to make up a passage of this sort to serve Leviticus 4 in particular.

Let us now turn to the classification of the units of discourse of which the *parashah* is composed. What we want to know is the structure of the *parashah* as a whole, where its largest subunits of thought begin and end and how they relate to one another. How shall we recognize a complete unit of thought? It will be marked off by the satisfactory resolution of a tension or problem introduced at the outset. A complete unit of thought may be made up of a number of subdivisions, many of them entirely spelled out on their own. But the composition of a complete unit of thought will always strike us as cogent, the work of a single conception on how a whole thought should be constructed and expressed. While that unitary conception drew upon already available materials, the main point is made by the composition as a whole, and not by any of its (ready-made) parts.

The single most striking recurrent literary structure of Leviticus Rabbah is what we may call the base-verse/intersecting verse construction. In such a construction, a base-verse, drawn from the book of Leviticus, is juxtaposed to an intersecting verse, drawn from any book other than a pentateuchal one. Then this intersecting verse is subjected to systematic exegesis. On the surface the exegesis is out of all relationship with the base-verse. But in a stunning climax, all of the exegeses of the intersecting verse are shown to relate to the main point the exegete wishes to make about the base-verse. What that means is that the composition as a whole is so conceived as to impose meaning and order on all of the parts, original as well as ready-made ones, of which the author of the whole has made use. For the one example in *Parashah* 5, the base-verse is Leviticus 4:3 and the intersecting verse Job 34:29-30.

The other two recurrent literary structures, besides the base-verse/intersecting verse construction (called type I), are the intersecting verse/base-verse construction (type II) and the clause-by-clause exegetical construction (type III), which invokes a broad range of intersecting verses only for narrowly illustrative purposes). Type IV encompasses miscellanies. We are confronted with these categories of units of discourse in numerical order, that is, type I is first, type II second, and type III third. We can see that, even though Leviticus Rabbah hardly exhibits, on the surface, the sort of rhetorical discipline we discerned in the Mishnah and in Sifra, once we take a close look we find a highly restricted repertoire of patterns of language, and, moreover, we notice that the available patterns are used in a fixed order. Clearly, we have in hand a coherent piece of writing, one that is characterized by a deliberate set of choices about rhetoric.

Having identified the rhetorical patterning of language, we ask about the modes of cogent discourse. How does our authorship set forth its propositions, and what makes me claim that it has chosen to present theological propositions of broad concern for Jewry, not systemic ones of limited concern to the natural philosophy of the sages' group itself? We turn first to the underlying logic by which sentences are made to compose paragraphs, and paragraphs completed thoughts. The framers of Leviticus Rabbah treat topics, not particular verses. They make freestanding generalizations. They express cogent propositions through extended compositions, not episodic ideas. The authorship so collects and arranges its materials that an abstract proposition emerges. That proposition is not expressed only or mainly through episodic restatements, assigned, as I said, to an order established by a base-text. Rather, it emerges through a logic of its own. This authorship makes the move from an essentially exegetical mode of logical discourse to a fundamentally philosophical one. It is the shift from discourse framed around an established (hence old) text to syllogistic argument organized around a proposed (hence new) theorem or proposition. What changes, therefore, is the way in which cogent thought takes place, as people move from discourse contingent on some prior principle of organization to discourse autonomous of a ready-made program inherited from an earlier paradigm.

Accordingly, when we listen to the framers of Leviticus Rabbah, we see how statements in the document at hand thus become intelligible not contingently, that is, not on the strength of an established text (i.e., the logic of fixed association that I explained in chapter 2), but *a priori*, that is, on the basis of a deeper logic of meaning and an independent principle of rhetorical intelligibility. How so? Leviticus Rabbah is topical, not exegetical. Each of its thirty-seven *parashiyyot* pursues its given topic and develops points relevant to that topic. It is logical, in that discourse appeals to an underlying principle of composition and intelligibility. An anthology of statements about a single subject becomes a composition of theorems about that subject. With Leviticus Rabbah, rabbis take up the problem of saying what they wish to say not in an exegetical but in a syllogistic and freely discursive logic and rhetoric, and they do so for

148 *The Ecology of Religion*

theological, not merely philosophical and systemic, purposes. Since I hypothesize that form and substance cohere, I start back with the points of formal cogency of the document. It is there, at the repeated literary structures, that I should be able to point to the evidences of a fundamentally coherent way of seeing things, a mode of thought expressed throughout. What people wished to say and the way in which they chose to say it together constituted the document as we now know it.

We revert to the paramount and dominant exegetical construction, the base-verse/intersecting verse exegesis characteristic of our document. In such an exercise we read one thing in terms of something else. To begin with, it is the base-verse in terms of the intersecting verse. But, as the reader will have observed in the text itself, it also is the intersecting verse in other terms—a multilayered construction of analogy and parable. The intersecting verse's elements always turn out to stand for, to signify, to speak of, something other than that to which they openly refer. If water stands for Torah and the skin disease for evil speech, if the reference to something stands for some other thing entirely, then the mode of thought at hand is simple. One thing symbolizes another; nothing says what it means. Everything important speaks metonymically, elliptically, parabolically, symbolically. All statements carry deeper meaning, which inheres in other statements altogether. The profound sense, then, of the base-verse emerges only through restatement within and through the intersecting verse—as if the base-verse spoke of things that, on the surface, we do not see at all. Accordingly, if we ask the single prevalent literary construction to testify to the prevailing frame of mind, its message is that things are never what they seem. All things demand interpretation. Interpretation begins in the search for analogy, for that to which the thing is likened, hence the deeper sense in which all exegesis at hand is parabolic. It is a quest for that for which the thing in its deepest structure stands.

Exegesis, here, consists of an exercise in analogical thinking, just as in the case of the Mishnah. That is to say, if something is like something else, it therefore evokes or symbolizes that which is quite outside itself. It may be the opposite of something else, in which case in the Mishnah it follows the opposite rule, and in the case of Leviticus Rabbah it conforms to the exact opposite of the rules that govern that something else. The reasoning is either analogical or contrastive, and the fundamental logic is taxonomic. The taxonomy rests on those comparisons and contrasts we should call, as I said, metonymic and parabolic. In that case, what lies on the surface misleads. What lies beneath or beyond the surface—there is the true reality, the world of truth and meaning. Thus, the tracts that allow classification serve only one purpose: to teach us to recognize what is beneath the surface. How shall we characterize people who see things this way? They constitute the opposite of those who call a thing as it is. Self-evidently, they have become accustomed to perceiving more—or less—than is at hand. Perhaps that is a natural mode of thought for the Jews of this period (and not only of this period), so long used to calling themselves God's first love, yet now seeing others with greater worldly reason claiming that same advantaged relationship.

This draws us toward the theological discourse undertaken in the document before us. For it is not in mind only, but still more in the politics of the world that the people that for more than three hundred years remembered its origins along with the very creation of the world and founding of humanity, that recalled how it alone served and serves the one and only God, had confronted a quite different existence. The radical disjuncture between the way things were and the way Scripture said things were supposed to be—and in actuality would some day become—surely imposed an unbearable tension. It was one thing for the slave born to slavery to endure. It was another for the free man sold into slavery to accept that same condition. The vanquished people, the nation that had lost its city and its temple, that had, moreover, produced another nation from its midst to take over its Scripture and much else, could not bear too much reality. That defeated people will then have found refuge in a mode of thought that trained vision to see other things otherwise than the eyes perceived them. Among the diverse ways by which the weak and subordinated accommodate to their circumstance, the one of iron-willed pretense in life is most likely to yield the mode of thought at hand: Things never are, because they cannot be, what they seem.

In this context we note in the case before us, as in numerous other passages in this writing, the recurrence of a list of events in

Israel's history, meaning, in this context, Israel's history solely in scriptural times, down through the return to Zion. The one-time events of the generation of the Flood. Sodom and Gomorrah, the patriarchs and the sojourn in Egypt, the Exodus, the revelation of the Torah at Sinai, the golden calf, the Davidic monarchy and the building of the Temple, Sennacherib, Hezekiah, and the destruction of northern Israel, Nebuchadnezzar and the destruction of the Temple in 586 B.C.E., the life of Israel in Babylonian captivity, Daniel and his associates, Mordecai and Haman—these events occur over and over again. They turn out to serve as paradigms of sin and atonement, steadfastness and divine intervention, and equivalent lessons. We find, in fact, a fairly standard repertoire of scriptural heroes or villains, on the one side, and conventional lists of Israel's enemies and their actions and downfall, on the other. The boastful, for instance, include the generation of the Flood, Sodom and Gomorrah, Pharaoh, Sisera, Sennacherib, Nebuchadnezzar, and the wicked empire (Rome), contrasted to Israel, despised and humble in this world. The four kingdoms recur again and again, always ending, of course, with Rome, with the repeated message that after Rome will come Israel. But Israel has to make this happen through its faith and submission to God's will. Lists of enemies ring the changes on Cain, the Sodomites, Pharaoh, Sennacherib, Nebuchadnezzar, and Haman.

Accordingly, the mode of thought brought to bear upon the theme of history remains exactly the same as in the Mishnah: *Listenwissenschaft* or list making, just as in the case of the Mishnah, with data exhibiting similar taxonomic traits drawn together into lists based on common monothetic traits or definitions. These lists, then, through the power of repetition make a single enormous point or prove a social law of history. The catalogues of exemplary heroes and historical events serve a further purpose. They provide a model of how contemporary events are to be absorbed into the biblical paradigm. Since biblical events exemplify recurrent happenings—sin and redemption, forgiveness and atonement—they lose their one-time character. At the same time and in the same way, current events find a place within the ancient, but eternally present, paradigmatic scheme. So no new historical events, other than exemplary episodes in lives of heroes, demand narration, because, through what is said about the past, what was happening in the times of the framers of Leviticus Rabbah would also come under consideration. This mode of dealing with biblical history and contemporary events produces two reciprocal effects. The first is the mythicization of biblical stories—their removal from the framework of ongoing, unique patterns of history and sequences of events and their transformation into accounts of things that happen all the time. The second is that contemporary events, too, lose all of their specificity and enter the paradigmatic framework of established mythic existence. So (1) the Scripture's myth happens every day, and (2) every day produces reenactment of the Scripture's myth.

We now turn to the substance of theological discourse as it is effected in response to—of all biblical writings!—the book of Leviticus. In seeking the substance of the mythic being invoked by the exegetes at hand, who read the text as if it spoke about something else and the world as if it lived out the text, we uncover a simple fact. At the center of the pretense, that is, the as-if mentality of Leviticus Rabbah and its framers, we find a simple proposition. Israel is God's special love. That love is shown in a simple way. Israel's present condition of subordination derives from its own deeds. It follows that God cares, so that Israel may look forward to redemption on God's part in response to Israel's own regeneration through repentance. When the exegetes proceeded to open the scroll of Leviticus, they found numerous occasions to state this proposition in concrete terms and specific contexts. The sinner brings on his own sickness, but God heals through that very ailment. The nations of the world govern in heavy succession, but Israel's lack of faith guaranteed their rule, and its moment of renewal will end it. Israel's leaders—priests, prophets, kings—fall into an entirely different category from those of the nations, as much as does Israel. In these and other concrete allegations, the same classical message comes forth.

The message of Leviticus Rabbah attaches itself to the book of Leviticus, as if that book had come from prophecy, interpreted history, and addressed the issue of salvation. But it came from the priesthood and spoke of sanctification. The paradoxical syllogism—the as-if reading, the opposite of how things seem—of the composers of Leviticus Rabbah therefore reaches simple formulation. In the very setting of sanctification we find the promise of salvation. In the topics of the cult and the priesthood we uncover the national and social issues of the moral life and redemptive hope of Israel. The repeated comparison and contrast of priesthood and prophecy, sanctification and salvation, turn out to produce a complement, which comes to most perfect union in the text at hand. Nearly all of Leviticus Rabbah deals with the national, social condition of Israel, and this in three contexts: (1) Israel's setting in the history of the nations, (2) the character of the inner life of Israel itself, (3) the future history of Israel. So the biblical book that deals with the holy Temple now is shown to address the holy people. Leviticus really discusses not the consecration of the cult but the sanctification of the nation—its conformity to God's will, laid forth in the Torah, and God's rules. When we review the document as a whole and ask what is that other thing that the base-text is supposed to address, it turns out that the sanctification of the cult stands for the salvation of the nation. The nation now is like the cult then, the ordinary Israelite now like the priest then. The holy way of life lived now, through acts to which merit accrues, corresponds to the holy rites then. The process of metamorphosis is full, rich, complete. When everything stands for something else, the something else repeatedly turns out to be the nation.

At the end, we must ask how systemic theology is worked out through exegetical form, since, as we can see, the document does not express these syllogisms in the form of arguments at all. Rather, they come before us as statements of fact, and the facts upon which numerous statements rest derive from Scripture. The appeal is to an autonomous realm, namely, reason confirmed by experience. The repeated claim is not that things are so merely because Scripture says what it says, but that things happened as they happened in accord with laws we may verify or test (as Scripture, among other sources of facts, tells us). The emphasis is on the sequence of events, the interrelationship exhibited by them. How does Scripture in particular participate? It is not *in particular* at all. Scripture serves as a source of information, much as any history of the world or of a nation would provide sources of information: facts. The conditional syllogisms of our composition over and over again run through the course of history. The effort is to demonstrate that the rule at hand applies at all times, under all circumstances. It is because the conditional syllogism must serve under all temporal circumstances. The recurrent listing of events subject to a single rule runs as often as possible through the course of all of human history, from creation to the fourth monarchy (Rome), which in Judaism is the end of time prior to the age that is coming. Accordingly, the veracity of rabbinic conditional arguments depends over and over again on showing that the condition holds at all times. The facts with which our authorship has worked are scriptural. The propositions it proposes to demonstrate through these facts, however, are eternal. That is why it found in exegesis the correct structure for the presentation of its theology.

In my view, the correct method for reading, writing, and revealing religion lies in the identification of the modes of thought that underlay discourse. What we have in Leviticus Rabbah in particular is the result of the mode of thought not of prophets or historians but of philosophers and scientists— hence, in the framework of religion, of theologians. The framers propose not to lay down but to discover rules governing Israel's life. As we find in the Mishnah's discourse the rules of nature by identifying and classifying facts of natural life, so we find in the discourse of Leviticus Rabbah rules of society by identifying and classifying the facts of Israel's social life. In both modes of inquiry we make sense of things by bringing together like specimens and finding out whether they form a species, then bringing together like species and finding out whether they form a genus—in all, classifying data and identifying the rules that make possible the classification. That sort of thinking lies at the deepest level of list making, which is, as I said, the work of offering a proposition and facts (for social rules), similar to outlining genus and species (for rules of nature). Once discovered, the social rules of Israel's national life yield explicit statements, of course, such as that God hates the arrogant and loves the humble. The logical status of these statements, in context, is as secure and unassailable as the logical status of statements about physics, ethics, or politics, as these emerge in philosophical—and therefore also theological—thought.

It suffices to observe that the method of rhetorical and logical analysis has done its work on three disparate pieces of writing: the Mishnah, Sifra, and Leviticus Rabbah. It has examined diverse data and in all three instances has shown that we deal with coherent writing. Texts read entirely on their own thus are shown to form coherent statements. But they are not closed systems, and in the nature of things systemic description involves more than the demonstration that the writings of a religious system can be read as freestanding statements, one by one. We have to find out how to read these writings in relationship with one another, or we are left not with a religious system but merely with its sherds and remnants. In the examination of the connections between autonomous texts, we are able to move outward from the writing toward that religious system that the writing now represents, and this we do in both diachronic and synchronic dimensions.

PART THREE

Context:

The Connection Between Texts

CHAPTER SIX

From Text to Context

Documents form testimony—not to private conception but to public religion—only when read in relationship with one another. For it is in that relationship, brought about by the decision of parties other than a single, original authorship, that we discern the intervention of that social entity for which the documents, transformed into and read as a canon, are made to speak. A social world, an audience, a readership, intervenes. For a book is not a religion, but at the moment an audience, a readership, receives and values discrete writings and joins them together into a larger formation, a canon is born.

Since it is the canon that points toward a religion as the result of a social act of persons beyond individual authorships, our task is to investigate the relationships between and among autonomous documents, which is to say, we have to put texts in their broader contexts. As before, we do this inductively, working with the smallest whole units at hand, starting with two documents at a time. These investigations, therefore, cannot take on a uniform character, since we may identify the shared, social context of two or more texts by more than a single indicative trait. Among what must be many more possibilities beyond my capacity to imagine, I discern three ways in which a text may lead beyond itself.

The first derives from the imagination of its authorship. By points of stress that are implicit and unstated, an authorship testifies to its conception of the world out there, beyond its own circle. When a text comments on the social world beyond, the comments may or may not attest to the context in which the text is composed. But when the authorship repeatedly asks one range of questions and ignores another, then it suggests a profound judgment on how things are perceived, an act of definition of critical issues, and that judgment draws us beyond the text, to the authorship's conception of the social world to which it proposes to address its text.

A second and quite different context for discerning connections between texts finds definition in the formal, documentary relationship between one text and another, for example, between a text and a document of amplification and augmentation of that text. If a later authorship receives and revises an earlier document, the shape and system imparted by the later authorship creates for the earlier document a connection, hence a context, beyond its own limits.

A third context, equally distinct from the first two, derives from a later authorship's implicit judgment upon and unarticulated relationship with the materials it has received and revised. This judgment may be laid down in more than a single way, but it is a judgment that is invariably imparted when the authorship receive and rework traditional materials.

Accordingly, we have at least three quite distinct ways in which we may investigate the connections that define the context of texts. First, we ask the rhetorical traits of a text's authorship to inform us about their perception of the world beyond. This we do in the present chapter, in the setting of the Talmud of the Land of Israel, or the Yerushalmi. Second, in chapter 7, we raise the quite separate question of how a text's authorship proposes to set forth not a statement *about* norms but a fully articulated representation of those norms. For that purpose we turn to The Fathers According to Rabbi Nathan, in its relationship with The Fathers. Finally, in chapter 8, we address a third distinct question, the classification of texts in relationship to systems, and this question will define our inquiry into the Yerushalmi of Babylonia, or Bavli. There I show how to describe the definitive traits of a document as systemic evidence. This point, expressed somewhat obscurely here, will become clear in chapter 8. In each of these inquiries into the context of texts, now read as connected to a broader frame of reference, I mean to exemplify methods of inquiry that I have worked out. These form three dimensions by which to take the measure of context, seen as the matter of the connection between texts.

While our focus of interest is on the points of stress and recurrent tensions in the Yerushalmi, it also presents us with a writing explicitly related to a prior one. Nearly every discourse of the Yerushalmi—perhaps 90 percent of the whole—addresses one main point: the meaning of the Mishnah. Here, the connection and focus bear their own meaning. For the Yerushalmi's authorship, the life of Israel reaches the level of analysis within the integument of the Mishnah. That is to say, the Mishnah is about life, while the Yerushalmi is about the Mishnah. This judgment, however, should not be confused with the historical fact concerning the circumstance of the authorship of the Yerushalmi. For, I must stress, we do not know how this authorship did its work over a long span of time. We have only the final result, the Yerushalmi itself. The world beyond, to which our authorship attests and which forms the context of the text, comes to us as a still shot of the moment of ultimate redaction.

The reason is that, on the surface, such evidence as we have, differentiating one authority from another, one period of work from another, one school from another, consists in only one fact. A great many sayings in the Yerushalmi are assigned to particular names. If we could demonstrate that what the Yerushalmi assigns to an authority really was said by him, then, on the face of it, we should have ample evidence of the history of the discussions ultimately preserved by the Yerushalmi. For if we knew that Rabbi X really said what he is supposed to have said, then we might assign to him (his day, school, town, and generation) the opinions he held. These opinions then might be differentiated from the ones belonging to Rabbi Y (at another time, in another school, town, and generation). Knowing what one man or group thought at one time, we might then compare and contrast that corpus of ideas and modes of thought with those presented by a different group of people at another place and time. The upshot would be the history of the reception and realization of the legacy of the Mishnah, both in its parts (individual laws) and as a whole: the formation of rabbinic Judaism upon the foundations of the Mishnah over a sequence of two hundred years. But we cannot show, and therefore do not know, that people really said what is attributed to them by the final document, and we cannot show and do not know that they really did what stories say they did. Accordingly, we see a tableau, not a stage in motion. We shall return to this problem in chapter 9.

The traits of the Yerushalmi viewed as phenomena out of all social and historical context nonetheless allow us access to the social imagination of the text's authorship. For the Yerushalmi speaks about the Mishnah in essentially a single voice, about fundamentally few things. Its mode of speech as much as of thought is uniform throughout. Diverse topics produce slight differentiation in modes of analysis. The same sorts of questions phrased in the same rhetoric—a dialectical argument, composed of questions and answers—turn out to pertain equally well to every subject and problem. The Yerushalmi's discourse, therefore, forms a closed system, akin to the logic of methodical analysis I introduced earlier. That is a stunning fact, for it clearly defines the choice at hand. The choices people made then announce, by implication, the views of the world that they held. And the "they" is a clear fact. For the Yerushalmi presents us with both a uniformity of discourse and a monotony of tone. The Yerushalmi speaks in a single voice that by definition is collective, not greatly differentiated by traits of individuals.

The Yerushalmi identifies no author or collegium of authors. When I say that the Yerushalmi speaks in a single voice, I mean to say that it everywhere speaks uniformly, consistently, and predictably. That explains why we may move from the text to the context imagined by the text's authorship. For in the case of this writing, the voice is the voice of a book. The message is one deriving from a community, the collectivity of sages for whom and to whom the book speaks. Overall, the document seems to intend to provide notes, an abbreviated script that anyone may use to reconstruct and reenact formal discussions of problems: about this, one says that. Curt and often arcane, these notes can be translated only by immense bodies of inserted explanation. All of this script of information is public and undifferentiated, not individual and idiosyncratic. We must assume that people took it for granted that, out of the signs of speech, it would be possible for anyone to reconstruct speech, doing so in accurate and fully conventional ways. So the literary traits of the document presuppose a uniform code of communication: a single voice. This fact justifies my claim that we may read the text in the context established by the collegium of its authorship. That single voice is a social voice, the collective comment of a society of sages upon a larger society to which it wished to speak: "all Israel," as it would have said.

The role of individuals in the Yerushalmi is unimportant. The paramount voice is that of "the Yerushalmi." The rhetoric of the Yerushalmi may be described very simply: a preference for questions and answers, and a willingness then to test the answers and to expand through secondary and tertiary amplification, achieved through further questions and answers. The whole gives the appearance of the script for a conversation to be reconstructed, or an argument of logical possibilities to be reenacted, in one's own mind. In this setting, of course, we shall be struck by the uniformity of the rhetoric, even though we need not make much of the close patterning of language, for example, Rab's and Yohanan's, where it occurs. The voice of "the Yerushalmi," moreover, authoritatively defines the mode of analysis. The inquiry is consistent and predictable; one argument differs from another not in supposition but only in detail. When individuals' positions occur, it is because what they have to say serves the purposes of "the Yerushalmi" and its uniform inquiry. The inquiry is into the logic and the rational potentialities of a passage. To these dimensions of thought, the details of place, time, and even of an individual's philosophy are secondary. All details are turned toward a common core of discourse. This, I maintain, is possible only because the document as a whole takes shape in accord with an overriding program of inquiry and comes to expression in conformity with a single plan of rhetorical expression. The upshot is that we may speak about "the Yerushalmi," its voice, its purposes, and its mode of constructing its view of the Israelite world.

The reason I claim that we may rely upon the Yerushalmi to testify to the viewpoint of its framers (we assume, a group of sages) at the end point in the Yerushalmi's formation is simple. We rely upon the document as a whole because it speaks, overall, in a uniform voice. It is not merely an encyclopedia of information, but, in general, a remarkably protracted, uniform inquiry into the logical traits of passages of the Mishnah. As I said, most of the Yerushalmi deals with the exegesis and amplification of the Mishnah's rules. Now, wherever we turn, that labor of exegesis and amplification, without differentiation in topics or tractates, conforms to a few simple rules in inquiry, repeatedly phrased, implicitly or explicitly, in a few simple rhetorical forms or patterns. So in the end, we know what the framers of the Yerushalmi want us to know, namely, the main lines of their vision of the social world in which their writing found its context.

If we want to know what concerns shaped the imagination of the makers of the Yerushalmi, the sages of the later fourth century, we must thus ask what they said about the Mishnah. For the Mishnah forms the center of their attention, the focus of nearly the whole of the Talmud's inquiry. In describing and later interpreting the testimony of the Yerushalmi about the formation of Judaism, therefore, we must locate the points of insistence, the recurrent questions, the patterns of thought, that, all together, tell us what, about the Mishnah in particular, confronted the Talmud's sages as issues of urgency. These then are to be generalized beyond the specificities of exegesis of the Mishnah.

If I have one lesson of method to teach, it is that while God lives in the details, God speaks about some few things obviously and repetitively: an effective author. So, too, do well-crafted texts, and by definition, a religious text that has survived has served its framers well indeed and effectively delivered their message. So we seek to discern not details but the character of the whole, even as we move from the text to its broader context and framework of connection.

The very character of the Yerushalmi tells us the sages' view of the Mishnah. The Mishnah presented itself to them as constitutive, the text of ultimate concern. That self-evident fact requires specification when we realize that to others of the same period, as well as to Israelites of an earlier time, discussions of law did not invariably yield secondary compositions upon an authoritative code outside of Scripture. To be sure, the legal texts of the Essene library at Qumran are framed as autonomous statements of ordinary rules and procedures, perhaps comparable with the Mishnah. But these do not elicit secondary expansion and development, the accretion of sustained discourse, such as the Yerushalmi reveals. A brief comparison to writings of other Judaisms makes the point clear. If, in the Essene community, another text besides Scripture was venerated, it was not the Manual of Discipline. Rules for an occasion such as those in the Manual of Discipline did not generate elaborate books of explanation and amplification. Books of ad hoc rules, so far as we know, were not venerated, and people who knew those rules and could apply them were not on that account alone treated as holy. Israelites could and did write down rules without making the rule book into a focus of intellectual obsession by creating a line-by-line exegesis for a text, the way the Talmud's sages exalted the phrases and words of the Mishnah and so vastly expanded the whole into something larger and deeper than what it originally had been.

Among many other candidates, whether the Mishnah, the Manual of Discipline, the Elephantine Papyri, or even the Holiness Code, the Priestly Code, and the Covenant Code of the Pentateuch (the mosaics of the written Torah) so far as we know, only the Mishnah received a Yerushalmi—two of them, in fact, as we recall. What separated the Mishnah from all other, earlier Israelite law codes must be located in the fact and circumstance of its formation and reception. But we should be carried far afield, to speculate on the comparisons in the diverse states of Israelite politics and culture revealed among the diverse circumstances in which the various codes, or even fragments, of law came to closure and reached a position of authority for the Jewish nation. It suffices to state the simple conclusion that, for the sages of the later fourth century (and for their predecessors as well, we must assume), the Mishnah, beyond Scripture, constituted Israel's single most important piece of writing. It is, at any rate, the document they cite after Scripture.

That fact is not difficult to interpret. The character of the Yerushalmi presents us with the definitive context. The Yerushalmi is a commentary written by philosopher-lawyers, men with extraordinary power to explain and amplify legal words and phrases, to generalize about rules, to theorize about matters of law as about mathematics. The reason that the sages deemed it urgent to do so, and to do so with such extraordinary vigor and energy, must surely be that the document in hand, the Mishnah, was the authoritative code for their courts. The exposition of the laws of the Mishnah demanded their best energies because the Mishnah's laws governed. Studied, therefore, in their circles of disciples, these laws defined both what was to be done and why sages in particular were the ones to do it. That they did indeed receive and rework the Mishnah is only known to us because we have the Yerushalmi. To state the obvious, the work was done by people who needed to do the work in just the way they did it. From that simple supposition all else follows. Philosophers (if that is what they were) were drawn to this text rather than some other because they were also lawyers.

These lawyers' profession centered upon an institution lacking analogy in our own world and hence also lacking a suitable name in our language. We call it simply an "institution." The institution was formed by masters with their disciples and subordinated specialists, such as professional memorizers of traditions. The institution in part intersected with the Jewish government of the country and so constituted a court or bureau of some sort. Certain activities of public administration are well represented. So the institution intersected also with the political system of the Jewish sector of the land of Israel and constituted a kind of inchoate municipality. But the institution did not encompass the Jewish government, which comprised other elements. The tales told about this same institution and the fantasies attached to its principal masters testify to yet another trait. The institution formed a center of supernatural power. So whatever we call it, the institution that received the Mishnah and produced the Yerushalmi turns out to have been protean and remarkably productive. It made Judaism. But in saying so, I have moved ahead of my story.

Since the Mishnah stands forth as the principal authority for the law and theology of Judaism, so far as the Yerushalmi portrayed both, one conclusion must follow. The Mishnah, not an institution or political authority but a book, constituted the stable foundation for certainty, the basis for authority, legitimating whatever the Talmudic sages did in their work of governing Israel in its land. The character of the Yerushalmi makes it clear that the Mishnah laid the foundation and set the goal of the Talmud's sages' quest for authority. This means that the character of Talmudic discourse tells us that sages believed that if they knew precisely what the Mishnah said and meant, they then knew what they were supposed to do, how things were supposed to be. So the proper interpretation of the Mishnah, in relationship to Scripture, served as the ultimate guarantee of certainty. We therefore should anticipate a splendid myth of the origin and authority of the Mishnah, on which, for the sages, all else rested. Yet, so far as I can see, the Yerushalmi presents no explicit theory of the Mishnah.

Implicitly, however, the Talmud's judgment of the Mishnah is self-evident, hardly demanding specification. After Scripture, the Mishnah is the authoritative law code of Israelite life—the center, the focus, the source from which all else flows. Beyond the Mishnah is only Scripture. At the same time, the very implicit character of the expression of this fundamental judgment is puzzling. While nearly every unit of discourse of the Yerushalmi—90 percent of the whole, as I said—pays its tribute to the importance of interpreting a cited law of the Mishnah, seldom does a passage of the Yerushalmi speak of the Mishnah as a whole, let alone of its origin and authority. It is rare to find an allusion to a complete tractate, or even to a chapter as such. Accordingly, if we want to know how the sages of the Yerushalmi explained to themselves the status of the Mishnah, we are at a loss to find out. All is implicit, with views of the whole rarely expressed.

There is ample evidence to allow a reliable description of how the Talmud's founders view the Mishnah. The Mishnah rarely cites verses of Scripture in support of its propositions. The Yerushalmi routinely adduces Scriptural bases for the Mishnah's laws. The Mishnah seldom undertakes the exegesis of verses of Scripture for any purpose. The Yerushalmi consistently investigates the meaning of verses of Scripture and does so for a variety of purposes. Accordingly, the Yerushalmi, subordinate as it is to the Mishnah, regards the Mishnah as subordinate to, and contingent upon, Scripture. That is why, in the Talmud's view, the Mishnah requires the support of prooftexts of Scripture. That fact can mean only that, by itself, the Mishnah exercises no autonomous authority and enjoys no independent standing or norm-setting status. The task of the framers of the Yerushalmi is not only to explain Mishnah-law but to prove through Scripture the facticity of the rules of the Mishnah. Accordingly, so far as the Yerushalmi has a theory about the Mishnah as such, as distinct from a theory about the exposition, amplification, and application to the court system of various laws in the Mishnah, it is quite clear. To state matters negatively (and the absence of articulate statements makes this the wiser choice), the Mishnah does not enjoy autonomous and uncontingent authority as part of the one whole Torah of Moses revealed by God at Sinai. The simple fact that one principal task facing the sages, as I just said, is to adduce prooftexts for the Mishnah's laws makes this conclusion ineluctable. It follows that without such texts the Mishnah's laws lack foundation.

Here is a fine instance of how the characteristics of a text inform us about the authorship's context, as they imagined it. If the sages of the second century, who made the Mishnah as we know it, spoke in their own name and in the name of the logic of their own minds, those who followed, certainly the ones who flourished in the later fourth century, took a quite different view. Reverting to ancient authority, like others of the age, they turned back to Scripture, deeming it the sole reliable source of certainty about truth. Unlike their masters in the Mishnah, theirs was a quest for a higher authority than the logic of their own minds. The shift from age to age, then, is clear. The second-century masters took commonplaces of Scripture, well-known facts, and stated them wholly in their own language and context. Fourth-century masters phrased commonplaces of the Mishnah or banalities of worldly wisdom, so far as they could, in the language of Scripture and its context.

The challenge of the Mishnah demanded more than a theory of the ultimate authority of the document and its various laws. It also involved a quite separate set of issues, generated by two things. One was the particular way in which the Mishnah had been formulated and handed on. The other was the peculiar character of the Mishnah's discussions. As to the former, the Mishnah was not published in the usual way, which was to place a single, authoritative text in an archive, so that all questions of wording in copies of the text might be referred to that one correct version. Rather, it was published through processes of oral formulation, transmitted through the memories of professional memorizers, who could be relied upon to repeat exactly the words they had learned. Second, the Mishnah is not a code of laws in which people are told what to do and not to do. It is a compilation of opinions on laws, in which various views of what people should and should not do are laid out. These two peculiarities inherent in the document, its form, and its character, produced the two most painful points of uncertainty: the exact wording of the text and the correct decision of the law. Accordingly, the Talmud's sages had these tasks when they approached any passage of the Mishnah: first, they needed to sort out the versions of the wording of a saying of the Mishnah; second, they had to determine the correct law in a case of dispute.

These two matters, together with the issue of authority, define principal themes of the thought of the Talmud's sages concerning the Mishnah. The principle expressed in both issues is the same: dogmatically rigid honesty, an absolutely critical approach to all allegations of fact. The sages of the Yerushalmi were confronted with a diversity of claims about matters of detail. Because it had been formulated and handed on through memorization and oral transmission, each passage of the Mishnah existed in numerous versions. Diverse possibilities for reading the text permitted a variety of decisions on the practical law. Accordingly, the condition of the Mishnah generated considerable uncertainty. The character of the document, with its incessant din of contradictory opinions, necessitated a predictable and reliable means of settling matters. So the Mishnah had to be turned into a law code.

As to the quest for accurate readings, the strong interest in testing statements in light of all available information, publicly shared and collectively evaluated, is illustrated in the following story. Here we see that a disciple was expected to study with another person, then to exercise supervision of reasoning and the traditions of the other. Idiosyncratic and eccentric traditions were dismissed, not trusted. A single individual's testimony to what an authority had said was not apt to be dismissed, but it also was not likely to be granted immediate credence. We deal with a highly collective labor of attaining certainty through consensus. The prejudice against engaging in processes of learning on one's own and by oneself was blatant, and that tells us that we deal with a document that conceives of religion as forming a social fact, not a private preserve of personal privilege:

Y: Nedarim 11:1:IV

P.   Judah of Husa hid in a cave for three days to inquire into the reason for the rule that the maintenance of the life of this town takes precedence over the maintenance of the life of another town.

Q.   He came to R. Yosé b. Halapta, saying to him, "I hid in a cave for three days to inquire into the reason for the rule that the maintenance of the life of this town takes precedence over the maintenance of the life of another town."

R.   He called R. Abba, his son, saying to him, "What is the reason for rule that the maintenance of the life of this town takes precedence over the maintenance of the life of another town?"

S.   He recited for him the following verse: "'These cities had each its pasture lands round about it; so it was with all these cities' (Josh. 21:42). [That is, each city was supplied with all its needs.]"

T.   He said to him, "What caused your ignorance? It was that you did not study with your fellow [but all by yourself]."

The most striking characteristic of the story just now reviewed is this: The same certainty sought in the reading of passages of the Mishnah was a matter of concern also in the formulation and assessment of versions of sayings assigned to sages themselves.

The treatment of the Mishnah serves to exemplify a more pervasive trait of mind, one expressed in approaches to the sayings of authorities of the day, not only of times past. Just as the Talmudic sages adduced verses of Scripture to validate a law of the Mishnah, so they pursued the same mode of exegesis in behalf of a legal or theological statement of their own times. Likewise, just as they assumed that the processes of accurate memorization of what had been orally formulated had brought the Mishnah from its point of origin to their own hands, so they took for granted that those same processes would carry forward an accurate account of what they would formulate in their own names for oral transmission. The sole point of differentiation was quite natural. What was given in their own names might originate either in what they said or in what they did, so they were careful to preserve a record of the source of what was given: observation and surmise, or actual formulation of ipsissima verba. But the purpose was the same.

Certainty depended upon disciplined, collective processes of framing and handing on reliable sayings. And that fact again points, within the text, to the broader context that the authorship conceived. What was deemed reliable was what could be shown to accord with laws originally laid down in Scripture. It follows that what the sages had in hand was an accurate account of what God had expressed as his will for Israel and revealed to Moses at Mount Sinai. While in the Yerushalmi the Torah-myth did not encompass the Mishnah in particular, the Torah-myth in general assuredly stands behind the disparate procedures and points of concern we have now surveyed: the search for scriptural proof for contemporary opinion and the scrutiny of the accuracy of transmission, from times of old or from the present day, of what was, to begin with, Torah. What that means is that, once more, the Mishnah in particular was never the issue. It was part of the answer, not of the question. The question came from elsewhere. Those troubled by the question addressed it to the Mishnah, among other things. At issue was the authority of the sage, the accuracy, back to Sinai, of his opinions, the certainty of his standing. The literary expression of this issue should not confuse us as to its origin and point of reference: men, not books. We deal with writing, but the writing attests to a social world of a particular order, a religious one, to which we return in chapter 10.

This brings us to a second critical trait of intellect facing society that the Yerushalmi's authorship reveals. Its concern with certainty, which drew its eyes upward to Sinai, involved yet another kind of certainty, this one concrete. For a quite distinct type of uncertainty derives from the failure of the Mishnah's text to specify clear and definite instructions on what to do and what not to do. The carefully exemplified principles, expressed through recurrent rules, yield a surface of differences of opinion on matters of detail. Consequently, the Mishnah generates the necessity to formulate principles for sorting out different viewpoints and so deciding what actually is to be done. For lawyer-philosophers, matters of mere speculation cannot have been especially urgent. We may assume that the reticence of the Mishnah's framers to specify solutions to their endless thought-problems implicitly expresses their own judgment on this point. Since they did not have to make concrete decisions, and had, indeed, slight power to effect them (they were merely employees of the local ethnarch), they also did not imagine the need to present their ideas as a practical code of law. This guess, at any rate, seems plausible when we consider what the Mishnah's heirs found it necessary to do. They framed a program of resolving Mishnaic disagreements that had given no significant hint as to the right answer and the ultimate decision. Whatever the reason for the Mishnah's peculiar character as a set of open-ended disputes, the fact is that in the period and circumstance represented by the Yerushalmi, people believed that decisions had to come forth, arguments had to reach solution, doubt had to be resolved.

One may suppose that the sages' program of settling disagreements and stating practical law constituted a criticism of the Mishnah's framers' policy. When we consider their insistence upon supplying prooftexts for propositions deemed by Our Holy Rabbi not to require them, it seems clear that a criticism of Rabbi's position was intended. But the opposite is made explicit. Disputes left unresolved served a valuable purpose and did not constitute a flaw in Rabbi's Mishnah; so Yannai:

Y. Sanhedrin 4:2

A. In property cases they decide by a majority of one, whether for acquittal or for conviction,

B. While in capital cases they decide by a majority of one for acquittal, but only with a majority of two [judges] for conviction.

I. A. Said R. Yannai, "If the Torah were handed down cut-and-dried [so that there were no possibility for disagreement in reasoning about the law and no need to make up one's mind], there would be no place [for the world] to stand. [We should not know how to decide a case.]"

B. What is the Scriptural basis for that statement?

C. "And the Lord spoke to Moses . . . ," [telling him the diverse arguments relevant to each law].

D. [Moses] said to him, "Lord of the World! Teach me the [practical] law [so that there will be no doubts about it]."

E. He said to him, "'. . . follow the majority to incline' [the law to a decision, that is, make a decision in the law by a majority of the judges' opinions] (Ex. 23:2).

F. "[If] those who declare innocent form the majority, declare the accused innocent. [If] those who declare the accused to be guilty, declare him to be guilty."

G. [This is] so that the Torah may be expounded in forty-nine ways on the side of a decision of uncleanness, and in forty-nine ways in favor of a decision of cleanness. ["Now if I reveal the law to you in all its finality, there will be no possibility for such a range of argument."]

H. And so it says, "The promises of the Lord are promises that are pure, silver refined in a furnace on the ground, purified seven times seven" (Ps. 12:6). [That is why there must be forty-nine arguments, G.]

I. And it says, "Rightly do they love you" (Song of Songs 1:4). [In argument to work out a right decision, they express their love for God.]

The importance of determining which authority's opinion should prevail as law self-evidently derived from the need to judge practical cases. An instance of the Talmud's portrayal of matters follows, in which we see that the tradition on the governing rule determined how to decide a particular case. How matters were worked out in courts in which those statements were not available or not deemed authority, is not clear.

Y. Ketubot 1:10

A. Said R. Yosé, "There was the precedent of a girl who went down to draw water from the well and was raped.

B. "Ruled R. Yohanan b. Nuri, 'If most of the men of the town marry off their daughters to the priesthood, lo, she may be married into the priesthood.' "

I. A. R. Judah in the name of R. Kahana, "The incident took place at the wagon-station of Sepphoris [where the wagons were parked for the marketplace, that is, in public domain.]"

B. Both R. Jeremiah, R. Hama bar Uqba say in the name of R. Hanina in the name of R. Yannai, "R. Joshua concurs in the case of a woman who was raped [that she is believed if she says it was by a man who has not invalidated her, by his act of sexual relations, from marriage into the priesthood]. [His position, that a licentious woman does not care with whom she has sexual relations and hence is not believed when she says it was with a valid man, does not apply in the present case.]"

C. R. Abbahu in the name of R. Yohanan: "R. Joshua concurs in the case of a woman who was raped."

D. R. Hiyya bar Ashi said in the name of Rab, "The law accords with the view of R. Yosé, which he stated in the name of R. Yohanan b. Nuri."

E. R. Zeira asked before R. Yosa, "How is a case to be judged?"

F. He said to him, "It is in accord with R. Yosé's view, which he stated in the name of R. Yohanan b. Nuri."

Two different kinds of disputes confronted the Talmud's sages. First, they had to work out the decided law when the correct version of the Mishnah's rule was represented by a named authority, on the one hand, and an anonymous statement, on the other (or one by a named authority as against "sages say"). Here the principle was laid down that the law follows the majority as against the minority, under nearly all circumstances. When that was not the case, it had to be specified and explained. Accordingly, the goal of resolving disputes was to uncover the consensus of the collegium of sages as a whole. Here are ways in which that paramount principle is expressed.

Y.Taanit 2:13:I

E. R. Mana raised the question before R. Yudan: "Did not R Hezekiah, R. Abbahu in the name of R. Eleazar [state]: 'In any case in which Rabbi [Judah the patriarch in the Mishnah] presented the law as subject to dispute, and then afterward he presented it without ascription, the law follows the version given without ascription'?"

F. He said to him, "It is not Rabbi [who taught it without a named authority]. But here we have a different situation. If Rabbi presented a dispute and then he taught the matter without ascription, the law follows the version not bearing the name of an individual authority.

G. "But in the case in which Rabbi, for his part, did not repeat the tradition as a dispute, but others presented it as a dispute, and Rabbi taught the matter without naming an authority, is it not an argument a fortiori that the law should follow the view of the anonymous version of the law?"

H. R. Hezekiah, R. Jacob bar Aha, R. Simeon bar Aba in the name of R. Eleazar: "And even if others taught the tradition as subject to dispute, while Rabbi taught it without ascription, the law accords with the version lacking a named authority."

I. In that case, why did [Yohanan] teach the law as it was given in the name of a single individual [rather than in accord with the anonymous version]?

J. R. Samuel bar Jonah in the name of R. Aha: "That which you have said applies to a case in which there is no dispute alongside the anonymous version of the law. But if there is a dispute alongside the anonymous version of the law, it is not in such a case that the law follows the anonymous version of the law."

K. R. Yosé b. R. Bun in the name of R. Aha: "That which you have said applies to the case in which there is a dispute of one individual with another individual. But in a case in which there is an individual as against sages, it is not in such a case that the law follows the opinion presented without the name of an individual authority, but rather anonymously."

Along these same lines, if we deal with opinions of individuals, one may join one's opinion with that of an individual and the master who taught that individual, and do the same on the other side. But if you have an individual against sages, there is no choice but to follow the sages (Y. Niddah 1:4, IV). A named saying is deemed idiosyncratic, an anonymous one authoritative. That is why Judah the Patriarch's mode of formulation of the Mishnah was understood to provide hints about the decided law. It goes without saying, therefore, that determining the exact state of affairs—whether an opinion was that of an individual or the anonymous consensus of the sages—involved sifting and resifting traditions on the matter. Statements originating in the Tosefta constituted a particularly valuable and authoritative source of information.

The same principles of resolving disagreements and settling the law pertained to disputes among contemporary authorities as well. First, people carefully followed available traditions, memorized with great precision. If a tradition from a disciple's master was in hand, that would govern the decision in his own court. On the other hand, where there was no such tradition, an authority would rely upon a consensus of sages, whether of his own day or otherwise. In the following, striking case, an authority made certain to join to his decision the authority of two others, so as to represent his view as that of a collegium of sages.

Y. Niddah 2:7.VI

L. R. Haninah was living in Sepphoris, and cases would come before him. Twice cases went forth [from his court]. Now R.

Yohanan and R. Simeon b. Laqish were living there, but he did
not add them to his court.

M. They said, "That old man is wise, and his knife is sharp."

N. One time he did join them [to his court, asking them to
share in deciding a case].

O. They said, "Why does Rabbi [after ignoring us so long] pay
attention to us today?"

P. He said to them, "May [something bad] come upon me, if it
is not so that every case that I bring forth from my court I judge in
accord with a law that I learned from my teacher as a valid law
[This I learned from him] as many times as there are hairs on my
head. [In addition I saw my teacher apply these laws] in practice
at least three times. And on that account I rely on my own
teaching [without your concurrence]. But this particular case did
not come before my teacher as a matter of law or practical
decision more than twice. On that account I have joined you with
me to make the decision."

We see, therefore, that the example of the master was decisive,
if the master's tradition on a disputed law had been confirmed
both in the wording of the law and in the actual practice of the
court. Then the disciple—himself a great authority—was
prepared to apply the law without further ado. But otherwise
the disciple was prepared to associate with himself other leading
authorities, so providing a firm precedent for further judges.

Finally, we see in this last instance, which follows, how both
reason and authority joined to settle the matter. When all parties
to a dispute were present, it was not so easy to close discussion
and reach a final decision merely by appealing to the number of
concurring authorities. Persuasion through reasonable argument in the end was all that could settle issues among the actual
participants.

Y. Sanhedrin 3:8.IV

G. [If] two say, "We saw a single hair on his privy parts," and
two say, "We saw a single hair on his belly"—

H. R. Yosé and R. Hoshaiah bar R. Shimi—once said, "He is
unfit [not yet mature]." The other said, "He is fit."

I. The one who said that he is unfit deems the testimony to be
equivalent to that of one who testifies concerning the appearance

of only part of the required sign [of maturity]. The one who said
he is valid [maintains], "I say that [there were two hairs, but one of
them] may have fallen out."

J. [If] one party says, "I saw two hairs on his privy parts," and
one says, "I saw two hairs on his belly,"

K. R. Ba said, "In the opinion of all parties, he is now valid
[fully mature], [since there is sure evidence that there are the
requisite two pubic hairs]."

L. Said R. Haggai, "In the opinion of all parties he is invalid."

M. R. Yosé says, "The matter is [still] subject to dispute."

N. Said R. [Yosé] to R. Haggai, "Lo, R. Yudan [my student]
ruled in accord with my view of the matter."

O. He said to him, "Now since I differ from his master, all the
more so do I disagree with him!"

P. Said R. Mana, "R. Haggai's ruling is quite sound. For if we
have a bond which bears four seals, and one party gives testimony
concerning two of them, while another gives testimony concerning two of them, and someone cavils at the value of the bond, is
the bond of any value whatsoever? [Hardly!] For does not each
seal require the validation of two witnesses [and two witnesses are
as sound as a hundred]? Here too each sign [of maturity] requires
the validation of two witnesses [who suffers for all purposes]."

Q. R. Hinena derived the same facts from the case of
[attesting to full use and enjoyment of a property] throughout the
years of usucaption [to which testimony must be brought]. [That
is, if one wishes to establish the claim of title through usucaption,
he must bring evidence that he has held and used the property
for a given number of years.] "Now if one witness testified that he
had enjoyed usucaption for the first, second, and third years, and
one witness testified that he had enjoyed usucaption for the
fourth, fifth, and sixth years, is it possible that such [joined]
testimony is worth a thing? [No!] Is it not so that each year of
usucaption must be attested by two witnesses? Here too each sign
[of maturity] requires the validation of two witnesses."

The point, then, is that where tradition provided certainty, it
sufficed. When it did not, then the sages had to appeal to reason
and the inner logic of the law, an unsteady guide indeed in the
setting of different views of reason and logic. It is no wonder,
then, that wherever possible, the authority of decided law,
established principles, and precedents should be called upon, in
preference to making things up fresh for a new day.

The vast majority of the Yerushalmi's units of discourse take up the exegesis and amplification of the laws of the Mishnah. But what the framers of discourse regarded as appropriate procedures of inquiry into the meaning of the statements of the Mishnah in no way differed from what they accepted as valid practice in analyzing positions taken in other documents besides the Mishnah, on the one hand, and in sayings of their own predecessors and contemporaries, on the other. The Mishnah appears to be the focus, and it is. But the Mishnah does not stand at the center of the Yerushalmi's modes of differentiation. That is to say, from the Yerushalmi's view, certainty about what is to be done depends not (merely) upon a correct understanding of what the Mishnah's rules require. Certainty derives (1) from Scripture, as against the mere assertions of the Mishnah's authorities; (2) from well-attested versions of statements, as against the plethora of possible wordings; and (3) from harmonious decisions of the sages as a collegium, as against an endless exploration of the potentialities of idiosyncratic principles and eccentric opinions.

These three criteria, applied to all matters of doubt, not only the Mishnah's exegesis, then promise a resolution to the unresolved issues of the ancient inheritance. The sages of the Yerushalmi seek certain knowledge about some few, practical things. They therefore reject—from end to beginning—the chaos of speculation, the plurality of possibilities even as to the choice of words, and, above all, the daring and confidence to address the world in the name, merely, of sagacity. True, the Yerushalmi preserves the open-ended discourse of sages, not reduced to cut-and-dried positions. But the Yerushalmi makes decisions.

Thus, the elegant classicism of the Mishnah gives way to another set of concerns entirely. Reasoned speculation is chaotic; a range of choices in phrasing matters is disconcerting; authority resting on little more than human reflection is insufficient. Therefore, speculation gave way to practical reason. This I take to be the intellectual context in which the text at hand finds its locus, and this further indicates the view of the social world that the text's authorship sets forth. What people now sought was how to know what they should do. Unlike Mishnaic sages, the authorship at hand no longer cared merely to ratiocinate on abstract principles, always leaving matters in a state of irresolution. What bound text to text in a common context was the Mishnah.

Even as it speaks of its most intimate and particular concerns in its exegesis of small passages of the Mishnah, the Yerushalmi's authorship testifies to a world beyond itself. The Yerushalmi's sages speak of the Mishnah and how to find certainty in its uncertain phrasing and mooted principles. But in doing so, they testify vividly about themselves and about their task. The text, therefore, directs us to its context: Why these particular points of stress? Discourse on the Mishnah, so peculiar to our Yerushalmi (as well as to the Talmud of Babylonia) carries us to a world altogether beyond the narrow province of the Mishnah and its exegesis. The reason is clear. If we proposed to describe the kind of Judaism revealed in the pages of the Yerushalmi solely out of what is in those pages, as we can and do describe the Judaism of the Mishnah upon the basis of the resources of the Mishnah alone, we should find ourselves at an impasse. Everything we learn, beyond the simple and trivial facts about what some people thought the Mishnah's rules said and meant, points to a system of Judaism—a world view, a way of life, expressed within a distinct social group—of which the Yerushalmi forms a partial expression, not the entire account.

That fact becomes especially clear when we realize that everything sages wished to say about and to do with a law of the Mishnah, they proposed to say and do also in regard to laws they themselves made up. If laws of the Mishnah were held to require prooftexts of Scripture, so, too, were positions on all manner of subjects in the names of Talmudic sages. If the exact text of the Mishnah had to be ascertained and carefully preserved, the same was true for the exact wording of statements by the Yerushalmi's authorities. If the disputes about laws presented in the Mishnah had to be resolved in accord with simple, predictable rules, these same rules applied without variation to disputes among the Yerushalmi's masters. The present (the situation of the fourth century, possibly also the third) was to be projected onto the past, whether the case involved the second century's work or the words of God to Moses over a millennium before. A world view, a way of life, produced within and for a distinct social group—a Judaism—clearly had taken shape. The

Yerushalmi points toward the context defined by the structure and dynamic of that Judaism. In the comparison of the earlier with the later document, the Mishnah and the Yerushalmi, we see how writing moves us outward toward religion. Another such comparison, to which we now turn, brings to vivid expression just what that religion means to say when it is realized in the person of a human being.

CHAPTER SEVEN

The Text
in Diachronic Context

T he chronological connection between documents that are
formed in a continuum (primary text and secondary text)
defines yet another occasion for the documentary reading of a
religious system. Here we compare writings that clearly are
meant to be continuous with one another and present evidence
of systemic development. The diachronic unfolding of a
connected system emerges from the connected texts, the later
commentary on the earlier document. To see how this kind of
documentary description is worked out in such a way as to
indicate the entry of new considerations into an established
systemic framework, we turn to Tractate Abot, The Fathers, and
its continuator, Abot deRabbi Nathan, The Fathers According
to Rabbi Nathan.

Attached to the Mishnah but given a date of about a half
century after the closure of the Mishnah (ca. c.e. 250), The
Fathers found its continuators in The Fathers According to
Rabbi Nathan, a document whose closest affinities place it in the
circle of the authorship of the Talmud of Babylonia, circa
seventh century. Here the connection between the two
documents is established much as it is between the Mishnah and
the Yerushalmi; that is, a later authorship presents its ideas in
the form of a commentary to the work of an earlier one. But the
comparison and contrast draws our attention from formal traits
to substantive characteristics, as a later writing shifts attention

from matters important to the earlier one to altogether fresh concerns. Systemic description and analysis is advanced by the connection, hence the legitimate comparison and contrast of these two related and sequential writings.

The connection between the two writings, accordingly, affords a firm basis for characterizing the second of the two as a systemic development. This is in two complementary aspects. First of all, we find in the later document, The Fathers According to Rabbi Nathan, the kind of story (defined presently) absent in The Fathers. Second, and more important, through that new genre of writing we also find brought to expression a set of systemic values not characteristic of the prior composition. Let me explain. The Fathers According to Rabbi Nathan provides a remarkable opportunity to investigate in the context of religious literature the entry of the story as an important medium for presenting a message in Judaism, because this document contains an unusually rich selection of stories about sages, whereas The Fathers does not. The Fathers contains no sustained narratives about sages and has very few narratives of other types. The narrative level pertaining to apothegms set in a "dramatic" framework is reached by "One day he saw . . . and saw . . . ," with the "one day" serving to establish the episodic character in which the saying is presented. Had the apothegm stated simply, "Whenever he saw a skull, he said . . . ," it would have obviated the need for the (pseudo-) narrative setting in which it presently appears. In the movement from The Fathers to The Fathers According to Rabbi Nathan, therefore, we are able to see how the framers of the later work of exegesis of an earlier writing found a place in their composition for a genre of materials not found appropriate for use as a paramount medium among prior framers or author-ships of canonical documents. Not only so, but the fresh message of the later document makes its appearance in the new medium presented there. What is new in The Fathers According to Rabbi Nathan, by comparison to The Fathers, is a doctrine concerning the sage, on the one hand, and history and eschatology, on the other. The medium that bears the new message is the story about the sage, which is in narrative form quite different from the story about the biblical hero, the parable, and the narrative setting for a saying. In the canonical history of ideas (a term explained in chapter 9) the facts adduced in the study of the context defined by the comparison of texts will provide a fine example of what can be attained in systemic analysis.

The initial writings had taken slight interest in the lives and persons of sages. The Mishnah (tractate Avot) and the Tosefta, for instance, contain only a few such stories. Later on, the canonical writings of Judaism, represented, for example, by the two Talmuds (but in particular by the Talmud of Babylonia) drew upon and made extensive use of a rich corpus of stories about sages. The story of an important event in the life of a sage, told, for example, in the Talmud of the Land of Israel at the end of the fourth century and in its successor two centuries later, took an important role in the presentation of the message of the Torah. But in the two Talmuds' fundamental principles of organization and structure, the sage-story did not play a prominent role. Although both Talmuds resort for their fundamental redactional structure to the Mishnah, and although, in addition, the Bavli appeals to sustained passages of Scripture as the basis for organizing its materials, neither of the two Talmuds formulates as a continuous (i.e., more than merely episodic) narrative a sequence of stories about a given authority. In The Fathers According to Rabbi Nathan, by contrast, the sustained story about the sage serves as one important structural and organizational basis for sustained discourse, in addition to sayings of The Fathers. Furthermore, the story about the sage became the paramount and critical medium for the presentation of what was new in the message of the document's framers. Accordingly, in the movement from The Fathers, which reached closure in the middle of the third century, to the formation of The Fathers According to Rabbi Nathan, concluded at some indeterminate point (probably in the same period as the Talmud of Babylonia in the sixth or seventh century), the story about a sage became the chosen medium for a very particular message. In moving from writing to religion, we have here a valuable methodological guideline.

I refer to a specific type of story, and hence, we have to begin with a taxonomy of narrative generated by The Fathers According to Rabbi Nathan. There I find five kinds of narrative, or to put it differently, five species of the genus *narrative*. I classify these species as (1) parable, (2) precedent, (3) narrative setting for a saying, (4) scriptural story, and (5) sage-story. Formal, not merely thematic (let alone subjectively perceived), differences justify the taxonomy at hand. That is, a story about a scriptural hero differs in its narrative qualities from a story about a sage hero. The sage-story forms the largest proportion by far of the narratives in the document at hand. Not only so, but the proportion of the species *sage-story* in The Fathers According to Rabbi Nathan constitutes a larger component of the narratives used in that document than in any other document. The reason why that fact is important has already been introduced. The fresh and new messages of The Fathers According to Rabbi Nathan, in contrast to the statement of The Fathers, come to expression in what we now see is a newly important medium, the sage-story.

The conventions exhibited in the stories about sages in our document, but not in other types of narratives in that same document, require movement, so that a problem and its solution are recorded through an account of what people not only said but also did (sometimes, to be sure, stated implicitly and not through detailed description). So I understand by *sage-story*— and it is the sage-story that bears the burden of the religious message and systemic judgment—a narrative with these distinctive and indicative (but by no means unique) traits: (1) a beginning, middle, and end; (2) tension and resolution; and (3) characterization accomplished through an account of the motivations of (4) a particular person and (5) an account of what that person said and did on a distinct and important occasion. A sage-story (6) rarely cites verse of Scripture and differs from a scriptural story in its omission of close attention to citations of verses of Scripture as a main focus of discourse. I derived the foregoing catalogue of the indicative traits of the sage-story from an inductive analysis of the sage-stories in The Fathers According to Rabbi Nathan, which exhibit no parallels or counterparts in other writings. I was able to distinguish this document's sage-stories from comparable narratives elsewhere by resort to the stated criteria for the definition of a story, meaning, a sage-story. For these distinctive and indicative traits do not characterize other stories, for example, ones about scriptural heroes, let alone parables, settings for sayings (in which nothing much happens), or legal precedents and

illustrations of the law through concrete accounts of circumstance.

None of the other kinds of narratives tells us about motivation
and characterization, none of them portrays a situation with
movement provided by tension and resolution, and, therefore,
none has a beginning, middle, and end. Ordinarily, the
narrative other than the sage-story portrays a stationary tableau.
The one exception, the parable, speaks of paradigms, not
persons, illustrating a teaching in a way rhetorically similar, if
more affecting, to a narrative setting for a saying. It is in The
Fathers According to Rabbi Nathan that the story about the sage,
with its stylistically indicative traits, forms the largest proportion
of narratives of any document among the principal writings in
the canon of Judaism in late antiquity. All the others resort to
narratives of various kinds in the service of making diverse
points. But our authorship is the one to employ the story about
the sage to make its two new and critical points, the one about the
supernatural character of the Torah-sage, the other about the
eschatological character of the teleology of the Judaism of the
dual Torah contained within the canonical writings before us.
The new messages of The Fathers According to Rabbi Nathan,
concerning the nation, enduring this age, and waiting for the
age to come, occur not only in sayings but also in stories. A
medium not utilized in The Fathers carries a new message. And
that fact makes possible the transformation of a literary fact into
a datum for the description of a religious system.

Let us first dwell on the typology of narratives, that is,
compositions that appeal for cogency to the teleological logic
outlined in chapter 2. A narrative will convey a message by
telling a sequential tale of things that happened through a
symbol that is described in an evocative way, rather than framing
a message in general and abstract language.

Let me expand on this point negatively, then positively.
"Someone came and said" does not constitute a narrative; "he
said to him . . . he said to him . . ." does not form the substrate
of implicit action, for what is said is ordinarily a position in
logical analysis and practical reason. But "someone came and
did, and the rabbi, seeing the action, ruled" does constitute a
narrative, though of a different sort from one in which a
sequence of sustained actions, with beginning, middle, and end,

constitutes the account and bears the main message. So, too, "walking along one day, he saw a skull in the water and said" forms a narrative, even though the narrative serves only to provide a setting for the saying. So the trait of all sustained narrative discourse, absent in all non-narrative discourse, is that a point is made by description of action, not merely and solely by report of a position or principle that is established through what is said. I emphasize that the description of action may be implicit in what is said, for example, "Why did you do such and so?" "Because I wanted . . ." But implicit action is different from the statement of a principle as, for example, "Why do you maintain so and so?" "Because the verse says . . . ," or "Because the established principle is . . . " That mode of discourse reports on a conversation, to be sure, but does not portray an event, tell a tale, evoke a pictorial tableau of completed action, or indicate something that someone has done.

The genus *narrative* may encompass diverse modes of the concrete portrayal of a message, of which, in our document, I find four as I said. Let me now spell out the species of the genus *narrative,* as these occur in The Fathers According to Rabbi Nathan.

A parable is like a story, in that the narrative is centered on things people do rather than on what they say, and the message is carried by the medium of described action, commonly with a point of tension introduced at the outset and resolved at the end. A parable is different from a story in that its author presents a totally abstract tale, neither mentioning specific authorities nor placing the action in concrete time and setting nor invoking an authoritative text (e.g., a prooftext of Scripture). Like a story, a parable will not serve to prove a point of law or supply a precedent. But while a story centers on a sage's exemplary actions as the point of tension and resolution, a parable ordinarily will focus on wisdom or morality, which the parable's narrator will propose to illustrate. A parable teaches its lesson explicitly, whereas a story about a sage is rarely explicit in specifying its lesson; and the implicit lesson is always the exemplary character of the sage and what he does—whatever it is, whatever its verbal formulation as a lesson. So there is a very considerable difference between the parable and the story. One example of a parable, so labeled in our document, is as follows:

I:XIII.2.   A. R. Simeon b. Yohai says, "I shall draw a parable for
you. To what may the first Man be compared? He was like a man
who had a wife at home. What did that man do? He went and
brought a jug and put in it a certain number of dates and nuts. He
caught a scorpion and put it at the mouth of the jug and sealed it
tightly. He left it in the corner of his house.

B. "He said to her, 'My daughter, whatever I have in the
house is entrusted to you, except for this jar, which under no
circumstances should you touch.' What did the woman do? When
her husband went off to market, she went and opened the jug and
put her hand in it, and the scorpion bit her, and she went and fell
into bed. When her husband came home from the market, he said
to her, 'What's going on?'

C. "She said to him, 'I put my hand into the jug, and a
scorpion bit me, and now I'm dying.'

D. "He said to her, 'Didn't I tell you to begin with, "Whatever
I have in the house is entrusted to you, except for this jar, which
under no circumstances should you touch."' He got mad at her
and divorced her.

E. "So it was with the first man.

F. "When the Holy One, blessed be he, said to him, *Of all the
trees of the garden you certainly may eat, but from the tree of knowledge of
good and evil you may not eat, for on the day on which you eat of it, you will
surely die* (Gen. 2:17),

G. "on that day he was driven out, thereby illustrating the
verse, *Man does not lodge overnight in honor* (Ps. 49:24)."

Simeon's point is that by giving man the commandment, God
aroused his interest in that tree and led man to do what he did.
So God bears a measure of guilt for the fall of man.

The trait of the parable that draws our attention is its
impersonality: The details of the narrative point toward the lesson
to be drawn and, it goes without saying, not to the specificities of
the name of the man and the day of the week and the place of the
event. These have no bearing, obviously, because the parable is
intended to state in a concrete narrative a general point. The
parable in its narrative traits is the opposite of a historical story,
such as we find told about sages. The one is general, universal,
pertinent to humanity wherever and whenever the narrated event
takes place. The other is specific, particular, relevant to a concrete
circumstance and situation and person.

What I call formal setting, or *precipitant,* for a saying merely portrays a situation to which a setting pertains, for example, "He saw a skull and said . . ." That hardly adds up to a substantial story, since nothing happens to draw out the significance of the event, ("he saw"), but it does demand classification as a narrative because something has happened, not merely been said. Such a formal setting for a saying may prove substantial, but it will not constitute a narrative in the way that a story does, because not the action but the saying forms the focus of interest, and the potentialities of tension and resolution constituted by the precipitating action ("one day he saw a skull and said . . .") are never explored. Here is an example of a story that provides merely a narrative setting for a saying. The setting for a saying is like a parable in its generality and exemplary character, but it is unlike a parable in that the burden of the narrative is carried not by what is done, as in the parable, but only by what is said. What follows materially differs in no way from that brief lemma.

I provide only part of the actual citation of Eleazar's speech, to indicate that the setting, the "narrative," has no bearing upon the substance of the "saying," that is, the speech. XVIII:I.4 (The Fathers) defines the redactional setting; then the setting for the saying, followed by the actual statement(s), is given:

XVIII:I.4. A. R. Eleazar b. Azariah he called a peddler's basket. . . .

XVIII:II.1. A. When R. Joshua got old, his disciples came to visit him. He said to them, "My sons, what was the new point that you had today in school?"

B. They said to him, "We are your disciples, and your water [alone] do we drink."

C. He said to them, "God forbid! it is impossible that there is a generation of sages that is orphaned [and without suitable guidance]. Whose week was it to teach?"

D. They said to him, "It was the week of R. Eleazar b. Azariah."

E. He said to them, "And what was the topic of the narrative today?"

F. They said to him, "It was the passage that begins, Assemble the people, the men and the women and the children (Deut. 31:12)."

G. He said to them, "And what did he expound in that connection?"

What follows works out the speech and never refers back to the narrative setting. The elaborate narrative setting has no impact upon the point of what is portrayed and from the viewpoint of the message is simply a formality.

A precedent narrates a case, often in the form of a tale of something that was done, not merely said. The setting is always discourse on the law, but what marks the precedent as different from a story is not its setting but its narrative quality. Specifically, the precedent will portray a tableau of completed action, in which the tension is established not by the action but by the ruling and in which the resolution of the tension is accomplished solely by the same component, the decision of the sage. There is rarely a beginning, middle, and end, such as there is in a parable and a story. The precedent, unlike the story, is paradigmatic and makes a general point, rather than being historical and particular to a distinctive situation. A precedent or illustration of the law is like a parable in that it presents no concrete details that allow us to identify a particular place or actor. The usual kind of precedent ties a story to a legal ruling, as in the following item. Here the narrative includes the name of the authority, as it must, but the personality and role of the named authority make no impact, since the narrative points toward J, the ruling, which occurs also at M. Baba Qamma 8:7, cited verbatim and here given in boldface type:

III:III.1.   A. There was a man who violated the instructions of R. Aqiba by pulling off a woman's hair-covering in the market place.

B. She brought complaint before R. Aqiba and he imposed on the man a fine of four hundred *zuz*.

C. The man said to him, "My lord, give me time [to pay up this substantial sum]."

D. He gave him time.

E. When the man left court, his friend said to him, "I'll tell you how you won't have to pay her even something worth a penny."

F. He said to him, "Tell me."

G. He said to him, "Go and get yourself some oil worth an *issar* and break the flask at the woman's door."

H. [He did so.] What did that woman do? She came out of her house and let her hair down in the marketplace and mopped up the oil with her hands and wiped it on her hair.

I. Now the man had set up witnesses and came back to R. Aqiba's court and said to him, "Should I pay off four hundred *zuz* to this contemptible woman? Now because of a mere issar's worth of oil, this woman could not forego the dignity owing to herself, but rather came out of her house and let her hair down in the marketplace and mopped up the oil with her hands and wiped it on her hair."

J. He said to him, "You have no legitimate claim at all. For **if a person inflicts injury on herself, even though one is not permitted to do so, she is exempt from penalty, others who do injury to that person are liable,** she who does injury to herself is exempt from penalty, while you, who have done injury to her [are liable]. Go and pay her the four hundred *zuz*."

The narrative points toward the ruling at J, and the details of the tale are so formed as to provide a concrete illustration for the abstract ruling. The narrator sets up the point of tension by the device of having the defendant ask for and be given time, with E-H providing the incident and the action. Then he works out the consequence and makes the point, with everything, as I said, finding resolution at J. The difference between this narrative precedent and the foregoing is less than meets the eye, since the former one also is so composed as to point toward the climactic ruling.

We come now to the story, both the scriptural and the sage-story. A story is like an illustration in that it presents a narrative. Story and illustration are also alike in their interest in the concrete and specific way of framing a point. But they are different in one fundamental and definitive way. A story's importance requires emphasis: *while meaning to provide a good example of how one should behave, the teller of a story always deals with a concrete person and a particular incident.* The person is concrete in that he (in our document there is not a single story about a woman) is always specified by name. It concerns a particular incident in that the viewpoint of the narrator makes clear the singularity and specificity of the event that is reported. The story always happens in historical time, and the point it wishes to make is subordinate to the description of action, the development of a point of tension, at which the story commences, and its resolution, at which the story concludes: beginning, middle, and end.

To begin the matter of the analysis of the story, we have first to distinguish the story from its closest analogue, the illustration. Both of these modes of narrative seem to deal with a concrete person and a particular incident, even though the illustration may not invoke the name of a sage, but a story commonly does. A particular set of materials in which a story-as-illustration and a story in the classic and definitive sense occur together will make this point abundantly clear. The difference between the species *story* and the illustration, categorized as a subspecies of the species *precedent* emerges in the striking contrast between the treatment of two sayings in the same pericope of The Fathers by The Fathers According to Rabbi Nathan, chapter 38.

XXXVIII:III.1.   A. Pestilence comes to the world on account of neglect of the requirement to leave in the fields the defective grape, the forgotten sheaf, and the corner of the field, as well as to separate tithe for the poor person.

XXXVIII:IV.1.   A. There is the case of a woman who lived in the neighborhood of a landlord, and her two sons went out to gather [the crops that are to be left for the poor], but did not find any produce in the field.

B. Their mother said, "When my sons come from the field, perhaps I'll find something in their hands to eat."

C. For their part, they were saying, "When we get home, perhaps we'll find something in mother's hands to eat."

D. She found nothing with them, nor they with her, to eat. They put their heads on their mother's lap and all three of them died on one day.

E. The Holy One, blessed be he, said to them, "You people have exacted from them their lives! By your lives! I shall exact from you your lives."

F. And so Scripture says, *Do not rob from the weak, because he is weak, nor crush the poor in the gate, for the Lord will plead their cause and take the life of those who despoil them* (Prov. 22:22-23).

We see that the saying about pestilence coming to the world because of neglect of the provision of gifts to the poor (corner of the field and the like) is illustrated in a concrete way. Yet the case of the woman is not particular to the rule, because E-F do not refer back to pestilence. Two facts are important in our classification of narratives: first, the use of the narrative of the woman and her children as a means of amplifying the general point (if not its particular expression); and second, the narrator's disinterest in concrete details, for example, the woman's name, where and when she lived, and the like. This brings us to a fine example of this narrative typology.

The story is told in the same setting as the illustration just now considered and concerns precisely the same proposition, yet it is different. First, by contrast to the illustration, it is exceedingly concrete and specific. Second, the storyteller is never bound by the requirements of a larger redactional purpose and intent. Since we cannot say that the story is told "for its own sake," since I cannot define the traits of a story told "for its own sake," we must conclude that the generative and definitive power of the story derives from internal interests and not extrinsic ones. That is, the storyteller wishes to compose the narrative along lines required by the generative tension of the story at hand, not those imposed by the redactional purpose supplied by the (planned) setting of the story. The power of the story—its definitive function—is intrinsic to the narrative and self-evident within the narrative. Any further point that the story serves to prove or illustrate lies outside of the imaginative framework.

In what follows, we are told that war ("a sword") comes because of perversion of justice or failings of the Torah-teachers. The story that is told takes up this second point. But now "sword" becomes specific to the story: One of the authorities has his head cut off by a sword. Yet a good illustration (or precedent) for the saying about "those who teach the Torah not in accord with the law" would tell us that a given master rejected the decided law and imposed his own heretical or dissenting view instead. The story at hand does not imagine such a point; rather, it has the holy rabbi put to death for taking pride in his office, and that hardly pertains to "teaching the Torah not in accord with the law," except, perhaps, in a most recondite setting. Although this illustration adequately relates to the teaching it is

meant to illustrate, we may hardly treat the following story from
The Fathers According to Rabbi Nathan in the same way. The
reason is that the point of the saying and the narrative focus of
the story do not intersect. (In the following, the saying cited from
The Fathers is in boldface type.)

**XXXVIII:V.1.   A. A sword comes into the world because of
the delaying of justice and perversion of justice, and because of
those who teach the Torah not in accord with the law.**
XXXVIII:V.2.   A. When they seized Rabban Simeon b. Gamaliel and R. Ishmael on the count of death, Rabban Simeon b.
Gamaliel was in session and was perplexed, saying, "Woe is us!
For we are put to death like those who profane the Sabbath and
worship idols and practice fornication and kill."

C. Said to him R. Ishmael b. Elisha, "Would it please you if I
said something before you?"

D. He said to him, "Go ahead."

E. He said to him, "Is it possible that when you were sitting at
a banquet, poor folk came and stood at your door, and you did
not let them come in and eat?"

F. He said to him, "By heaven [may I be cursed] if I ever did
such a thing! Rather, I set up guards at the gate. When poor folk
came along, they would bring them in to me and eat and drink
with me and say a blessing for the sake of Heaven."

G. He said to him, "Is it possible that when you were in
session and expounding [the Torah] on the Temple mount and
the vast populations of Israelites were in session before you, you
took pride in yourself?"

H. He said to him, "Ishmael my brother, one has to be ready
to accept his failing. [That is why I am being put to death, the
pride that I felt on such an occasion.]"

I. They went on appealing to the executioner for grace. This
one [Ishmael] said to him, "I am a priest, son of a high priest, kill
me first, so that I do not have to witness the death of my
companion."

J. And the other [Simeon] said, "I am the patriarch, son of
the patriarch, kill me first, so that I do not have to witness the
death of my companion."

K. He said to him, "Cast lots." They cast lots, and the lot fell
on Rabban Simeon b. Gamaliel.

L. The executioner took the sword and cut off his head.

M. R. Ishmael b. Elisha took it and held it in his breast and wept and cried out: "Oh holy mouth, oh faithful mouth, oh mouth that brought forth beautiful gems, precious stones and pearls! Who has laid you in the dust, who has filled your mouth with dirt and dust.

N. "Concerning you Scripture says, *Awake, O sword, against my shepherd and against the man who is near to me* (Zech. 13:7)."

O. He had not finished speaking before the executioner took the sword and cut off his head.

P. Concerning them Scripture says, *My wrath shall wax hot, and I will kill you with the sword, and your wives shall be widows, and your children fatherless* (Ex. 22:23).

XXXVIII:V.3. A. Since it is said *I will kill you with the sword*, do I not know that *your wives shall be widows*?

B. They will be widows but not really widows, for they will not find witnesses [that you have died, so as] to permit them to remarry.

C. The example is Betar, from which not a single one escaped so as to give testimony that someone has died and his wife may remarry.

D. Since it is said, *your wives shall be widows*, do I not know that *your children will be fatherless*?

E. But they will be fatherless and not fatherless [for the same reason as before], so that the property they are to inherit will remain in the domain of their father, with the result that they will not be permitted to inherit and to transact business with that property [being unable to settle the estate].

I included XXXVIII.V.3 because it shows where the redactor enters in and the narrator of the story pulls out. The prooftext, Exodus 22:23, bears its own amplification, and that is given at XXXVIII:V.3. The contrast to the foregoing, of course, is self-evident.

The story about the execution by the sword of the two great rabbis surely cannot illustrate the notion that they were responsible for a delay of justice or the perversion of justice or taught the Torah not in accord with the law. It is simply tacked on as a story about how people died by the sword. The power and nobility of the story testify to the narrator's intent, and it is not to tell us how a rabbi took pride in his public reception. That is why I distinguished intrinsic narrative purpose from extrinsic use. The broader redactional plan requires assembling thematically relevant, but substantively autonomous, materials around a tangential topic—death by the sword, in this case. The storyteller has told the story for his own purpose, involving the moving action within, not merely the illustrative tableau pointing to an external truth. The interchange, the search for the hero's motive—the soul's honesty in recognizing its guilt—yield a quite powerful polemic in favor of God's ultimate and perfect justice. The story vindicates God's justice—nothing less. It furthermore portrays affecting heroes. These are given personality, character, even the elements of biography. In these indicative aspects the story readily differs from the illustration, the precedent, the parable, and other modes of narrative. (The secondary expansion of the exegesis of the prooftext points to that same conclusion.) From the viewpoint of the classification of diverse narratives, comparing the narrative about the widow and her children and the story about the execution of the two rabbis yields solid reason for treating the two as distinct species of the genus *narrative*.

Now that we recognize differences among the four specified species of narrative, noting in particular what makes the story different from the other three, we turn to the instances of the story in The Fathers According to Rabbi Nathan. Our particular point of interest remains whether the new and different medium bears a message that also proves distinct from that of the other kinds of narratives. A survey of the stories at hand yields in detail ample justification for the claim that, as the medium is different, so, too, is the religious message, to which we shall presently turn. First, let me summarize numerous obvious differences in narrative convention dictating the technique of telling stories about sages in particular. Three are definitive:

1. The story about a sage has a beginning, middle, and end, and the story about a sage also rests not only on verbal exchanges ("he said to him . . . , he said to him . . .") but also on (described) action.
2. The story about a sage unfolds from a point of tension and conflict to a clear resolution and remission of the conflict.
3. The story about a sage rarely invokes a verse of Scripture

and never serves to prove a proposition concerning the meaning of a verse of Scripture.

The traits of stories about scriptural figures and themes (surveyed in *Judaism and Story: The Evidence of The Fathers According to Rabbi Nathan*) prove opposite:

1. In the story about a scriptural hero, there is no beginning, middle, and end, and little action. The burden of the narrative is carried by verbal exchanges. Described action is rare and plays a slight role in the unfolding of the narrative. Often the narrative consists of little more than a setting for a saying, and the point of the narrative is conveyed not through what is told but through the cited saying.
2. The story about a scriptural hero is worked out as a tableau, with description of the components of the stationary tableau placed at the center. There is little movement, no point of tension that is resolved.
3. The story about a scriptural hero always invokes verses from Scripture and makes the imputation of meaning to those verses the center of interest.

As to religion, stories on sages in The Fathers According to Rabbi Nathan yield a single message: People may begin the study of the Torah at any point in life, and if they work hard, they will achieve success, riches, and fame. If they cut off their ties from their family, they will end up inheriting their family's estate, and if their wives tolerate their long absences and support them and their family, their wives will share in their success, riches, and fame. It follows that the stories on the common theme of the origins of great masters, as preserved in The Fathers According to Rabbi Nathan, address the question of the breakup of the families of mature men who choose to study the Torah and respond by promising success, riches, and fame, for those who in mature years do convert to study of the Torah. The lesson of the origins of the great masters is to give up home and family in favor of the Torah.

In conclusion, let me answer the questions with which I began. First, does the subject matter—sages—generate its own narrative literary conventions, differing from those that guide writers of stories about scriptural figures? Second, do we find propositions emerging from stories on sages? The answers to both questions decidedly favor the affirmative. The distinctive narrative conventions make one cogent and critical point. The sage learns through study of the Torah, which is accomplished solely by service of the master, to be patient and affable and forbearing. The story about a sage has a beginning, a middle, and an end, and the story about a sage also rests not only on verbal exchanges but on (described or implicit) action. The story about a sage unfolds from a point of tension and conflict to a clear resolution and remission of the conflict; it rarely invokes a verse of Scripture. That means that where a distinct subject comes into view, the narrator of stories about sages will nonetheless follow a fixed set of everywhere applicable narrative conventions.

The sage plays a public, not solely a private, role. Within the genealogical theory of Israel as one extended family, the sage as supernatural father forms the critical element in the history of this family. That history, of course, is defined by the encounter with Rome in particular. Rome will be represented by its persona, just as is Israel, and that can only be the emperor. That is why, in addition to the theme of Torah-study, the story bears a second important burden, namely, that of history and eschatology, this age and the age to come. All stories in The Fathers According to Rabbi Nathan that do not deal with the lives and deeds of sages concern the large historical question facing Israel: what will be its history in this world and its destiny in the world to come.

History finds its definition in a single event, the encounter with Rome, involving two aspects: first, the destruction of the Temple and the sages' role in dealing with that matter; second, the (associated, consequent) repression of Torah-sages and their study. Israel's history in this world works itself out in the encounter with Rome, Israel's counterpart and opposite, and that history in the world coming soon will see a reversal of roles. The centrality of study of the Torah in securing Israel's future forms the leitmotif of the stories at hand.

We take up one important story about the destruction of the Temple. This protracted story finds its setting in an exegesis of the saying in The Fathers that the world stands on deeds of loving-kindness. These, then, are found by the exegete at Hosea 6:6, and the intrusion of that verse carries in its wake a narrative—not a story but a narrative setting for a saying—about Yohanan ben Zakkai and his disciple, Joshua, in the ruins of the Temple. Only at the end of the matter do we find the major historical story of the destruction.

    IV:V.1. A. . . . on deeds of loving kindness: how so?

    B. Lo, Scripture says, *For I desire mercy and not sacrifice, [and the knowledge of God rather than burnt offerings]* (Hos. 6:6).

    C. To begin with the world was created only on account of loving kindness.

    D. For so it is said, *For I have said, the world is built with loving kindness, in the very heavens you establish your faithfulness* (Ps. 89:3).

    IV:V.2. A. One time [after the destruction of the Temple] Rabban Yohanan ben Zakkai was going forth from Jerusalem, with R. Joshua following after him. He saw the house of the sanctuary lying in ruins.

    B. R. Joshua said, "Woe is us for this place which lies in ruins, the place in which the sins of Israel used to come to atonement."

    C. He said to him, "My son, do not be distressed. We have another mode of atonement, which is like [atonement through sacrifice], and what is that? It is deeds of loving kindness.

    D. "For so it is said, *For I desire mercy and not sacrifice, [and the knowledge of God rather than burnt offerings]* (Hos. 6:6)."

    IV:V.3. A. So we find in the case of Daniel, that most desirable man, that he carried out deeds of loving kindness.

    B. And what are the deeds of loving kindness that Daniel did?

    C. If you say that he offered whole offerings and sacrifices, do people offer sacrifices in Babylonia?

    D. And has it not in fact been said, *Take heed that you not offer your whole offerings in any place which you see but in the place which the Lord will select in the territory of one of the tribes. There you will offer up your whole offerings* (Deut. 12:13-14).

    E. What then were the deeds of loving kindness that Daniel did?

    F. He would adorn the bride and make her happy, join a cortege for the deceased, give a penny to a pauper, pray three times every day,

G. and his prayer was received with favor,

H. for it is said, *And when David knew that the writing was signed,
he went into his house—his windows were open in his upper chamber
toward Jerusalem—and he kneeled upon his knees three times a day and
prayed and gave thanks before his God as he did aforetime* (Dan. 6:11).

This entire construction serves as a prologue to what will now
follow, an account of the destruction of the Temple, which
forms the background to IV:VI.1. We have not a story but a
narrative that forms a setting for a saying in IV:V.2. From
IV:V.2.A we are given the occasion on which the colloquy of B-C
took place. Still, there is a narrative side to matters that emerges
from the implicit movement from B to C. But classifying the
passage as a story seems to me not justified.

IV:VI.1.   A. Now when Vespasian came to destroy Jerusalem,
he said to [the inhabitants of the city,] "Idiots! why do you want to
destroy this city and burn the house of the sanctuary? For what do
I want of you, except that you send me a bow or an arrow [as
marks of submission to my rule], and I shall go on my way."

B. They said to him, "Just as we sallied out against the first
two who came before you and killed them, so shall we sally out
and kill you."

C. When Rabban Yohanan ben Zakkai heard, he proclaimed
to the men of Jerusalem, saying to them, "My sons, why do you
want to destroy this city and burn the house of the sanctuary? For
what does he want of you, except that you send him a bow or an
arrow, and he will go on his way."

D. They said to him, "Just as we sallied out against the first
two who came before him and killed them, so shall we sally out
and kill him."

E. Vespasian had stationed men near the walls of the city,
and whatever they heard, they would write on an arrow and shoot
out over the wall. [They reported] that Rabban Yohanan ben
Zakkai was a loyalist of Caesar's.

F. After Rabban Yohanan ben Zakkai had spoken to them
one day, a second, and a third, and the people did not accept his
counsel, he sent and called his disciples, R. Eliezer and R. Joshua,
saying to them, "My sons, go and get me out of here. Make me an
ark and I shall go to sleep in it."

G. R. Eliezer took the head and R. Joshua the feet, and toward sunset they carried him until they came to the gates of Jerusalem.

H. The gate keepers said to them, "Who is this?"

I. They said to him, "It is a corpse. Do you not know that a corpse is not kept overnight in Jerusalem."

J. They said to them, "If it is a corpse, take him out," so they took him out and brought him out at sunset, until they came to Vespasian.

K. They opened the ark and he stood before him.

L. He said to him, "Are you Rabban Yohanan ben Zakkai? Indicate what I should give you."

M. He said to him, "I ask from you only Yavneh, to which I shall go, and where I shall teach my disciples, establish prayer [Goldin: a prayer house], and carry out all of the religious duties."

N. He said to him, "Go and do whatever you want."

O. He said to him, "Would you mind if I said something to you."

P. He said to him, "Go ahead."

Q. He said to him, "Lo, you are going to be made sovereign."

R. He said to him, "How do you know?

S. He said to him, "It is a tradition of ours that the house of the sanctuary will be given over not into the power of a commoner but of a king, for it is said, *And he shall cut down the thickets of the forest with iron, and Lebanon* [which refers to the Temple] *shall fall by a mighty one* (Is. 10:34)."

T. People say that not a day, two or three passed before a delegation came to him from his city indicating that the [former] Caesar had died and they had voted for him to ascend the throne.

U. They brought him a [Goldin:] catapult and drew it up against the wall of Jerusalem.

V. They brought him cedar beams and put them into the catapult, and he struck them against the wall until a breach had been made in it. They brought the head of a pig and put it into the catapult and tossed it toward the limbs that were on the Temple altar.

W. At that moment Jerusalem was captured.

X. Rabban Yohanan ben Zakkai was in session and with trembling was looking outward, in the way that Eli had sat and waited: *Lo, Eli sat upon his seat by the wayside watching, for his heart trembled for the ark of God* (1 Sam. 4:13).

Y. When Rabban Yohanan ben Zakkai heard that Jerusalem

had been destroyed and the house of the sanctuary burned in flames, he tore his garments, and his disciples tore their garments, and they wept and cried and mourned.

IV:VI.2. A. Scripture says, *Open your doors, O Lebanon, that the fire may devour your cedars* (Zech. 11:1).

B. That verse refers to the high priests who were in the sanctuary [on the day it was burned].

C. They took their keys in their hands and threw them upward, saying before the Holy One, blessed be he, "Lord of the world, here are your keys which you entrusted to us, for we have not been faithful custodians to carry out the work of the king and to receive support from the table of the king."

IV:VI.3. A. Abraham, Isaac, and Jacob, and the twelve tribes were weeping, crying, and mourning.

IV:VI.4. A. Scripture says, *Wail, O cypress tree, for the cedar is fallen, because the glorious ones are spoiled, wail, O you oaks of Bashan, for the strong forest is come down* (Zech. 11:2).

B. *Wail, O cypress tree, for the cedar is fallen* refers to the house of the sanctuary.

C. . . . *because the glorious ones are spoiled* refers to Abraham, Isaac, and Jacob, and the twelve tribes [who were weeping, crying, and mourning].

D. . . . *wail, O you oaks of Bashan* refers to Moses, Aaron, and Miriam.

E. . . . *for the strong forest is come down* refers to the house of the sanctuary.

F. *Hark the wailing of the shepherds, for their glory is spoiled* (Zech. 11:3) refers to David and Solomon his son.

G. *Hark the roaring of young lions, for the thickets of the Jordan are spoiled* (Zech. 11:3) speaks of Elijah and Elisha.

The story unfolds in a smooth way from beginning to end. It serves, overall, as an account of the power of the Torah to lead Israel through historical crises.

The storyteller at three points—the comparisons of Vespasian and Yohanan with the Jewish troops, Vespasian and Yohanan in their direct encounter, then, at the end, the destruction itself—places the sage into the scale against the emperor, Israel against Rome. Then the Torah makes the difference, for, in the end, Israel will outweigh Rome. The story's themes all form part of the larger theme of Torah-learning. The centerpiece is

Yohanan's knowledge that the Temple was going to be destroyed. This he acquired in two ways. First of all, his observation of the conduct of the Israelite army led him to that conclusion. But, second and more important, his knowledge of the Torah told him the deeper meaning of the event, which was in two parts. The one side had Rome get a new emperor. The other, and counterpart, side had Israel get its program for the period beyond the destruction. The opening unit of the story, A-T, is seamless. I can point to no element that could have been omitted without seriously damaging the integrity of the story. I see no intrusions of any kind. If that is a correct judgment, then the climax must come only at S, confirmed by T and what follows. That is to say, it is the power of the sage to know the future because of his knowledge of the Torah. Establishing a place for the teaching of disciples and the performance of other holy duties forms a substrate of the same central theme. And yet, deeper still, lies the theme of the counterpart and opposite: Israel and Rome, sage and emperor. That motif occurs first at A and C, which have Vespasian and Yohanan say precisely the same thing, with one difference. Vespasian calls the Jewish army "idiots," and Yohanan calls the troops "my sons." Otherwise, the statements are the same. And the replies, B and D, are also the same. So the first episode sets the emperor and the sage up as opposites and counterparts.

The second episode has the people unwilling to listen to the sage—the emperor has no role here—leading the sage to conclude that it is time to "make an ark and go to sleep in it." If I had to choose a point of reference, it would be not the sleep of death—then Yohanan would have wanted a bier—but the ark of Noah. Yohanan then forms the counterpart, in the storyteller's choice of the word at hand, to Noah, who will save the world beyond the coming deluge. F-G should then be viewed as a chapter in a complete story. E, on the one side, and H-J, on the other, link that cogent chapter to the larger context. E prepares us to understand why Vespasian recognizes Yohanan, an important detail added precisely where it had to come, and H-J forms the necessary bridge to what is coming.

The next component of the unitary story again places Vespasian in the balance against Yohanan. Now Yohanan tells Vespasian what is going to happen. Each party rises to power as a

direct outcome of the destruction of the Temple: sage versus
emperor, one in the scale against the other. The colloquy with
Vespasian, L-S, forms the only part of the story to rely upon
verbal exchanges. The point, of course, is clear. Then comes the
necessary denouement, in two parts. First, the Temple actually
was destroyed; second, we are told how, T-W, Yohanan
responded in mourning, X-Y. Here, too, we have that same
counterpart and opposite: Rome, then Israel, with Israel
represented by the sage, Rome by the emperor. What follows of
course is not narrative, let alone story. IV:VI.2 provides an
exegesis A-B, followed by a colloquy. IV:VI.3 is a singleton, and
IV:VI.4 joins the destruction of the Temple to the history of
Israel and its heroes, all of whom wept as did Yohanan. But I do
not see in the inclusion of IV:VI.4 an attempt to compare
Yohanan to the named heroes. This is virtually certain, since the
story itself at IV:VI.1.X invokes the figure of Eli, who is
noteworthy for his omission in IV:VI.4. The stories we have
reviewed establish the following propositions:

1. **IV:VI.1:** The sage had the foresight that would have
   prevented the destruction of the Temple. All that was
   required was to give the Gentile monarch a sign of
   submission.
2. **IV:VI.1:** The sage had the foresight to know that
   Vespasian would be made emperor. This he learned
   through his deep knowledge of the Torah.
3. **IV:VI.1:** The sage had the foresight to plan even before
   the destruction of Jerusalem for the life of Israel
   afterward. That life would involve study of the Torah by
   master and disciples, the saying of prayer, and the
   fulfilment of religious duties.
4. **IV:VI.1:** Israel and Rome weigh in the balance against one
   another, the emperor and the sage.
5. **XVII:III.1** (not reproduced here): The destruction of the
   Temple placed Israel under the rule of despicable nations.
6. **VI:IX.1** (not reproduced here): Divine grace will produce
   a miracle for someone who takes risks in behalf of the
   community at large. This is not a Torah-study story, and it
   is not told about a sage.

These propositions yield a simple point: Through knowledge of the Torah, the sage leads Israel to the age to come, when Israel will supplant Rome. The leadership of zealots on the battlefield led to the destruction of the Temple, to the senseless destruction of the food supply of Jerusalem, to the calamity that had overtaken Israel. The leadership of the sages, armed with foresight and backed by God, will show the right way.

The fresh topic—the sages and history—does not require the invention of modes of narrative different from those that served to deal with the sages' origins, on the one hand, and their correct personality and sagacity, on the other. As before, we find the same narrative conventions: The story about a sage (1) has a beginning, a middle, and an end; (2) rests not only on verbal exchanges but on (described or implicit) action; (3) unfolds from a point of tension and conflict to a clear resolution and remission of the conflict; and (4) never serves to prove a proposition concerning the meaning of a verse of Scripture. Does the subject matter—sages—generate its own narrative literary conventions, that differ from those that guide writers of stories about scriptural figures? Indeed so. But these conventions apply to all types of stories about sages. Do we find cogent propositions emerging from stores on sages? Yes, we do, and these propositions intersect, whether the story concerns the origin of the sage, his particular sagacity, or his role in the history of Israel.

Let us now review points of emphasis in The Fathers According to Rabbi Nathan lacking all counterpart in the Fathers: (1) One should study the Torah and other things will take care of themselves—a claim of a more supernatural character than the one in The Fathers. (2) Sages seemed to be portrayed as supernatural figures rather than mainly as political leaders, eager to conciliate and reconcile the other. (3) The later document imparts to the teleological question an eschatological answer altogether lacking in the earlier one. This third point underlines the main proposition at hand, which is that in The Fathers According to Rabbi Nathan, deeds make a difference, and therefore narrative in the form of the story emerges as a principal medium of stating the authorship's message. The definitive category here is social, therefore national, raising the issue not of the private person but of holy Israel, not of the private life and destiny but of the national history and future of Israel. The concern, then, is what will happen to the nation in time to come, meaning the coming age, not the coming life of the resurrection.

The systemic teleology shifts its focus to the holy people, and, alongside, to the national history of the holy people—now and in the age to come. The Fathers According to Rabbi Nathan is consistent and one-sided when it addresses not so much the individual as the nation and promises not the life of the world to come. The framers of The Fathers According to Rabbi Nathan redefine the teleology at hand and focus it upon historical and social categories, rather than upon those that emerge from the life and death of the individual.

These points strike me as critical: (1) The sage is now—in The Fathers According to Rabbi Nathan but not in The Fathers—not judge and teacher alone but also a supernatural figure. (2) Study of the Torah in preference to making a living promises freedom from the conditions of natural life; that is, it creates a new family, new father and brothers, in the place of the old. (3) Israel as the holy people seen as a supernatural social entity takes center-stage, with the sage as leading actor in behalf of Israel. To these propositions the stories we have reviewed turn out to fit quite symmetrically. Specifically, stories about sages represent the study of the Torah as the source for success, riches, and fame. The sage stands at the center of the national life and fate; his knowledge of the Torah gives him foresight into the future. The sage marks the transition of Israel from this age to the coming age, weighing in the balance against the emperor just as Israel and Rome take opposite sides of the scale. To state the matter simply: The stories about the sage make those very points in detail that, in general, mark the message and propositions that turn out to be specific to The Fathers According to Rabbi Nathan.

Sayings in The Fathers scarcely allude to the destruction of the Temple and say nothing about Rome, but the stories told in The Fathers According to Rabbi Nathan begin with that simple fact. Were we to rely upon The Fathers for knowledge of the world in which Israel lived, the circumstances in which the sayings before us are to be carried out, we should know nothing whatsoever. The burden and message of the story are twofold: the centrality of the sage and his Torah in the supernatural life of Israel, and the critical role of the sage in the movement of the age from this world, with Rome in command, to the coming age, the time of Israel and sages. Where the story tells us something that sayings have not told us—and cannot have told us—it concerns history. The medium fits the message: Story carries the burden of history. It would be difficult to produce more striking evidence concerning the formation and reformation of religious systems than is supplied through the comparison and contrast of the connected documents before us. Establishing the context of texts by comparing related documents and showing their connections therefore forms a fundamental step in moving from writing to religion.

CHAPTER EIGHT

The Text
in Synchronic Context

An indicative trait of a religious system, critical to interpreting its character, derives from the way in which systemic framers represent their work. For the representation of a system I see two possibilities, each bearing its own apologia for the systemic composition seen as a whole. A religious system's framers present their system as a tradition, exhibiting the marks of the increment of the ages. Then it bears the fundament of truth from its point of origination, and its validation lies in its claim to the accurate transmission of what was revealed in historical continuity. The representation of a system as a tradition then constitutes one indicative trait of that system, in its given formulation. Or a system may find representation as a cogent statement, a well-crafted set of compelling answers to urgent questions, well-proportioned principles of a well-constructed world. Then the system is represented as truth because of the ineluctable and correct propositions that it presents, without special appeal to point of origin (though that may form an incidental claim of the system). Argument, well-composed and correctly demonstrated propositions—these form the components of the systemic apologia. On the one hand, then, a system may represent itself as true because it is tradition; on the other, true because it is logical. The program of systemic analysis sorts out systems portrayed as factual history as against systems set forth as cogent philosophy. But what evidence do we seek in the process of analysis? It will be revealed by the system's definitive writing, by the principal documentary statement identified by systemic authorities as normative.

Let me set forth the alternatives as to both fact and representation of the fact. A religious tradition in its writing covers whatever the received sedimentary process has handed on. A religious system through its documentary statement addresses in an orderly way a world view, a way of life, and a defined social entity. And both processes of thought, the traditional as well as the systematic and systemic, obey each its own rules. In the comparison and contrast of writing, therefore, we will find the view that the life of the religious intellect commences morning by morning. Or we may locate the conception that the religious mind joins a flow in an on-going process of thought, in which one day begins where yesterday left off, and one generation takes up the task left to it by its predecessors. A system of thought by definition starts fresh, defines first principles, and augments and elaborates them in balance, proportion, and, above all, logical order. In a traditional process, by contrast, we never start fresh but always pick and choose, in a received program, the spot we choose to augment. The former process, the systematic one, works in an orderly, measured, and proportioned way to produce a cogent, and neatly composed statement—a philosophy, for instance. Tradition by its nature is supposed to describe not a system, whole and complete, but a process of elaboration of a given, received truth: exegesis, not fresh composition. And, in the nature of thought, what begins in the middle is unlikely to yield order and system and structure laid forth *ab initio*. In general terms, systematic thought is philosophical in its mode of analysis and explanation, and traditional thought is historical in its manner of drawing conclusions and providing explanations.

System and tradition as modalities of religious world-construction not only describe incompatible modes of thought but also generate results that cannot be made to cohere, in the aggregate. For the conflict between traditional and system requires us to choose one mode of thought about one set of issues and to reject the other mode of thought. And that choice bears profound consequences for the shape of mind. So far as "tradition" refers to the matter of process, it invokes, specifically, an incremental and linear process that step by step transmits out of the past statements and wordings that bear authority and are subject to study, refinement, preservation and transmission.

The one thing a traditional thinker in religion, as against a system-builder in religion, knows is that he or she stands in a long process of thought, with the sole task of refining and defending received truth. The systematic thinker, on the other hand, affirms the task of starting fresh and seeing things all together, all at once, in the right order and proportion, as a composition, not merely a composite, held together by an encompassing logic. A tradition requires exegesis, a system, exposition.

In the case of the Judaism of the dual Torah, it is universally acknowledged, that we deal not with a system but with a tradition, and Judaism is invariably described as a traditional religion. While I shall argue to the contrary, there can be no doubt that, from the Bavli (ca. c.e. 600) onward, the Jewish intellect flowed along traditional lines, making its contribution from generation to generation as commentary, not as fresh composition. Every available history of Jewish thought, academic and vulgar alike, represents the principal modality of intellect as the refinement, adaptation, or adjustment of a received increment of truth. However new and lacking all precedent, Judaic systems find representation as elaborations of received Torah, imputed to verses of Scripture, and not as a sequence of fresh and original beginnings of systematic and orderly statements of well-composed and cogent principles.

As between the fresh and perfect classicism of the well-proportioned Parthenon and the confused and disorderly alleyways of the streets below, the Jewish intellect made its residence in the side-alleys of the here and now, in an ongoing, therefore by definition never neatly constructed, piazza. The Jewish intellect carried on its work through receiving and handing on the inheritance of the ages, not through thinking it through in a fresh and fundamental way. It sought to preserve the sediment of truth and to add its layer, not to dig down to foundations and build afresh.

But is that how things were at the closure of the Bavli? That is to say, is the writing produced as the ultimate systemic statement of the Judaism of the dual Torah in its actual traits, as distinct

from its superficial ones, fundamentally traditional and historical or essentially systematic and philosophical? We shall know
the answer in two ways, the one formal, the other conceptual.
The first, the merely formal, of course, is the simpler. When an
authorship extensively cites received documents and makes its
statement through citing or clearly alluding to statements in
those documents, then, on the face of it, that authorship wishes
to present its ideas as traditional. It claims through its chosen
form of expression (merely) to continue, (only) to amplify, to
extend, to apply truth received, not to present truth discovered
and demonstrated. That authorship then proposes to present its
ideas as incremental, secondary, merely applications of available
words. Moreover, that authorship will always situate itself in
relationship to a received document—in the case of all Judaisms,
of course, in relationship to the Pentateuch. We may state flatly
that the Bavli presents a writing that, in form, is rigidly
traditional. Everything that the authorship presents it links to a
prior text. The larger part of its large-scale compositions links
discrete materials to the amplification of the Mishnah, now the
Oral Torah. The smaller part does the same for Scripture, now
the Written Torah. So in form, the Bavli presents a completely
traditional statement.

But what about the facts of the matter? For to study a religion,
our task is not merely to paraphrase the evidence set forth by
that religion. It is to analyze that evidence and to form an
autonomous judgment of its indicative traits. And that brings us
to the second indicator, the conceptual. Evidences as to the
intellectual modalities of the Bavli prove the more subtle but also
the more telling. The criteria for judging the evidence are
readily at hand. When an authorship takes over from prior
documents the problem and program worked out by those
documents, contributing secondary improvements to an established structure of thought, then we may confidently identify
that authorship as derivative and traditional. We realize that this
is how matters were represented, in theory at least, by the
framers of The Fathers, which text's opening statement is
"Moses received Torah at Sinai and handed it on to Joshua." So,
a piece of writing stands in a chain of handing on, receiving, and
handing on again in the context of a Judaism, of course, from
Sinai.

Now what sort of indicator tells us that we have a system, not a tradition? A systematic and, by nature, philosophical statement or document presents its ideas as though they began with its author or authorship, rather than by alluding to, let alone citing in a persistent way, a prior writing, such as Scripture. The form of a systematic statement ordinarily will be autonomous. The order of discourse will begin from first principles and build upon them. The presentation of a system may, to be sure, absorb within itself a given document, citing its materials here and there. But—and this forms the indicator as to conception, not form alone—the authorship in such a case imposes its program and its problem upon received materials, without the pretense that the program and order of those inherited materials ("traditional, "authoritative," "scriptures" has made any impact whatsoever upon its presentation.

The basic criterion of the systematic character of a document or statement derives from a distinct trait. It is the authorship's purpose, and whether (and how) a statement serves that purpose. How do we know that a statement, a sizable composition, for instance, is meant to be systematic? In a well-composed system, every detail will bear the burden of the message of the system as a whole. Each component will make, in its terms, the statement which the system as a whole is intended to deliver. In order to understand that fact, we have to appreciate an important distinction in the analysis of systems: It is between a fact that is systemically vital, and one that is inert. A system of religious thought, comprising a world view, a way of life, and a definition of the social entity meant to adopt the one and embody the other, makes ample use of available facts. In order to make their statement, the authors of the documents of such a system speak in a language common to their age. Some of these facts form part of the background of discourse. They are, if important, inert, because they bear no portion of the burden of the systemic message. Others of these facts form centerpieces of the system; they may or may not derive from the common background, yet their importance to the system forms part of the statement and testimony of that system.

Now, in a well-composed system, every systemically generated fact will bear in its detail the message of the system as a whole, and, of course, inert facts will not. What I mean is simply illustrated. It is clear to any reader of Plato's *Republic,* Aristotle's *Politics* (and related corpus, to be sure), the Mishnah, or Matthew's gospel, that these writers propose to set forth a complete account of the basic truth concerning their subject, beginning, middle, and end. Accordingly, they so frame the details that the main point is repeated throughout. At each point in the composition, the message as a whole, in general terms, will be framed in all due particularity. The choices of topics will be dictated by the requirements of that prevailing systemic attitude and statement. We can even account, ideally, for the topical components of the program, explaining (in theory at least) why one topic is included and another not. A topic will find its place in the system because only through what is said about that *particular* topic can the system make the statement it wishes to make. Silence on a topic requires explanation, as much as we must supply a systemic motive or reason for the selection of, and substantial disquisition on, some other topic.

My criterion for whether a document is traditional or systematic therefore allows us to test our judgment by appeal to facts of verification or falsification. For the importance of recognizing the systemically generative facts is obvious. When we can account for both inclusion and exclusion, we know not merely the topical program of the system but its fundamental intent and method, and we may assess the system-builders' success in realizing their program. A well-composed system will allow us to explain what is present and what is absent. Consequently, we may come to a reasonable estimation of the system's coverage, its realization of its program and full, exhaustive, presentation of its encompassing statement. Not only so, but a well-crafted systemic statement will by definition form a closed system, and the criterion of whether or not a statement stands on its own or depends upon other sources (for example, information not contained within its encompassing statement but only alluded to by that statement) serves as a second major indicator for taxonomic purposes.

Now, in all that I have said, I have treated as an axiom the formal and putative autonomy of systemic thought, which is so represented as if it begins *de novo* every morning, in the mind, imagination, and also conscience of the system-builders. But what about other systems and their literary, as well as their social, detritus? Let us turn to the relationships to prior writings exhibited by systematic and traditional authorships, respectively. How do we know the difference between a system and a tradition in respect to the reception of received systems and their writings? The criteria of difference are characterized very simply.

A systematic authorship will establish connections to received writings, always preserving its own autonomy of perspective. A traditional authorship will stand in a relationship of continuity, commonly formal but always substantive and subordinate, with prior writings. It will make use of its materials essentially in its own way. It will cite and quote and refine those received writings but will ordinarily not undertake a fundamentally original statement of its own, framed in its own terms and resting on a set of issues defined separately from the received writings or formulations. The appeal of a systematic authorship is to the ineluctable verity of well-applied logic, to practical reason tested and retested against the facts, whether deriving from prior authorities or emerging from examples and decisions of leading contemporary authorities.

A traditional authorship, accordingly, will propose to obliterate lines between one document and another, whereas a systematic authorship in the form of its writing will ordinarily not merge with prior documents. It *cites* the received writing as a distinct statement—a document "out there"—and does not merely allude to it as part of an internally cogent statement—a formulation of matters "in here." The systematic authorship begins by stating its interpretation of a received writing in words made up essentially independently of that writing—for example, different in language, formulation, syntax, and substance. The marks of independent, autonomous interpretation are always vividly imprinted upon the systematic authorships' encounter with an inherited document. Nothing out of the past can be shown to have dictated the systematic program, which is essentially the work of its authorship. Therefore, the system begins where reason reigns. Its inexorable logic and order govern supremely and alone, revising the received materials and restating into a compelling statement the entirety of the prior heritage of information and thought. From the Pentateuch to the Bavli, Judaic authorships presented not stages or chapters in an unfolding tradition but closed systems, each one of them constituting a statement at the end of a sustained process of rigorous thought and logical inquiry, applied logic and practical reason. The only way to read a reasoned and systematic statement of a system is defined by the rules of general intelligibility, the laws of reasoned and syllogistic discourse about rules and principles. And the correct logic for a systematic statement is philosophical and propositional, whether syllogistic or teleological. By contrast, the way to read a traditional and sedimentary document lies in the *ad hoc* and episodic display of instances and examples, layers of meaning and eccentricities of confluence, intersection, and congruence. But tradition and system cannot share a single throne, and a crown cannot sit on two heads. Diverse statements of Judaisms will be seen upon examination to constitute not traditional but systemic religious documents, with a particular hermeneutic of order, proportion, and, above all, reasoned context, to tell us now to reach each document. We cannot read these writings in accord with two incompatible hermeneutical programs; accordingly, I argue in favor of the philosophical and systemic, rather than the agglutinative and traditional, hermeneutic.

The contrast between thought received as truth and transmitted through a process of tradition and thought derived from active rationality carries us to the analysis of the Bavli. We ask whether that writing constitutes a tradition and derives from a process of traditional formulation and transmission of an intellectual heritage, facts and thought alike, or whether it makes a statement of its own, cogent and defined within the requirements of an inner logic, proportion, and structure, and imposes that essentially autonomous vision upon whatever materials its authorship has received from the past. We shall know the answer through a sequence of tests, one of which derives from the principal method illustrated in this part of the book: establishing connections between documents so as to compare and contrast the connected documents. What I shall show is that the Judaism of the dual Torah knows not traditions to be recited and reviewed but merely sources, to be honored always but to be used only when pertinent to a quite independent program of thought. The Bavli's authorship does not take over, rework, and repeat what it has received out of prior writings but makes its own statement, on its own program, in its own terms, and for its own purposes.

The authorship does not pursue anyone else's program, excepting only that of the Mishnah. It does not receive and refine writings concluded elsewhere. It takes over a substantial heritage and reworks the whole into its own sustained and internally cogent statement—and that forms not the outcome of a process of sedimentary tradition but the systematic statement of a cogent and logical order. I want to show this fact by comparing the whole of the exegesis of Mishnah-tractate Sukkah chapter 1 accomplished by the authorship of the Yerushalmi with the complete exegesis of that same chapter produced by its counterparts in the Bavli. I want to know whether the Bavli authorship has taken over and improved upon a received source, or whether it has made up what is essentially its own tradition, to be handed over to the future. We shall see that what earlier authorships wished to investigate in the Mishnah has little or nothing in common with the points of special concern systematically worked out by the authorship of the Bavli. The Bavli's authorship at about 600 c.e. approaches Mishnah-exegesis with a program distinct from that of the Yerushalmi's authority of about 400 c.e., and the Bavli's authorship reads a critical verse of Scripture within a set of considerations entirely separate from those of interest to the authorships of Leviticus Rabbah and Pesiqta de Rab Kahana of about 450 to 500 c.e. Any notion that the Bavli's authorship has taken as its principal task the restatement of received ideas on the Mishnah-topics and Scripture verses at hand derives no support to speak of from the following sample we shall examine.

That finding will contradict familiar convictions concerning the character of the Bavli and of the Judaism of the dual Torah, that is to say, the larger canonical corpus of which it forms a principal representative. Reaching the world of commonly held opinions in the song *Tradition*, this conviction leads us to expect the principal document of Judaism to say pretty much what had been said before, beginning at Sinai. That corpus is held to form a continuous statement, beginning in an earlier writing and standing behind, generating, and therefore continuing in a later one. Consequently, the corpus is called "traditional," in the sense that one document leads to the next, and all of the documents come to their climax and conclusion in the final one of late antiquity. To the documents of the Torah—oral and written— are imputed not only the status of tradition in the sense just now defined but also a relationship of continuity that we may call *imputed canonicity*. Thus, we are told, we may freely cite a passage from one document alongside a counterpart from another, treating them as part of a single—hence, continuous—statement and, in theological terms, a canonical one (though our issue is not to be confused with canonical research). And that claim of *traditionality* for the Bavli and the literature prior to it bears with it not merely theological but also literary implications about the nature of the documents and the correct way of reading them. Because of those implications, we can test the claim at hand and ask whether it indeed so describes the documents as to find substantiation in literary facts.

To state the issue simply, if the Bavli carries forward the exegetical program of its predecessor, the Yerushalmi, repeating, refining, restating that received plan of Mishnah-commentary, then the Bavli stands in a traditional relationship to the Yerushalmi. A single, unbroken chain of tradition reaches into the Bavli. If, on the other hand, the authorship of the Bavli can be shown to have made its own decisions, worked out its own program, and so to have made a statement in its own behalf upon an entire, received heritage, the Bavli will emerge not as traditional in intent and execution but as systemic and singular. The document will stand not at the end of a long line of tradition but at the outset of a fresh program entirely—and that despite the undeniable fact that the Bavli makes ample use of prior documents, Scripture and the Mishnah in particular, as well as, to a lesser extent, the Tosefta. But use of what is in hand does not signify traditional intent and program, any more than a composer's working within the received canon of harmony or an artist's utilizing a familiar palette attests to traditionalism.

Since the Bavli forms the second of the two Talmuds that undertake the systematic exegesis of Mishnah-tractates and the restatement, in encompassing terms, of the Torah's message on their respective topics, the Bavli's relationship to its predecessor provides indicative data. If we wish to assess the Bavli's use of

prior sources, therefore, we ask first of all about the relationship
of the Bavli to the Yerushalmi. Does the Bavli carry forward the
exegetical program of the Yerushalmi? Or does the authorship
of the Bavli invent its own, altogether singular and distinctive
topical-exegetical program for the same chapter of the
Mishnah? What we see is that the Bavli is autonomous, singular,
distinctive. Its authorship delivers its message in a way that is its
own and work out an exegetical program, on precisely the same
chapter of the Mishnah, that is particular to itself and not
dictated by the prior Talmud's treatment of the same materials.
The Bavli, therefore, is, in substantial measure, distinct from the
other Talmud. The Bavli is far more than a secondary
development of the Yerushalmi.

We need hardly dwell on the simple fact that both the
Yerushalmi and the Bavli organize their materials as comments
on Mishnah sentences or paragraphs. A further important but
equally obvious fact is that the two compositions differ from all
other documents of the rabbinic canon, both in their focus—the
Mishnah—and in their mode of discourse. That is to say,
Mishnah exegesis and expansion find their place, in the entire
corpus of rabbinic writings of late antiquity, solely in the two
Talmuds. What is shared between the two Talmuds and the
remainder of the canon deals with Scripture exegesis, on the one
hand, and deeds and sayings of sages, on the other. To give one
example, while Leviticus Rabbah contains exegeses of Scripture
found also in one or another of the two Talmuds, not a single
passage of the Mishnah is subjected in Leviticus Rabbah to
modes of analysis commonplace in the two Talmuds, even
though on rare occasions a Mishnah sentence or paragraph may
find its way into Leviticus Rabbah. So the two Talmuds stand
together as well as take up a position apart from the remainder
of the canon. These two facts make the definitive points in
common sufficiently clear, so we may address the more difficult
issue of whether and how the two Talmuds differ from each
other—that is, where and how the authorship of the Bavli has
accepted the program of its predecessors and so given us the seal
of tradition, and where that authorship has gone its own way and
so given us its own systemic statement.

To unpack and explore that issue, we shall entertain a series of propositions and examine evidence marshaled to test those propositions. We begin from the simplest point and move to the more complex and subtle ones. I can imagine no more obvious and self-evident point of entry than this: The two Talmuds not only treat the Mishnah paragraphs in the same order, but they also say much the same thing about them. Hence, the simplest proposition, set forth in two antithetical statements, reads:

A. The two Talmuds say basically the same thing in the same words. The Bavli, coming later, depends upon and merely amplifies or augments the Yerushalmi.

B. The two Talmuds treat the Mishnah paragraph in distinct and distinctive ways. They use different language to make their own points. Where they raise the same issue, it derives from the shared text (the Mishnah), and its logic. Both Talmuds respond to the Mishnah; the Bavli does not depend overall on a conventional program supplied by the Yerushalmi.

The sample at hand will decisively settle matters in favor of B. In what follows, I compare and contrast the exegetical program of the Yerushalmi, given on the left-hand column, against that of the Bavli, given on the right. My précis of each unit of discourse deals only with the issue at hand: What did the exegetes of the Mishnah paragraph wish to ask? Unless there is a clear reproduction of the same discussion in both Talmuds, I do not present the actual texts. The system of division and signification worked out in my translation of the Yerushalmi as well as of Bavli Sukkah (identified in the bibliography) is followed throughout. It has the merit of consistent principles of division, so we are comparing passages that, in a single, consistent way, are identified as whole and complete. Where passages are congruent, I indicate this in the Bavli column by a reference to the Yerushalmi unit. Where they intersect, I indicate this with an equal sign (=). I present the Mishnah-passages in italics.

Yerushalmi and Bavli on Mishnah-Tractate Sukkah 1:1A-F
1:1A-F
A. *A sukkah [booth for use on the Festival of Tabernacles] that is taller than twenty cubits is invalid.*

B. R. *Judah declares it valid.*

C. *And one which is not ten handbreadths high,*

D. *one which does not have three walls,*

E. *or one, the light of which is greater than the shade of which,*

F. *is invalid.*

Yerushalmi

I. Basis for Judah's dispute with rabbis: analogy to the Temple's dimensions. M.Er. 1:1.

II. Why sages regard a sukkah that is too tall as invalid.

III. Rab: A larger sukkah is valid even if it is very tall.

IV. Hoshaiah: If one builds an intervening floor, so diminishing the distance from roof to floor in part of a sukkah, what is the status of the space unaffected by the intervening floor?

V. If one lowered the sukkah roof by hanging garlands, does that lower the roof to less than the acceptable height?

VI. How do we know that air space ten handbreadths above the ground constitutes a domain distinct from the ground? M. Shab. 1:1.

VII. Rabbi, Simeon, Judah: Sukkah must be given dimension in length, breadth, and must have four walls. Dispute.

VIII. Hiyya-Yohanan: Sukkah is valid if it has two walls of normal size and a third of negligible dimensions.

IX. A braided wall as a partition.

X. M. Kil. 4:4.

XI. Tips of lathes that protrude from sukkah roofing are treated as part of the sukkah.

Bavli

I. Relationship of M. Suk. 1:1 to M. Er. 1:1: what differentiates sukkah from erub law. = Y.I.

II. Scriptural basis for position of sages at M. 1:1A. [cf. Y.I.]

III. If sukkah roofing touches walls of sukkah, the sukkah may be higher than twenty cubits.

IV. Dispute of Judah/sages + precedent supplied by T. Suk. 1:1A–E = Y. III.

V. Sukkah must hold person's head and greater part of his body. Discourse: M. Suk. 2:7.

VI. Who stands behind view that house not 4x4 cubits is not regarded as a house. = Y. II.

VII. Diminishing the height of a sukkah by raising the floor. [cf. Y. IV.]

VIII. Diminishing the height of a sukkah by lowering the roof with hangings. = Y. V.

IX. Putting sukkah roofing on posts.

X. M. 1:1C: Scriptural basis for rule that sukkah less than ten handbreadths in height is invalid.

XI. Continues X.

XII. Continues X.

XIII. Sukkah has to have three walls, with the third of negligible [cf. Y. VIII] dimensions. = Y. VII-VIII.

XIV. Where does builder set the little wall?

XII. Citation and discourse on M. 1:1E-F: If light is half and half, it is valid/invalid.

XV. Continues foregoing.
XVI. M. 1:1E-F: definition of valid roofing = Y.XII.
XVII. Sukkah must be permanent, not temporary, in character. Various authorities who take that view.
XVIII. Continues XVII.
XIX. Two sukkah, one inside the other.
XX. Sukkah built for gentiles, women, cattle, Samaritans is valid, if the roofing is valid.

Before proceeding to the comparison of the two Talmud's treatments of the same passage, let us briefly review how, overall, each one has composed its materials. The following discussion may prove a bit technical, but the main point, that the two authorships follow their own program, is best made to register in details, not merely as a generality. The documentary method, after all, serves concrete and specific writings, which often prove technical.

Yerushalmi to M. Sukkah 1:1A-F. The Yerushalmi provides a substantial discussion for each of the Mishnah's topical clauses in sequence, furthermore bringing together parallel rulings in other tractates to enrich the context for discussion. It would be difficult to point to a more satisfactory inquiry, on the part of either Talmud, into the Mishnah's principles and problems. Unit I takes up the noteworthy parallel between M. 1:1A and M. Er. 1:1A. The main point in both cases is the scriptural basis for the dimensions specified by the law. The effort to differentiate is equally necessary. Hence the difference between one sort of symbolic gateway and another, or between one wall built for a given purpose and another wall built for some other purpose, has to be specified. Unit II undertakes a complementary discourse of differentiation. It is now between a sukkah and a house. The two are comparable, since a person is supposed to dwell in a sukkah during the festival. Unit III, continuous with the foregoing, further takes up the specified measurement and explains it. Unit IV raises a difficult question, dealing with the theory, already adumbrated, that we extend the line of a wall or a roof or a cornice in such a way as to imagine that the line comes down to the ground or protrudes upward. At unit IV we seem to have a sukkah roofing at an angle, extending from the middle of a sukkah outward, above the limit of twenty cubits. Unit V asks about lowering the sukkah roofing by suspending decorations from it or raising the sukkah floor by putting straw or pebbles on it. Both produce the effect of bringing the sukkah within the required dimensions of its height. Unit VI does not belong at all; it is primary at Y. Shab 1:1. I assume it was deemed to supplement M. 1:1C. Unit VII takes up the matter of the required walls for the sukkah, M. 1:1D. Once again, the scriptural basis for the rule is indicated. Unit VIII carries forward this same topic, now clarifying the theoretical problems in the same matter. At unit IX we deal with an odd kind of partition, a braid partition. This discussion is primary to Y. Er. 1:9 and is inserted here because of IX and X. The inclusion of unit X is inexplicable, except as it may form a continuous discourse with unit IX. It is primary at Y. Er. 1:8. Units XI and XII are placed where they are as discussions of M. 1:1E. But only unit XII takes up the exegesis of the Mishnah's language.

Bavli to M. Sukkah 1:1A-F. The protracted Bavli passage serving M. 1:1A-F not only works its way through the Mishnah paragraph but systematically expands the law applicable to that paragraph by seeking out pertinent principles in parallel or contrasting cases of law. When a unit of discourse abandons the theme or principle connected to the Mishnah paragraph, it is to take up a secondary matter introduced by a unit of discourse that has focused on that theme or principle. Unit I begins with an analysis of the word choice at hand. At the same time, it introduces an important point, M. Er. 1:1, namely, the comparison between the sukkah and a contraption erected also on a temporary basis and for symbolic purposes. Such a contraption is a symbolic gateway that transforms an alley entry into a gateway for a courtyard and so alters the status of the alley and the courtyards that open on to it, turning them into a single domain. As one domain, they are open for carrying on the Sabbath, at which time people may not carry objects from one domain (e.g., private) to another (e.g., public). That comparison is repeatedly invoked. Units II and III then move from language to scriptural sources for the law. Unit IV stands in the same relationship to unit III, and so does unit V. Unit VI reverts to an issue of unit V. Thus, the entire discussion, II-VI, flows out of the exegetical requirements of the opening lines of the Mishnah paragraph. But the designated unit-divisions seem to mark discussions that could have stood originally by themselves. Unit VII then reverts to the original topic, the requisite height of the sukkah (= Y. IV-V). It deals with a fresh problem, namely, artificially diminishing or increasing the height of the sukkah by alterations to the inside of the hut. One may raise the floor to diminish the height or lower the floor to increase it. Unit VIII pursues the same interest. It further introduces principles distinct from the Mishnah's rules but imposed upon the interpretation of those rules or the amplification of pertinent cases. This important exercise in secondary expansion of a rather simple rule through the introduction of fresh and rather engaging principles—"curved wall," fictional extension of walls upward or downward, and the like—then proceeds in its own terms. Unit IX is continuous in its thematic interest with unit VIII. Unit X reverts to the Mishnah paragraph, now M. 1:1C, and asks the question usually raised at the outset about the scriptural authority behind the Mishnah's rule. This leads us into a sizable digression on scriptural exegesis, with special interest in establishing the analogy between utensils in the Temple and dimensions pertinent to the sukkah. The underlying conception, that what the Israelite does on cultic occasions in the home responds to what is done in the cult in the Temple, is familiar. Units XI and XII pursue the same line of thought. Then unit XIII reverts once more to the Mishnah's rule, M. 1:1D. Now we take up the issue of the walls of the sukkah. These must be three, in the rabbi's view, and four in Simeon's. Each party concedes that one of the requisite walls may be merely symbolic. The biblical source for the required number of walls forms the first object of inquiry. Unit XIV then takes up the symbolic wall. Unit XV reverts to a statement on Tannaite authority given in unit XIII.

There are diverse kinds of sukkah buildings. One, we know, is a sukkah erected to carry out the religious duty of the festival. But a person may build a sukkah to extend the enclosed and private area of his home. If he places such a sukkah by the door, the area in which it is permitted to carry objects—private domain—covers not only the space of the house but also the space of the sukkah. That sukkah, erected in connection with Sabbath observance, is compared to the sukkah erected for purposes of keeping the festival. The issue is appropriate here, since the matter concerns the character of the walls of the sukkah built for Sabbath observance. Unit XVI then returns to the Mishnah paragraph. Unit XVIII moves back from the Mishnah's statements and deals with the general principle, taken by some parties, that the sukkah must bear the qualities of a permanent dwelling. That issue intersects with our Mishnah paragraph in connection with Judah's and Simeon's views on the requirement that there be a roof of a certain height and four walls. But the construction as a whole stands independent of the Mishnah paragraph and clearly was put together in its own terms. Unit XVIII takes up XVII.M. Units XIX and XX evidently are miscellaneous—the only such units of discourse in the entire massive construction. I cannot point to a more thorough or satisfying sequence of Babylonian Talmudic units of discourse in which the Mishnah's statements are amplified than the amplifications themselves worked out on their own. The whole is thorough, beautifully articulated, and cogent until the very end.

Since, intersecting in topic and problematic, the Bavli goes over the ground of the Yerushalmi at several points, pursuing essentially the same problem, we have to ask about possible borrowing by the Bavli from the Yerushalmi, not of theses or conventions of interpretation but of whole constructions. To show the points of word-for-word correspondence, such as they are, let us now consider side by side a single suggestive item, which is marked, in my system, as Y.1:1. III = B.1:1. IV.

Y.1:1

B. 1:1

III.A. [As to the invalidity of a sukkah more than twenty cubits high,] R. Ba in the name of Rab: "That applies to a sukkah that will hold only the head and the greater part of the body of a person and also his table.

B. "But if it held more than that, it is valid [even at such a height]."

C. [Giving a different reason and

IV.A. [The specification of the cited authorities, II.A, C, E, on the minimum requirements of the sukkah, now comes under discussion in its own terms.] The following objection was raised:

B. A sukkah which is taller than twenty cubits is invalid.

C. R. Judah declares it valid [M. 1:1A-B], even up to forty or fifty cubits.

qualification,] R. Jacob bar Aha in the name of R. Josiah. "That applies [further] when the walls do not go all the way up with it [to the top, the roofing] but if the walls go all the way up with it to the roofing, it is valid."

D. [Proving that C's reason, not A-B's, is valid, we cite the following:]

E. Lo, the following Tannaite teaching differs [in T.'s version]: Said R. Judah, "M'SH B: The sukkah of Helene was twenty cubits tall, and sages went in and out, when visiting her, and not one of them said a thing."

F. They said to him, "It was because she is a woman, and a woman is not liable to keep the commandment of sitting in a sukkah."

G. He said to them, "Now did she not have seven sons who are disciples of sages, and all of them were dwelling in that same sukkah!" [T. Suk. 1:1].

H. Do you then have the possibility of claiming that the sukkah of Helene could not hold more than the head and the greater part of the body and the table of a person? [Surely, someone of her wealth would not build so niggardly a sukkah.]

I. Consequently, the operative reason is that the sides of the sukkah do not go all the way up [to the sukkah roofing at the top, leaving a space].

J. It stands to reason, then, that what R. Josiah has said is so.

K. [And the Tannaite teaching] does not differ [from sages' view], for it is the way of the rich to leave a

D. Said R. Judah, "M'SH B: The sukkah of Helene in Lud was twenty cubits tall, and sages went in and out, when visiting her, and not one of them said a thing."

E. They said to him, "It was because she is a woman, and a woman is not liable to keep the commandment of sitting in a sukkah."

F. He said to them, "Now did she not have seven sons [who are disciples of sages, and all of them were dwelling in that same sukkah]" [T. Suk. 1:1A-E].

G. "And furthermore, everything she ever did was done in accord with the instruction of sages.' "

H. Now what need do I have for this additional reason: "Furthermore, everything she ever did was done in accord with the instructions of sages"?

I. This is the sense of what he said to them: "Now, if you say that the sons were minors, and minors are exempt from the religious duty of dwelling in the sukkah, since she had seven sons, it is not possible that among them was not a single one who no longer needed his mother's tending [and so would be required to dwell on his own in the sukkah]."

J. "And if, further, you should maintain that a minor who no longer needs his mother's tending is subject to the law only on the authority of rabbis, and that woman paid no attention to rules that rested only on the authority of the rabbis, come and note the following: 'And furthermore, everything she ever did was done in accord with the instructions of sages.'"

small bit of the wall out beneath the sukkah roofing itself, so that cooling air may pass through.

K. [We now revert to the issue with which we began, namely, the comparison of the story at hand to the reasons adduced by the authorities at unit III:] Now with reverence to the one who said, the dispute applies to a case in which the walls of the sukkah do not touch the sukkah roofing, would a queen dwell in a sukkah, the walls of which do not touch the sukkah roofing?

L. [3A] [Indeed so! The reason is that] the space makes possible good ventilation.

M. But in the view of the one who has said that the dispute pertains to a small sukkah, would a queen ever dwell in a small sukkah?

N. Said Rabbah bar R. Ada, "At issue in the dispute is solely a case of a sukkah which is made with many small cubbies."

O. But would a queen take up residence in a sukkah that was subdivided into many small cubbies?

P. Said R. Ashi, "At issue is only [a large sukkah which had] such recesses.

Q. "Rabbis take the view that the queen's sons were dwelling in a sukkah of absolutely valid traits, while she dwelled in the recesses on account of modesty [i.e., not showing her face among the men], and it was on that account that rabbis said nothing to her [about her dwelling in what was, in fact, an invalid part of the sukkah].

R. "And R. Judah maintains the position that her sons were dwelling along with her [in the cubbyholes of

the sukkah], and even so, the rabbis
did not criticize what she was doing
[which proves that the small cubbies
of the sukkah were valid]."

Again, the reader may find the following a bit technical, but
the details are required to establish the main point. The issue of
Y.1:1. III.A and B.1:1. IV.A is the same. Tosefta's precedent,
marked in boldface, is used differently in each Talmud. In the
Bavli it makes a point relevant to B. IV.A, the height of the
sukkah. It is entirely relevant to the purpose for which it is
adduced. The sukkah of the queen was high, so sustaining
Judah's view. The secondary issue, IV.K, links the precedent to
unit III. The whole is integrated and well composed. By
contrast, the Yerushalmi's use of the precedent is odd. The
passage is explicit as to the large size of the hut, so Y.III.H is
somewhat jarring. It really contradicts Y.III.G. Y.III.I then
revises matters to force the precedent to serve Y.III.C. We
cannot imagine that Bavli's author has depended on Yerushalmi's composition. He has used the precedent for his own inquiry
and in his own way. Where, therefore, Yerushalmi and Bavli
share materials, the Bavli's use of those materials—if this case is
suggestive—will not depend upon the Yerushalmi's. Both refer
back to the Mishnah and to the Tosefta, responding to the
former in terms (here) of the exegetical program precipitated by
the contents available in the latter. There is no reason to belabor
the obvious. When the two Talmuds wish to deal with the same
issue, the overlap is in conception; but there is no point of verbal
contact, let alone of intersection. Each Talmud undertakes its
own analysis in its own way. Each Talmud bases its discussion on
the common source (the Mishnah, sometimes also the Tosefta),
but each one builds its discussion on the basis of points made by
its selection of authorities and pursues matters in terms of its
own established conventions of rhetoric.

The Bavli and the Yerushalmi assuredly stand autonomous
from one another. The authorship of the Bavli in its own way
works out a singular and independent program of exegesis and
amplification of the Mishnah. Word-for-word correspondences
are few and, on the whole, peripheral. But in all instances of
shared language or conventional hermeneutics, the framers of

the Bavli worked things out on their own. They in no way accepted the Yerushalmi as a model for how they said things, let alone for the bulk of what they said. What is shared derives principally from the Mishnah. It comes, secondarily, from some sort of conventional program (partly encapsulated, also, in the Tosefta). The Tosefta has not dictated to the Bavli's authorship a topical or logical program; it has merely contributed occasional passages for systematic analysis, much as the Mishnah has contributed a much larger volume of passages for systematic analysis. In any event, the Bavli's authors developed inherited intellectual conventions in a strikingly independent way. That fact leads us to see the Bavli's authorship's composition as an essentially autonomous statement, standing on its own, borrowing from prior compilations only what suited its purpose.

On the other hand, the Bavli and the Yerushalmi most certainly do form a cogent part of a larger, continuous statement, that of "the one whole Torah of Moses, our rabbi" or, in modern theological language, a canon, that is, Judaism. That premise of all study of the canon of formative Judaism stands firm. Nothing we have reviewed leads us to doubt its validity for those documents. The particular aspect of continuity at hand, however, requires specification. How is the Bavli continuous with the Yerushalmi? *The Bavli meets the Yerushalmi in the Mishnah.* The two also come together, in markedly diminished measure, in the Tosefta and, to a lesser degree, in some shared phrases deriving from post-Mishnaic authorities (e.g., those of the third-century masters Yohanan and Simeon b. Laqish). So in one specific way the two documents not only intersect but prove at one with each other and therefore continuous.

In somewhat more general ways, too, they wish to do much the same thing, which is to subject the Mishnah to a process of explanation and amplification. While the authors of the Bavli developed their own principles of hermeneutics, composition, and redaction, still, the upshot of their work, the Bavli as a whole, in the heavenly academy cannot have baffled their predecessors, who had earlier created the Yerushalmi. Apart from disagreements on tertiary details, the later of the two sets of authorities found themselves entirely at home in the conceptions, rhetoric, and documents created by their antecedent counterparts. That seems self-evident proof of the continuity of the Bavli with the Yerushalmi. If the two then turn out to be autonomous from, as well as continuous with one another, the real problem of nuance and differentiation is presented by matters of connection. These have forthwith to be divided into two parts: first, the connection of one document to the other; second, the connection of both documents to other components of the larger rabbinic canon.

The connection of the Bavli to the Yerushalmi brings us back to our main point, the systemic characterization represented by an authorship, as against the traits of the system produced by that authorship, hence, the issue of the traditionality of the Bavli. What we want to know concerns the Bavli in particular. Does the Bavli bear a message of its own? Or does the document essentially rest upon, and continue, the work of the Yerushalmi? If the Yerushalmi dictates the program and policy—the hermeneutics and rhetoric—of the Bavli, then we cannot speak of the Bavli as a document on its own. Its logic, its mode of inquiry, its rhetoric, its mode of thought—all these will turn out to belong to its precursors. What would define the Bavli, then, would be its authors' ability to do better or so say at greater length what others had already done and said. In that case, the Bavli would have to take its place as a secondary and subordinate component of that sector of the canon of Judaism defined, for all time, by the concerns and the circumstances of the framers of the Yerushalmi. In terms of the choices before us, the Bavli would emerge as traditional and not an essentially fresh systemic construction.

The contrary proposition is that while the Bavli shares with the Yerushalmi a common program and purpose, its authors carry out that program in their own way. By this thesis, they should appear to define that purpose in response to interests shaped in their distinct context and framework. Then we may claim that the Bavli presents its own message, a systemic statement of an original character, much as in reshaping and reconstituting received conventions, the composer or the artist accomplishes something fundamentally original. Stated simply, this other proposition will maintain that the authorship of the Bavli accomplishes its own goals. True, its logic, its inquiry, its mode of thought may run parallel to those of the Yerushalmi.

But that is only because they derive from sources common to both documents. In terms of this second hypothesis, the Bavli flows not from the Yerushalmi but from the Mishnah. According to this second proposition, the Bavli is not secondary. It is not subordinate to the Yerushalmi in that larger sector of the canon of Judaism defined by the Mishnah.

As between these two propositions, the materials we have examined decisively settle the question in favor of the second. At point after point, we found the two documents connected not only *to* the common source but mainly or solely *through* that source. Where they go over the same problems, it is because the shared source presented these problems to the authors of both documents. In our comparison of the two documents, we found that the rhetoric and literary program of the Bavli owed remarkably little to that of its predecessor. The comparisons of actual texts yielded decisive evidence for several propositions.

First, there is remarkably little verbatim correspondence. The Bavli's authors scarcely ever made use of extensive constructions and only rarely of brief formulations also found in the Yerushalmi. So far as our modest sample suggests, they never did so when it came to detailed expository arguments and analyses. Where there is verbatim sharing, it is a Mishnah paragraph or Tosefta passage that is held in common, on the one side, or a prior, severely abbreviated lemma of an earlier Amoraic authority, on the other. Where the two sets of authors deal with such a shared lemma, however, each group does exactly what it wishes, imputing words to the prior authority (as if the said authority had actually spoken those words) simply not known to the other group.

Second and more important, what the framers of the Bavli wished to do with a saying of an earlier Amoraic authority in no way responded to the policy or program of the Yerushalmi's authors. Quite to the contrary, where both sets of authors shared sayings of Yohanan and Simeon b. Laqish, we noted that each set went its own way. In no aspect did the Yerushalmi's interest in these shared sayings affect the Bavli's treatment of them. The point in common was that prior authorities explained the same passage of the Mishnah. From that simple starting point, the Bavli's authors went in a direction not imagined by the Yerushalmi's. The power and intellectual force of the Bavli's authors in that context vastly overshadowed the capacities of the Yerushalmi's.

What the systematic analysis of part of a single chapter tells us, therefore, may be stated very briefly. The Yerushalmi and the Bavli are alike in their devotion to the exegesis and amplification of the Mishnah. Viewed as literary constructions, they share, in addition, a basic exegetical program, which flows from the Mishnah and in fundamental ways is defined by the inner logic and cogency of the Mishnah. In relationship to the Yerushalmi, therefore, the Bavli's framers pursued their own interests in their own way. They reveal independence of mind and originality of taste. It must follow that the Bavli is sufficiently unlike the Yerushalmi to be judged as an autonomous document, disconnected from and unlike its predecessor in all the ways that matter. True, in general the Bavli falls into the same classification as does the Yerushalmi. But in detail, it presents its own message in its own way. The genus is the same, the species not. The opening hypothesis has yielded a negative result. When confronting the exegesis of the mishnah, which is its indicative trait and definitive task, the authorship of the Bavli does not continue and complete the work of antecedents. Quite to the contrary, that authorship made its statement essentially independently of its counterpart and earlier document.

The Bavli is simply not a traditional document, in the plain sense that most of what it says in a cogent and coherent way expresses the well-crafted statement and viewpoint of its authorship. Excluding, of course, the Mishnah, to which the Bavli devotes its sustained and systematic attention, little of what our authorship says derives cogency and force from a received statement, and most does not. Why not? Because, as our brief comparison shows, the system comes first. In the present context, that means that the logic and principle of orderly inquiry take precedence over the preservation and repetition of received materials, however holy. The mode of thought defined, the work of applied reason and practical rationality may get underway. First in place is the system that the Bavli as a whole expresses and serves in stupefying detail to define. Only then comes that selection, out of the received materials of the past, of topics and even concrete judgments, facts that serve the Bavli's authorship in the articulation of its system. Nothing out of the past can be shown to have dictated the Bavli's program, which is essentially the work of its authorship. In this context, the Mishnah forms no exception, for the work of the Bavli's authorship began with the selection of tractates to study and the designation of those to ignore.

The Bavli constitutes a statement of a sustained process of rigorous thought and logical inquiry, applied logic and practical reason. The only way to read a reasoned and systematic statement of a system is defined by the rules of general intelligibility, the laws of reasoned and syllogistic discourse about rules and principles. As I said at the outset, the way to read a traditional and sedimentary document by contrast lies in the ad hoc and episodic display of instances and examples, layers of meaning and eccentricities of confluence, intersection, and congruence. The formative writing of the Judaism of the dual Torah shows that the religious system in its definitive document constitutes not a traditional but a systemic religious statement, with a hermeneutic of order, proportion, and above all, reasoned context, to tell us how to read each document and therefore also how to describe, analyze, and interpret the religious system to which the writings speak.

PART FOUR

Matrix:
From Writing Through History to Religion

CHAPTER NINE

The Documentary History
of Ideas

I f we propose to translate writing into religion, we hardly conclude our task when all we discern is the religious world lived wholly within the mind and imagination of a textual community. Religion forms a public and a social fact, so the movement from writing to religion carries us across the bounds of the private and individual world, an interior world of imagination and sensibility. Beyond the limit of an authorship or a textual community, a world awaits attention, its urgent and critical problems demanding consideration. The premise that the reading of a document identifies evidence for the composition of a religious system defines the third and final task in my documentary method in the study of religion. It is to move yet a third step from the documents' parts, beyond the writing read whole and complete, past the perimeters of the intersecting circles of authorships represented by texts that are connected to one another, to the world beyond.

The matrix of a text read in context, the nourishing world that formed the authorships whose work we have in hand and that sustained them, has also to take its place in discourse on religion. We therefore have to ask how we may read writing and gain entry into the world to which that writing is addressed. How are we to determine the particular time and circumstance in which a writing took shape, and how shall we identify the generative problems, the urgent and critical questions, that informed the intellect of an authorship and framed the social world that nurtured that same authorship? Lacking answers to these questions, we find our work partial, and, if truth be told, stained by sterile academicism. Accordingly, the documentary method requires us to situate the contents of writings into particular circumstances, so that we may read the contents in the context of a real time and place. It is by reference to the time and circumstance of the closure of a document, that is to say, the conventional assignment of a piece of writing to a particular time and place, that we proceed outward from context to matrix.

Judaic scholars often simply take at face value attributions of sayings to particular authorities and interpret what is said as evidence of the time and place in which the cited authorities flourished. When studying topics in the Judaism of the sages of the rabbinic writings from the first through the seventh centuries, they routinely cite sayings categorized by attribution rather than by document. That is to say, they treat as one group of sayings whatever is assigned to Rabbi X. This is without regard to the time of redaction of the documents in which those sayings occur or to similar considerations of literary context and documentary circumstance. The category defined by attributions to a given authority furthermore rests on the premise that the things given in the name of Rabbi X really were said by him, as we noted in chapter 6. Commonly, the next step is to treat those sayings as evidence of ideas held, if not by that particular person, then by people in the age in which the cited authority lived. Once more, the premise that the sayings go back to the age of the authority to whom they are attributed underlies the inquiry. Accordingly, scholars cite sayings in the name of given authorities and take for granted that those sayings were said by the authority to whom they were attributed and, of course, in the time in which that authority flourished. By contrast, in my method of the documentary study of Judaism, I treat the historical sequence of sayings only in accord with the order of the documents in which they first occur, because although the attributions cannot be validated, the books can.

The first of the two principles by which I describe the matrix that defines the context in which texts are framed is that we compose histories of ideas of the Judaism of the dual Torah in accord with the sequence of documents that, in the aggregate, constitute the corpus and canon of the Judaism of the dual Torah. And those histories set forth dimensions of the matrix in which that Judaism, through its writings, is to be situated for broader purposes of interpretation. Documents reveal the system and structure of their authorships and, in the case of religious writing, allow us to compose an account of the authorship's religion: a way of life, a world view, a social entity meant to realize both. Read one by one, documents reveal the interiority of the intellect of an authorship, and that inner-facing quality of mind inheres even when an authorship imagines that it speaks outward, toward and about the world beyond. Even when set side by side, moreover, documents illuminate the minds of intersecting authorships.

The presently paramount way of determining the matrix of a text is simply to take at face value the allegation that a given authority, whose time and place we may identify, really said what is attributed to him, and that if a writing says something happened, what it tells us is not what its authorship thought happened, but what really happened. That reading of writing, for purposes of not only history but also of religious study, is in fact commonplace. It characterizes all accounts of Judaism, prior to mine, and it remains a serious option for all those outside of my school and circle. Accordingly, let me characterize the prevailing way of determining the historical and religious matrix of texts and then proceed to explain my alternate mode for answering the question of what is to be learned, from within a piece of writing, about the religious world beyond.

In historical study, we gain access to no knowledge *a priori*. All facts derive from sources correctly situated, which means classified, comprehensively and completely described, dispassionately analyzed, and evaluated. Nothing can be taken for granted. What we cannot show, we do not know. These simple dogmas of all historical learning go back to the very beginnings of Western critical historical scholarship, to the age of the Renaissance. But all historical and religious-historical scholarship on the documents of the Judaism of the dual Torah in its formative age, except for mine and for that of a very few others, ignores the canons of criticism that govern academic scholarship. Everyone in the past and many even now take for granted that almost everything they read is true—except what they decide is not true. They cannot and do not raise the question of whether an authorship knows what it is talking about, and they do not address the issue of the purpose of a text: historical or imaginative, for example. For them, the issue is always history, namely, what really happened, and that issue was settled, so to speak, at Sinai: It is all true (except, on an episodic basis, what is not true, which the scholars somehow know instinctively). The fundamentalists in the talmudic academies, rabbinical seminaries, and Israeli universities take not only as fact but at face value everything in the holy books. In their opinion, "Judaism" is special and need not undergo description, analysis, and interpretation in accord with a shared and public canon of rules of criticism.

The operative question facing anyone who proposes to translate writing into religion is the historical one: How do you know exactly what was said and done, that is, the history that you claim to report about what happened long ago? Specifically, how do you know it has really been said? And if you do not know that it has really been said, how can you ask the questions that you ask, which have as their premise the claim that you can say what happened or did not happen?

Let me list the range of uncertainty that necessitates this fresh approach I am advocating. First, if the order of the documents was fully sound and the contents representative of rabbinical opinion, then the result would be a history of the advent of the idea at hand and the development and articulation of that idea in formative Judaism. We should then have a fairly reliable picture of ideas at hand, as these unfolded in orderly sequence. But we do not know that the canonical history corresponds to the actual history of ideas. Furthermore, we cannot even be sure that the order of documents presently assumed in scholarly convention is correct. Second, if a rabbi really spoke the words attributed to him, then a given idea would have reached expression within Judaism *prior* to the redaction of the document. Dividing things up by documents will tend to give a later date and thus a different context for interpretation to opinions held earlier than we can presently demonstrate. Third, although we are focusing upon the literature produced by a particular group, again, we have no clear notion of what people were thinking outside of that group. We therefore do not know how opinions held by other groups or by the Jewish people in general came to shape the vision of rabbis. When, for example, we note that there also existed poetic literature and translations of Scriptures character- istic of the synagogue worship, we cannot determine whether the poetry and most translations spoke for rabbis or for some quite different group.

For these reasons, I have chosen to address the contextual question within the narrow limits of the canon. Obviously, if I could in a given formulation relate the appearance of a given idea to events affecting rabbis in particular or to the life of Israel in general, the results would be exceedingly suggestive. But since we do not know for whom the documents speak, how broadly representative they are, or even how comprehensive is their evidence about rabbis' views, we must carefully define what we do and do not know. So for this early stage in research, the context in which a given idea is described, analyzed, and interpreted is the canon. But this first step alone carries us to new territory. I hope that in due course others will move beyond these limits, which, at the moment, seem to me to mark the farthest possible advance.

Let me now explain the alternative, which I call the documentary history of ideas. It is a mode of relating writing to religion through history, that is, through close attention to the circumstance in which writing reached closure. It is accom- plished, specifically, by assessing shifts exhibited by a sequence of documents and appealing to the generally accepted dates assigned to writings in explaining those shifts. In this way I propose to confront questions of cultural order, social system and political structure, to which the texts respond explicitly and constantly.

Confronting writings of a religious character, we err by asking questions of a narrowly historical character: What did X really say on a particular occasion, and why? Not only are these questions not answerable on the basis of the evidence in hand, but they are also trivial and irrelevant to the character of the evidence. What strikes me as I review the writings just now cited is how little of real interest and worth we should know, even if we were to concede the historical accuracy and veracity of all the many allegations of the scholars we have surveyed. How little we should know—but how much we should have *missed* if that set of questions and answers were to encompass the whole of our inquiry.

If we are to trace the unfolding of a given theme or the ideas on a given problem in the sources of formative Judaism, the order in which we approach the several books, that is, components of the entire canon, gives us the sole guidance on sequence, order, and context, that we are apt to find. Lacking firm evidence in a sage's own, clearly assigned writings, or even in writings redacted by a sage's own disciples and handed on among them in the discipline of their own community, we have for chronology only a single fact. It is that a document, reaching closure at a given time, contains the allegation that Rabbi X said statement Y. So we know that people at the time the document reached closure took the view that Rabbi X said statement Y. We may then assign to statement Y a position, in the order of the sequence of sayings, defined by the location of the document in the order of the sequence of documents. The several documents' dates, as is clear, all constitute guesses. But the sequence explained in the Appendix—Mishnah, Tosefta, Yerushalmi, Bavli for the exegetical writings on the Mishnah—is absolutely firm and beyond doubt. The sequence for the exegetical collections on Scripture, namely, Sifra, the Sifrés, Genesis Rabbah, Leviticus Rabbah, the Pesiqtas, and beyond, is not entirely sure. Still, the sequence of the Sifra and the two Sifrés at the head, followed by Genesis Rabbah, then Leviticus Rabbah, then Pesiqta deRab. Kahana and Lamentations Rabbati and some related collections, seems likely.

What are the canonical mainbeams that sustain the history of ideas as I propose to trace that history? The formative age of Judaism is the period marked at the outset by the Mishnah, taking shape from sometime before the Common Era and reaching closure at circa 200 C.E., and at the end by the Talmud of Babylonia, which reached closure at circa 600 C.E. In between these dates, two streams of writings developed, one legal, explaining the meaning of the Mishnah, the other theological and exegetical, interpreting the sense of Scripture. The high points of the former set of writings come with tractate Abot (which is the Mishnah's first apologetic); the Tosefta, a collection of supplements circa 300 C.E.; the Talmud of the Land of Israel, circa 400 C.E.; and the Babylonian Talmud. The latter set of writings comprise compositions on Exodus, in Mekilta attributed to R. Ishmael and of indeterminate date; Sifra on Leviticus; Sifré on Numbers; and another Sifré on Deuteronomy, at a guess to be dated at circa 300 C.E.; Genesis Rabbah, circa 400 C.E., Leviticus Rabbah, circa 425 C.E.; and at the end, Pesiqta de Rab Kahana, Lamentations Rabbati, and some other treatments of biblical books, all of them in the fifth or sixth centuries. These books and some minor related items together form the canon of Judaism as it had reached its definitive shape by the end of late antiquity.

If we lay out these writings in the approximate sequence in which they reached closure, we gain what I call "canonical history." This is, specifically, the order of the appearance of ideas when the documents, read in the outlined sequence, address a given idea or topic. The consequent history consists of the sequence in which a given statement on the topic at hand was made (early, middle or late) in the unfolding of the canonical writings.

To illustrate the process, what does the authorship of the Mishnah have to say on the theme? Then how does the compositor of Abot deal with it? Then the Tosefta's compositor's record comes into view, followed by the materials assembled in the Talmud of the Land of Israel, alongside those now found in the earlier and middle ranges of compilations of scriptural exegeses, and, as always, the Talmud of Babylonia at the end. In the illustrative exercise that follows, we shall read the sources in exactly the order outlined here. I produce a picture of how these sources treat an important principle of the Judaism of the dual Torah. We shall see important shifts and changes in the unfolding of ideas on the symbol under study.

So, in sum, this story of continuity and change rests upon the notion that we can present the history of the treatment of a topical program in the canonical writings of that Judaism. I do not claim that the documents represent the state of popular or synagogue opinion. I do not know whether the history of the idea in the unfolding official texts corresponds to the history of the idea among the people who stand behind those documents. Even less do I claim to speak about the history of the topic or idea at hand outside of rabbinical circles, among the Jewish nation at large. All these larger dimensions of the matter lie wholly beyond the perspective of this book. The reason is that the evidence at hand is of a particular sort and hence permits us to investigate one category of questions and not another. The category is defined by established and universally held conventions about the order in which the canonical writings reached completion.

We trace the way in which ideas were taken up and spelled out in these successive stages in the formation of the canon. *When we follow this procedure, we discover how, within the formation of the rabbinical canon of writings, the idea at hand came to literary expression, and how it was then shaped to serve the larger purposes of the nascent canonical system as a whole.* By knowing the place and uses of the topic under study within the literary evidences of the rabbinical system, we gain a better understanding of the formative history of that system. Yet neither the condition of the people at large nor the full range and power of the rabbinical thinkers' imagination comes to the fore. About other, larger historical and intellectual matters, we have no direct knowledge at all. Consequently, we claim to report only what we learn about the canonical literature of a system evidenced by a limited factual base. No one who wants to know the history of a given idea in all the diverse Judaisms of late antiquity, or the role of that idea in the history of all the Jews in all parts of the world in the first seven centuries of the Common Era, will find it here.

In order to understand the documentary method, we must again underline the social and political character of the documentary evidence presented. These are public statements, preserved and handed on because people have adopted them as authoritative. The sources constitute a collective, and therefore official, literature. All of the documents took shape and attained a place in the canon of the rabbinical movement as a whole. None was written by an individual in such a way as to testify to personal choice or decision. Accordingly, we cannot provide an account of the theory of a given individual at a particular time and place. We have numerous references to what a given individual said about the topic at hand. But these references do not reach us in the authorship of that person, or even in his language. They come to us only in the setting of a *collection* of sayings and statements, some associated with names, others unattributed and anonymous. By definition, the collections were composed under the auspices of rabbinical authority—a school or a circle. They tell us what a group of people wished to preserve and hand on as authoritative doctrine about the meaning of the Mishnah and Scripture. The compositions reach us because the larger rabbinical estate chose to copy and hand them on. Accordingly, we know the state of doctrine at the stages marked by the formation and closure of the several documents.

We follow what references we find to a topic in accord with the order of documents just now spelled out. In this study we learn the order in which ideas came to expression in the canon. We begin any survey with the Mishnah, the starting point of the canon. We proceed systematically to work our way through tractate Abot, the Mishnah's first apologetic, then the Tosefta, the Yerushalmi, and the Bavli at the end. In a single encompassing sweep, we finally deal with the entirety of the compilations of the exegeses of Scripture, arranged in the order that I have now explained. Let me expand on the matter of my heavy emphasis on the order of the components of the canon.

We have to ask not only what documents viewed whole and all at once ("Judaism") tell us about our theme. In tracing the order in which ideas make their appearance, we ask about the components in sequence ("history of Judaism") so far as we can trace the sequence. Then, and only then, shall we have access to issues of *history*, that is, of change and development. If our theme makes its appearance early on in one form (so one set of ideas predominates in a document that reached closure in the beginnings of the canon) and then that theme drops out of public discourse or undergoes radical revision in writings in later stages of the canon, that fact may make considerable difference. Specifically, we may find it possible to speculate on where and why a given approach proved urgent, and also on the reasons why that same approach receded from the center of interest.

In knowing the approximate sequence of documents and therefore the ideas in them (at least so far as the final point at which those ideas reached formal expression in the canon), a second possibility emerges. What if—as is the case—we find pretty much the same views, treated in the same proportion and for the same purpose, yielding the same message, early, middle, and late in the development of the canon? Then we shall have to ask why the literature remains so remarkably constant. Given the consideration shifts in the social and political condition of Israel in the land of Israel as well as in Babylonia over a period of more than four hundred years, that evident stability in the teachings for the affective life will constitute a considerable fact for analysis and interpretation. History, including the history of religion, done rightly thus produces two possibilities, both of them demanding sustained attention. Things change. Why? Things do not change. Why not? We may well trace the relationship between the history of ideas and the history of the society that holds those same ideas. We follow the interplay between society and system—world view, and way of life, addressed to a particular social group—by developing a theory of the relationship between contents and context, between the world in which people live and the world which people create in their shared social and imaginative life. When we can frame a theory of how a system in substance relates to its setting, of the interplay between the social matrix and the mode and manner of a society's world view and way of life, then we may develop theses of general intelligibility.

The story of continuity and change rests upon the notion that we can present the history of the treatment of a topical program in the canonical writings of that Judaism. I do not claim that the documents represent the state of popular or synagogue opinion. I do not know whether the history of the idea in the unfolding official texts corresponds to the history of the idea among the people who stand behind those documents. Even less do I claim to speak about the history of the topic or idea at hand outside of rabbinical circles, among the Jewish nation at large. All these larger dimensions of the matter lie wholly beyond the perspective of this book. The reason is that the evidence at hand is of a particular sort and hence permits us to investigate one category of questions and not another. The category is defined by established and universally held conventions about the order in which the canonical writings reached completion. Therefore, we trace the way in which matters emerge in the sequence of writings followed here. We trace the way in which ideas were taken up and spelled out in these successive stages in the formation of the canon. When we follow this procedure, we discover how, within the formation of the rabbinical canon of writings, the idea at hand came to literary expression and how it was then shaped to serve the larger purposes of the nascent canonical system as a whole.

I will give an example of the result of the method I have outlined. For that example, I take the documentary history of the single critical symbol of the Judaism of the dual Torah, namely, (the) Torah. That documentary history traces the story of how "the Torah" lost its capital letter and definite article and ultimately became "torah." What for nearly a millennium had been a particular scroll or book came to serve as a symbol of an entire system. When a rabbi spoke of torah, he no longer meant only a particular object, a scroll and its contents. Now he used the word to encompass a distinctive and well-defined world view and way of life. Torah had come to stand for something one does. Knowledge of the Torah promised not merely information about what people were supposed to do, but ultimate redemption or salvation.

In the Judaism of the dual Torah as it emerged from its formative age, everything was contained in that one thing, "Torah." It connotes a broad range of clearly distinct categories of noun and verb, concrete fact and abstract relationship alike. "Torah" stands for a kind of human being, for a social status and a social group. It refers to a type of social relationship. It further denotes a legal status and differentiates among legal norms. As symbolic abstraction, the word encompasses things and persons, actions and statuses, points of social differentiation and legal and normative standing, as well as "revealed truth." In all, the main points of insistence of the whole of Israel's life and history come to full symbolic expression in that single word. If people wanted to explain how they would be saved, they would use the word Torah. If they wished to sort out their parlous relationships with Gentiles, they would use the word Torah. Torah stood for salvation and accounted for Israel's this-worldly condition and the hope, for both individual and nation alike, of life in the world to come. Therefore, the word Torah stood for everything. When, therefore, we wish to describe the unfolding of the definitive doctrine of Judaism in its formative period, the first exercise consists in paying close attention to the meanings imputed to a single word. Every detail of the religious system at hand exhibits essentially the same point of insistence, captured in the simple notion of the Torah as the generative symbol, the total, exhaustive expression of the system as a whole.

If we start back with the Mishnah, which later on formed the oral part of the one whole Torah, written and oral, revealed by God to Moses at Sinai, we look in vain for a picture of the Mishnah as (part of) the Torah. For the Mishnah provided no account of itself. Unlike biblical law codes, the Mishnah begins with no myth of its own origin. It ends with no doxology. Discourse commences in the middle of things and ends abruptly. What follows from such a laconic approach is that the exact status of the document required definition entirely outside the framework of the document itself. The framers of the Mishnah gave no hint of the nature of their book, so the Mishnah reached the political world of Israel without a trace of self-conscious explanation or any theory of validation. The framers of the Mishnah nowhere claim, implicitly or explicitly, that what they have written forms part of the Torah, enjoys the status of God's revelation to Moses at Sinai, or even systematically carries forward secondary exposition and application of what Moses wrote down in the wilderness. Later on, some two hundred years beyond the closure of the Mishnah, the need to explain the standing and origin of the Mishnah led to two postulates: First, God's revelation of the Torah at Sinai encompassed the Mishnah as much as Scripture; second, the Mishnah was handed on through oral formulation and oral transmission from Sinai to the framers of the document as we have it.

As for the Mishnah itself, however, it contains not a hint that anyone has heard any such tale. The earliest apologists for the Mishnah, represented in Abot and the Tosefta, know nothing of the fully realized myth of the dual Torah of Sinai. Only the two Talmuds reveal that conception—alongside their mythic explanation of where the document came from and why it should be obeyed. So the Yerushalmi marks the change. A survey of the uses of the word Torah in the Mishnah provides us with an account of what the framers of the Mishnah, founders of what would emerge as rabbinic Judaism, understood by that term. But it will not tell us how they related their own ideas to the Torah, nor shall we find a trace of evidence of that fully articulated way of life—the use of the word Torah to categorize and classify persons, places, things, relationships, all manner of abstractions—that we find fully exposed in some later redacted writings.

The next document in sequence beyond the Mishnah—Abot,

The Fathers—draws into the orbit of Torah-talk the names of authorities of the Mishnah. But Abot does not claim that the Mishnah forms part of the Torah, any more than the document imputes supernatural standing to sages, as we saw in chapter 7. Nor, obviously, does the tractate know the doctrine of the two Torahs. Only in the Talmuds do we begin to find clear and ample evidence of that doctrine. Abot, moreover, does not understand by the word Torah much more than the framers of the Mishnah do. Not only does the established classification scheme remain intact, but the sense also essentially replicates already familiar usages, producing no innovation. On the contrary, I find a diminution in the range of meanings. Yet Abot in the aggregate does differ from the Mishnah. The sixty-two tractates of the Mishnah contain Torah-sayings here and there. But they do not fall within the framework of Torah-discourse. They speak about other matters entirely. Abot, by contrast, says a great deal about Torah-study. The claim that Torah-study produces a direct encounter with God forms part of Abot's thesis about the Torah. In Abot, Torah is instrumental. The figure of the sage, his ideals and conduct, forms the goal, focus, and center. To state matters simply: Abot regards study of Torah as what a sage does. The substance of Torah is what a sage says. That is so whether or not the saying relates to scriptural revelation. The content of the sayings attributed to sages endows those sayings with self-validating status. The sages usually do not quote verses of Scripture and explain them, nor do they speak in God's name. Yet, it is clear, sages talk Torah.

Accordingly, Abot treats Torah-learning as symptomatic, an indicator of the status of the sages, hence, as I said, as merely instrumental. The instrumental status of the Torah, as well as of the Mishnah, lies in the net effect of their composition: the claim that through study of the Torah sages enter God's presence. So study of Torah serves a further goal, that of forming sages. The theory of Abot pertains to the religious standing and consequence of the learning of the sages. To be sure, a secondary effect of that theory endows the things sages say with the status of revealed truth. But then it is because they say them, not because they have heard them in an endless chain back to Sinai. The fundament of truth is passed on through sagacity, not through already formulated and carefully memorized truths. The single most important word in Abot also is the most common, the word *says*.

The Mishnah is held in the Yerushalmi to be equivalent to Scripture (Y. Horayot 3:5). But the Mishnah is not called Torah. Still, once the Mishnah entered the status of Scripture, it would take but a short step to a theory of the Mishnah as part of the revelation at Sinai—hence, oral Torah. In the Yerushalmi we find the first glimmerings of an effort to theorize in general, not merely in detail, about how specific teachings of Mishnah relate to specific teachings of Scripture. The citing of scriptural prooftexts for Mishnah propositions, after all, would not have caused much surprise to the framers of the Mishnah; they themselves included such passages, though not often. But what conception of the Torah underlies such initiatives, and how do the Yerushalmi sages propose to explain the phenomenon of the Mishnah as a whole? The following passage gives us one statement. It refers to the assertion at M. Hagigah 1:8D that the laws on cultic cleanness presented in the Mishnah rest on deep and solid foundations in the Scripture.

Y. Hagigah 1:7

[V.A] The laws of the Sabbath [M. 1:8B]: R. Jonah said R. Hama bar Uqba raised the question [in reference to M. Hag. 1:8D's view that there are many verses of Scripture on cleanness], "And lo, it is written only, 'Nevertheless a spring or a cistern holding water shall be clean; but whatever touches their carcass shall be unclean' (Lev. 11:36). And from this verse you derive many laws. [So how can M. 8:8D say what it does about many verses for laws of cultic cleanness?]"

[B] R. Zeira in the name of R. Yohanan: "If a law comes to hand and you do not know its nature, do not discard it for another one, for lo, many laws were stated to Moses at Sinai, and all of them have been embedded in the Mishnah."

The truly striking assertion appears at B. The Mishnah now is claimed to contain statements made by God to Moses. Just how these statements found their way into the Mishnah, and which passages of the Mishnah contain them, we do not know. That is hardly important, given the fundamental assertion at hand. The passage proceeds to a further, and far more consequential, proposition. It asserts that part of the Torah was written down and part was preserved in memory and transmitted orally. In context, moreover, that distinction must encompass the Mishnah, thus explaining its origin as part of the Torah. Here is a clear and unmistakable expression of the distinction between two forms in which a single Torah was revealed and handed on at Mount Sinai, part in writing, part orally.

While the passage below does not make use of the expressions *Torah-in-writing* and *Torah-by-memory*, it does refer to "the written" and "the oral." I feel fully justified in supplying the word Torah in square brackets. The reader will note, however, that the word Torah likewise does not occur at K, L. Only when the passage reaches its climax at M does it break down into a number of categories—Scripture, Mishnah, Talmud, laws, lore. It there makes the additional point that everything comes from Moses at Sinai. So the fully articulated theory of two Torahs (not merely one Torah in two forms) does not reach final expression in this passage. But short of explicit allusion to Torah-in-writing and Torah-by-memory, which (so far as I am able to discern) we find mainly in the Talmud of Babylonia, the ultimate theory of Torah of formative Judaism is at hand in what follows.

Y. Hagigah 1:7

[V. D] R. Zeirah in the name of R. Eleazar: "'Were I to write for him my laws by ten thousands, they would be regarded as a strange thing' (Hos. 8:12). Now is the greater part of the Torah written down? [Surely not. The oral part is much greater.] But more abundant are the matters which are derived by exegesis from the written [Torah] than those derived by exegesis from the oral [Torah]."

[E] And is that so?

[F] But more cherished are those matters which rest upon the written [Torah] than those which rest upon the oral [Torah]. . . .

[J] R. Haggai in the name of R. Samuel bar Nahman, "Some teachings were handed on orally, and some things were handed on in writing, and we do not know which of them is the more precious. But on the basis of that which is written, "And the Lord said to Moses, Write these words; in accordance with these words I have made a covenant with you and with Israel' (Ex. 34:27), [we conclude] that the ones which are handed on orally are the more precious."

[K] R. Yohanan and R. Yudan b. R. Simeon—One said, "If you have kept what is preserved orally and also kept what is in writing, I shall make a covenant with you, and if not, I shall not make a covenant with you."

[L] The other said, "If you have kept what is preserved orally and you have kept what is preserved in writing, you shall receive a reward, and if not, you shall not receive a reward."

[M] [With reference to Deut. 9:10: "And on them was written according to all the words which the Lord spoke with you in the mount,"] said R. Joshua b. Levi, "He could have written, 'On them,' but wrote, 'And on them.' He could have written, 'All,' but wrote, 'According to all.' He could have written, 'Words,' but wrote 'The words.' [These then serve as three encompassing clauses, serving to include] Scripture, Mishnah, Talmud, laws, and lore. Even what an experienced student in the future is going to teach before his master already has been stated to Moses at Sinai."

[N] What is the Scriptural basis for this view?

[O] "There is no remembrance of former things, nor will there be any remembrance of later things yet to happen among those who come after" (Qoh. 1:11).

[P] If someone says, "See, this is a new thing," his fellow will answer him, saying to him, "this has been around before us for a long time."

Here we have absolutely explicit evidence that people believed part of the Torah had been preserved not in writing but orally. Linking that part to the Mishnah remains a matter of implication. But it surely comes fairly close to the surface, when we are told that the Mishnah contains Torah-traditions revealed at Sinai. From that view it requires only a small step to the allegation that the Mishnah is part of the oral part of the Torah.

To define the category of the Torah as a source of salvation, as the Yerushalmi states matters, I point to a story that explicitly states the proposition that the Torah constitutes a source of salvation. In this story we shall see that because people observed the rules of the Torah, they expected to be saved. And if they did not observe these rules, they accepted their punishment. So the Torah now stands for something more than revelation and life of study, and (it goes without saying) the sage now appears as a holy, not merely a learned, man. This is because his knowledge of the Torah has transformed him. Accordingly, we deal with a category of stories and sayings about the Torah entirely different from what has gone before.

Y. Taanit 3:8

[II. A] As to Levi ben Sisi: troops came to his town. He took a scroll of the Torah and went up to the roof and said, "Lord of the ages! If a single word of this scroll of the Torah has been nullified [in our town], let them come up against us, and if not, let them go their way."

[B] Forthwith people went looking for the troops but did not find them [because they had gone their way].

[C] A disciple of his did the same thing, and his hand withered, but the troops went their way.

[D] A disciple of his disciple did the same thing. His hand did not wither, but they also did not go their way.

[E] This illustrates the following apothegm: You can't insult an idiot, and dead skin does not feel the scalpel.

What is interesting here is how taxa into which the word Torah previously fell have been absorbed and superseded in a new taxon. The Torah is an object: "He took a scroll. . . ." It also constitutes God's revelation to Israel: "If a single word. . . ." The outcome of the revelation is to form an ongoing way of life, embodied in the sage himself: "A disciple of his did the same thing. . . ." The sage plays an intimate part in the supernatural event: "His hand withered. . . ." Now, can we categorize this story as a statement that the Torah constitutes a particular object or a source of divine revelation or a way of life? Yes and no. The Torah here stands not only for the things we already have catalogued. It also represents one more thing that takes in all the others. Torah is a source of salvation. How so? The Torah stands for, or constitutes, the way in which the people Israel saves itself from marauders. This straightforward sense of salvation would not have surprised the author of Deuteronomy.

In the canonical documents up to the Yerushalmi, we look in vain for sayings or stories that fall into such a category. True, we may take for granted that everyone always believed that, in general, Israel would be saved by obedience to the Torah. That claim would not have surprised any Israelite writers from the first prophets down through the final redactors of the Pentateuch in the time of Ezra and onward through the next seven hundred years. But, in the rabbinical corpus from the Mishnah forward, the specific and concrete assertion that by taking up the scroll of the Torah and standing on the roof of one's house, confronting God in heaven, a sage in particular could take action against the expected invasion—that kind of claim is not located, so far as I know, in any composition surveyed so far.

The belief that the Torah in the hands of the sage constituted a source of magical, supernatural, and hence salvific power must have existed even before circa 400 C.E. We cannot show it, hence we do not know it. All we can say with assurance is that no stories containing such a viewpoint appear in any rabbinical document associated with the Mishnah. So what is critical here is not the generalized category—the genus—of conviction that the Torah serves as the source of Israel's salvation. It is the concrete assertion—the speciation of the genus—that in the hands of the sage and under conditions specified, the Torah may be utilized in pressing circumstances, as Levi, his disciple, and the disciple of his disciple used it. This is what is new.

This stunningly new usage of Torah found in the Yerushalmi emerges from a group of stories not readily classified in our established categories. All of these stories treat the word Torah (whether scroll, contents, or act of study) as source and guarantor of salvation. Accordingly, evoking the word Torah forms the centerpiece of a theory of Israel's history, on the one hand, and an account of the teleology of the entire system, on the other. Torah indeed has ceased to constitute a specific thing or even a category or classification, when stories about studying the Torah yield not a judgment as to status (i.e., praise for the learned man) but promise for supernatural blessing now and salvation in time to come.

The key to the first Talmud's theory of the Torah lies in its conception of the sage, to which that theory is subordinate. Once the sage reaches his full apotheosis as Torah incarnate, then, but only then, the Torah becomes (also) a source of salvation in the present concrete formulation of the matter. That is why we traced the doctrine of the Torah in the salvific process by elaborate citation of stories about sages, living Torahs exercising the supernatural power of the Torah and serving, like the Torah itself, to reveal God's will. Since the sage embodied and revealed the Torah, the Torah naturally came to stand for the principal source of Israel's salvation, not merely a scroll, on the one hand, or a source of revelation, on the other. The history of the symbolization of the Torah proceeds from its removal from the framework of material objects, even from the limitations of its own contents, to its transformation into something quite different and abstract, quite distinct from the document and its teachings. The Torah stands for something more, specifically, when it comes to be identified with a living person, the sage, and is endowed with those particular traits that the sage claimed for himself. While we cannot say that the process of symbolization leading to the pure abstraction at hand moved in easy stages, we may still point to the stations that had to be passed in sequence. The word Torah reached the apologists for the Mishnah in its long-established meanings: Torah-scroll, contents of the Torah-scroll. But even in the Mishnah itself, these meanings provoked a secondary development, status of Torah as distinct from another (lower) status, hence, Torah-teaching as opposed to scribal-teaching. With that small and simple step, the Torah ceased to denote only a concrete and material thing—a scroll and its contents. It now connoted an abstract matter of status. And once made abstract, the symbol entered a secondary history beyond all limits imposed by the concrete object, the Torah-scroll, including its specific teachings.

It can be assumed that Abot stands at the beginning of this process. In the history of the word Torah as abstract symbol, a metaphor serving to sort out one abstract status from another regained concrete and material reality of a new order entirely. For the message of Abot, as we saw, was that the Torah served the sage in that the Torah indicated who was a sage and who was not. Accordingly, the apology of Abot for the Mishnah was that the Mishnah contained things sages had said. What sages said formed a chain of tradition extending back to Sinai. Hence, it was equivalent to the Torah. The upshot is that words of sages enjoyed the status of the Torah. The small step beyond was to claim that what sages said was Torah, as much as what Scripture said was Torah. And, a further small step (and the steps need not have been taken separately or in the order here suggested) moved matters to the position that there were two forms in which the Torah reached Israel: one [Torah] in writing, the other [Torah] handed on orally, that is, in memory. The final step, fully revealed in the Talmud at hand, brought the conception of Torah to its logical conclusion: what the sage said was in the status of the Torah, was Torah, because the sage was Torah incarnate. So the abstract symbol now became concrete and material once more. We recognize the diverse ways in which the Talmud stated that conviction. Every passage in which knowledge of the Torah yields power over this world and the next, the capacity to coerce to the sage's will the natural and supernatural worlds alike, rests upon the same viewpoint. The first Talmud's theory of the Torah carries us through several stages in the processes of the symbolization of the word Torah. First transformed from something material and concrete into something abstract and beyond all metaphor, the word Torah finally emerged once more in a concrete aspect, as the encompassing and universal mode of stating the whole doctrine, all at once, of Judaism in its formative age.

The documentary history of the symbol, Torah, raises more questions than it settles. Once we recognize that shifts and turnings in the treatment of a fixed topic or symbol characterize the movement from one writing to the next, we want to explain the change. And in the nature of things, we wonder what has happened in the world beyond that has led to the reconsideration of the generative symbol of a system such a this one. Identifying the documentary matrix of an idea or a symbol directs our attention not to but beyond the sequence of writings. We want to ask about the world beyond the system. The method set forth in this book addresses that final question when it asks about the interplay between system and circumstance, the ideas of an authorship and the issues of the world in which that authorship did its work. Once more, we consider the method and then an application of the method.

CHAPTER TEN

Religious Writings in the Matrix
of History

The last step in the documentary method in the study of Judaism leads us to read documents not only as a whole but all together and all at once, in their three dimensions—autonomy, connection, continuity—as these correspond to text, context, and matrix. For transforming writing into religion requires that we make the effort to hear that whole statement as response, an answer to a question. That is to say, the final task of the documentary method is to offer an interpretation of the system as a self-evidently valid answer to a pressing and critical question. In this concluding stage in the exposition of the documentary method, I provide an example from the Mishnah of the way in which I propose to read the writings of religion in the setting of history. In that way I interpret religion as an independent variable in the formation of the society and politics of a social entity, as I claimed in chapter 1 I would do in order to translate writing into religion.

A Judaism seen as a religious system of a social entity—that is, as ethos, ethics, and ethnos, all together in writing—serves a purpose that is political and social. It is therefore fair to ask how a system solves a problem of a common culture or, in our context, answers through a self-evidently right doctrine a question that none can escape or ignore. But how are we to identify the question that a systemic statement answers? It is, once more, by working our way back from writing to the context in which the writing takes place, and by context I mean the historical context rather than the religious-systemic one, on which we have concentrated to this point. The goal of reading documents as wholes, in context and in reference to a matrix, is achieved by reverting at the end to the text itself, asking whether we can find in a given document a cogent statement, which then is to be seen as answer to a question. For a statement forms both affirmation and denial, and the making of a statement responds to a generative question, one that precipitates cogent thought and requires a coherent expression of the result of thought.

Putting documents together, then, allows a set of statements to be seen as a cogent response to an urgent question. For every Judaic system, seen whole, turns out to repeat in many ways a single encompassing proposition. Once the question is defined, the exegetical process takes over, with its infinite capacity to make details repeat a basic premise or proposition. But the systemic statement as a whole obsessively reviews a set of seemingly ineluctable questions. What we have to identify in seeing systems as wholes is what the authorships represent as self-evident, the truths that demand no articulation, no defense, no argument. What is self-evident and a datum of all discourse forms the system and defines its generative exegetical principles. And if I want to know what people find self-evident, I have to uncover the questions they confront and cannot evade. These questions will dictate the program of inquiry, the answers to which then follow after the fact. If I know what issues of social existence predominate, I can also uncover the point—the circumstance—of origin of a Judaism. Accordingly, a system forms a closed circle, just as do documents, in that everything is made to say one thing, and that one thing turns out to be the only thing that needs to be said. These traits of systems emerge from the reading of documents as autonomous statements, in relationship to other documents, that is, in the context of comparison and contrast, and, finally, in the matrix of the systemic writings as a whole, that is, as statements continuous with one another and with the larger setting that contains them.

At issue in seeing systems as wholes and in context is how particular religious systems relate to the political circumstances of the people who find urgent the questions answered by those systems. For, as I argued in chapter 1, religion as a fact of politics constitutes a principal force in the shaping of society and imagination alike, whereas politics for its part profoundly affects the conditions of religious belief and behavior. In the period under study, two political events, very well documented in a variety of writings and also in archaeology, defined the circumstances in which all Jews lived and therefore in which all Judaisms took shape. Hence, in the case of the first of these two shifts, which I spell out here, we see in the details of the Judaism of the dual Torah how a stunning shift in the political circumstance of a religion affected that religion's thought about perennial questions. The first shift was represented by the destruction of the second temple in C.E. 70 and the complete defeat three generations later, in 135, of Bar Kokhba, who tried to reconstruct the Temple. The second shift was accomplished by two events: first, the conversion of the Roman Empire to Christianity, beginning with Constantine's conversion and adoption of Christianity in 312; second, the unsuccessful attempts, under Emperor Julian, in 361–362 to adopt paganism in place of Christianity as the religion of the Roman Empire and to rebuild the Temple of Jerusalem for Judaism.

The Mishnah comes to closure at the end of the second century, and, I shall suggest, forms a sustained response to the crisis of that age. In other studies, based on the same method as I originally applied to the Mishnah, I have shown how the Yerushalmi and its associated writings were brought to conclusion at the end of the fourth century and I maintain, present a system that takes account of the calamity represented by the conversion of Rome to Christianity and the failure to rebuild the temple in that same period. Accordingly, two facts, which still need to be proved, serve as premises for all I have done in the systemic analysis of the writings of Judaism in its formative age. The first is that the Mishnah came to closure at circa C.E. 200, the second, that the Yerushalmi reached its conclusion at circa C.E. 400. These two facts define everything else that follows, and both of them rest solely on what is today's scholarship consensus. Should the consensus shift, the entire interpretation that yields this picture of religious writings in the matrix of history will fall away, even though the method I apply remains entirely valid. Here we focus on the first of the two facts, that the Mishnah took shape about three generations after the defeat of Bar Kokhba by the Roman government.

For purposes of spelling out how a method works, a single example suffices. Seeing the Mishnah whole requires us to return to the formal traits of the document, that is to say, to its authorship's way of saying things. That is the one fact we know for certain, and it is the relationship between that one fact and the datum that the authorship did their work after Bar Kokhba's defeat that defines the work of reading religious writings in the matrix of history. Beginning with how they used language, we hope to learn something about them and their world view. The formal rhetoric of the Mishnah is empty of content, which is proved by the fact that pretty much all themes and conceptions can be reduced to a few formal patterns. These patterns, I have shown, are established by syntactical recurrences, as distinct from repetition of sounds. Long sequences of sentences fail to repeat the same words—that is, syllabic balance, rhythm, or sound—yet they do establish a powerful claim to order and formulary sophistication and perfection. The arrangement of the words, not their substance, is indicative of pattern. Accordingly, while we have a document composed along what clearly are mnemonic lines, the document's susceptibility to memorization rests principally upon the utter abstraction of recurrent syntactical patterns, rather than on the concrete repetition of particular words, rhythms, syllabic counts, or sounds. Even though the Mishnah is to be memorized and handed on orally, it expresses a mode of thought attuned to abstract relationships rather than concrete and substantive forms. The formulaic, not the formal, character of Mishnaic rhetoric yields a picture of a subculture that speaks of immaterial things. In this subculture the relationship, rather than the thing or person which is related, is primary and constitutes the principle of reality. The thing in itself is less than the thing in cathexis with other things; so, too, the person. The repetition of form creates form. But what is repeated here is not form but formulary pattern, a pattern effected through persistent grammatical or syntactical relationships and affecting an infinite range of diverse objects and topics. Form and structure emerge not from concrete, formal things but from abstract and unstated, but ubiquitous and powerful, relationships.

The Mishnah's authorship implicitly maintains that a wide range of things fall within the territory mapped out by a limited number of linguistic conventions, grammatical sentences. What is grammatical can be said and therefore constitutes part of the reality created by Mishnaic word. What cannot be contained within the grammar of the sentence cannot be said and therefore falls outside of the realm of Mishnaic reality. Mishnaic reality consists in those things that can attain order, balance, and principle. Chaos, then, lies without. But all things can be said by formal revision. Everything can be reformed, reduced to the order and balance and exquisite sense for the just-match characteristic of the Mishnaic pericope. There are no thematic limitations of Mishnaic formalized speech.

Implicit in the rhetoric of our document is the notion of deep regularities, which in principle unite cases, just as regularities in rhetoric unite cases. What is abstract need not be spelled out and instantiated endlessly because it already is spelled out through recurrent, implicit relationships among words, among cases. We may say that the thinking about matters of detail within a particular pattern of cognitive constructions treats speculation and thought as themselves capable of informing and shaping being, not merely expressing its external traits. Language becomes ontology. That is to say, the character of language forms a statement of being. What the limitation of Mishnaic language to a few implicit relational realities accomplished, therefore, is the reduction of the world to the limits of language. In ritual grammar, the world therein contained and expressed attains formalization among, and simplification by, the unstated but remarkably few principles contained within, and stated by, the multitudinous cases that correspond to the world. Mishnaic language makes possible the formalization of the whole of the everyday, workaday world. It accomplishes the transformation of all things in accord with that sense for perfect form and unfailing regularity that once were distinctive to the operation of the cult. Mishnaic language explores the possibility of containing and creating a new realm of reality, one that avoids abstractions and expresses all things only through the precision of grammatical patterns, that is, through the reality of abstract relationships alone.

To impose upon those sayings an underlying and single

structure of grammar corresponding to the inner structure of reality is to transform the structure of language into a statement of ontology. Once our minds are trained to perceive a principle among cases and a pattern within grammatical relationships, we further discern in the concrete events of daily life both principle and underlying autonomous pattern. The form of the Mishnah is meant to correspond to the formalization perceived within, not merely imposed upon, the conduct of concrete affairs, principally, the meaning and character of concrete happenings among things, in the workaday life of people. The matter obviously is not solely ethical, but the ethical component is self-evident. It also has to do with the natural world and the things that break its routine. Here all things are a matter of relationship, circumstance, fixed and recurrent interplay. *If X, then Y, if not X, then not Y*—that is the datum by which minds are shaped.

There is a perfect correspondence between what the Mishnah proposes to say and the way in which it says it. An essential part of the ethos of Mishnaic culture is its formal and formulaic sentence, the means by which it makes its cognitive statements and expresses its world view. Not only does ethos correspond to world view, but world view is expressed in style as much as in substance. In the case of Mishnaic form, the ethos and world view come together in the very elements of grammatical formalization, which, never made articulate, express the permanence and paramount character of relationship, the revelatory relativity of context and circumstance. Life attains form in structure. It is structure that is most vivid in life. The medium for the expression of the world view is the ethos. But for the Mishnah, ethos neither appeals to nor, so far as I can see, expresses emotion. Just as there is no room for nuance in general in the severe and balanced sentences of the Mishnah, so there is no place for the nuance of emotion of commitment in general. How so? The rhetoric of our document makes no appeal to emotion or to obedience, describing, not invoking, the compelling and ineluctable grounds for assent. Law is law, despite the accidents of workaday life, and facts are facts. The bearer of facts, the maker of law, is the relationship, the pattern by which diverse things are set into juxtaposition with one another, whether subject and predicate or dead creeping thing

and loaf of heave-offering. What is definitive is not the thing but
the context and the circumstance, the time, the condition, the
intention of the actor. All things are relative to all things.

World view and ethos are synthesized in language. The
synthesis is expressed in grammatical and syntactical regularities. What is woven into some sort of ordered whole is not a
cluster of sacred symbols. The religious system is not discerned
within symbols at all. Knowledge of the conditions of life is
imparted principally through the description of the commonplace facts of life, which symbolize nothing beyond themselves
and their consequences for the clean and the unclean. That
description is effected through the construction of units of
meaning, intermediate divisions composed of cognitive elements. The whole is balanced, explicit in detail but reticent about
the whole, balanced in detail but dumb about the character of
the balance. What is not said is as eloquent and compelling as
what is said. The medium of patterned speech conveys the
meaning of what is said. This is how language becomes ontology.

Precisely what systemic message comes to expression in the
medium of the language just now described? The system of the
Mishnah delivers the message that through order—through the
reordering of Israelite life—Israel attains that sanctification that
inheres in its very being. The Mishnah is divided into six
divisions, covering sixty-three tractates and containing 531
chapters, and encompasses six large topics. This brings us to a
cursory survey of the several parts of the system, the six divisions
and their sixty-two tractates.

The Division of Agriculture treats two topics: first, producing
crops in accord with the scriptural rules on the subject, and
second, paying the required offerings and tithes to the priests,
the Levites, and the poor. The principal point of the Division is
that the land is holy because God has a claim both on it and upon
what it produces. God's claim must be honored by setting aside a
portion of the produce for those for whom God has designated
it. God's ownership must be acknowledged by observing the
rules God has laid down for use of the land. In sum, the Division
is divided along these lines: (1) rules for producing crops in a
state of holiness—tractates Kilayim, Shebiit, Orlah; (2) rules for
disposing of crops in accord with the rules of holiness—tractates

Peah, Demai, Terumot, Maaserot, Maaser Sheni, Hallah, Bikkurim, Berakhot.

The Division of Appointed Times forms a system in which the advent of a holy day, like the Sabbath of creation, sanctifies the life of the Israelite village through imposing on the village rules on the model of those of the Temple. The purpose of the system, therefore, is to bring into alignment the moment of sanctification of the village and the life of the home with the moment of sanctification of the Temple on those same occasions of appointed times. The underlying and generative theory of the system is that the village is the mirror image of the Temple. If things are done in one way in the Temple, they will be done in the opposite way in the village. Together the village and the Temple on the occasion of the holy day therefore form a single continuum, a completed creation, thus awaiting sanctification.

This Division is made up of two quite distinct sets of materials. The first addresses what one does in the sacred space of the Temple on the occasion of sacred time, as distinct from what one does in that same sacred space on ordinary, undifferentiated days (which is a subject worked out in the Division of Holy Things). The second set defines how for the occasion of the holy day one creates a corresponding space in one's own circumstance and what one does within that space during sacred time. The issue of the Temple and cult on the special occasion of festivals is treated in tractates Pesahim, Sheqalim, Yoma, Sukkah, and Hagigah. Three further tractates, Rosh Hashshanah, Taanit, and Megillah, are necessary to complete the discussion. The matters of the rigid definition of the outlines in the village, of a sacred space, delineated by the limits within which one may move on the Sabbath and the festival, and of the specification of those things one may not do within that space in sacred time, is in Shabbat, Erubin, Besah, and Moed Qatan. While the twelve tractates of the division appear to fall into two distinct groups joined merely by a common theme, they do, in fact, relate through a shared, generative metaphor. It is the comparison, in the context of sacred time, of the spatial life of the Temple to the spatial life of the village upon the common occasion of the Sabbath or festival. The Mishnah's purpose, therefore, is to correlate the sanctity of the Temple with the restrictions of space and of action which make the life of the village different and holy, as defined by the holy day.

The Division of Women defines women in the social economy of Israel's supernatural and natural reality. Women acquire definition wholly in relationship to men, who impart form to the Israelite social economy. The status of women is effected through both supernatural and natural action. What men and women do on earth provokes a response in heaven, and the correspondences are perfect. So women are defined and secured both in heaven and here on earth, and that position is invariably relative to men. The principal interest for the Mishnah is the points at which a woman becomes (and ceases to be) holy to a particular man, that is, marriage and divorce. These transfers of women are the dangerous and disorderly points in the relationship of woman to man, and therefore, as the Mishnah states, in society as well.

The formation of the marriage comes under discussion in Qiddushin and Ketubot, as well as in Yebamot. The rules for the duration of the marriage are scattered throughout, but derive especially from parts of Ketubot, Nedarim, and Nazir, on the one hand; they are the paramount constituents of Sotah, on the other. The dissolution of marriage is dealt with in Gittin, as well as in Yebamot. Issues of the transfer of property, along with women, are covered in Ketubot and to some measure in Qiddushin, and the proper documentation of the transfer of women and property is treated in Ketubot and Gittin. The critical issues, therefore, turn upon legal documents such as writs of divorce and the legal recognition of changes in the ownership of property, for example, through the collection of the settlement of a marriage contract by a widow, through the provision of a dowry, or through the disposition of the property of a woman during the period in which she is married. Within this orderly world of documentary and procedural concerns, a place is made for the disorderly conception of the marriage not formed by human volition but decreed in heaven, the levirate connection. Yebamot states that supernature sanctifies a woman to a man (under the conditions of the levirate connection). What it says by indirection is that man sanctifies, too: Man, like God, can sanctify that relationship between a man and a woman and can also effect the cessation of the sanctity of that same relationship. Five of the seven tractates of the Division of

Women are devoted to the formation and dissolution of the marital bond. Of them, three treat what is done by man here on earth, that is, the formation of a marital bond through betrothal and marriage contract and its dissolution through divorce: Qiddushin, Ketubot, and Gittin. One of them is devoted to what is done by woman here on earth: Sotah. And Yebamot, greatest of the seven in size and in formal and substantive brilliance, deals with the corresponding heavenly intervention into the formation and end of a marriage: the effect of death upon both forming the marital bond and dissolving it through death. The other two tractates, Nedarim and Nazir, draw into one the two realms of reality, heaven and earth, as they work out the effects of vows, perhaps because vows taken by women and subject to the confirmation or abrogation of the father or husband make a deep impact upon the marital life of the woman who has taken them.

The Division of Damages comprises two subsystems, which fit together in a logical way. One part presents rules for the normal conduct of civil society. These cover commerce, trade, real estate, and other matters of everyday intercourse, as well as mishaps, such as damages by chattels and persons, fraud, overcharge, interest, and the like, in that same context of everyday social life. The other part describes the institutions governing the normal conduct of civil society, that is, courts of administration, and the penalties at the disposal of the government for the enforcement of the law. The two subjects form a single tight and systematic dissertation on the nature of Israelite society and its economic, social, and political relationships, as the Mishnah envisages them.

The main point of the first of the two parts of this Division is expressed in the sustained unfolding of the three Babas: Baba Qamma, Baba Mesia, and Baba Batra. It is that the task of society is to maintain perfect stasis, to preserve the prevailing situation, and to secure the stability of all relationships. To this end, in the interchanges of buying and selling, giving and taking, borrowing and lending, it is important that there be an essential equality of interchange. No party in the end should have more than what it had at the outset, and none should be the victim of a sizable shift in fortune and circumstance. All parties' rights in this stable and unchanging economy of society are to be preserved. When the condition of a person is violated, so far as possible the law will secure the restoration of the antecedent status.

An appropriate appendix to the Babas is Abodah Zarah, which deals with the orderly governance of transactions and relationships between Israelite society and the outside world—the realm of idolatry, relationships which are subject to certain special considerations. These are generated by the fact that Israelites may not derive benefit (e.g., through commercial transactions) from anything that has served in the worship of an idol. Consequently, commercial transactions suffer limitations on account of extrinsic considerations of cultic taboos. While these cover both special occasions, like fairs and festivals of idolatry, and general matters, that is, what Israelites may buy and sell, the main practical illustrations of the principles of the matter pertain to wine.

The Mishnah supposes that Gentiles routinely make use, for a libation, of a drop of any sort of wine to which they have access. It therefore is taken for granted that wine over which Gentiles have had control is forbidden for Israelite use and also that such wine is prohibited for Israelites to buy and sell. This other matter—ordinary, everyday relationships with the Gentile world, with special reference to trade and commerce—concludes what the Mishnah has to say about all those matters of civil and criminal law that together define everyday relationships within the Israelite nation and between that nation and all others in the world.

The other part of this Division describes the institutions of Israelite government and politics. Two aspects are important: first, the description of the institutions and their jurisdiction, with reference to courts, conceived as both judicial and administrative agencies; second, the extensive discussion of criminal penalties. The penalties are three: death, banishment, and flogging. There are four ways by which a person convicted of a capital crime may be put to death: strangling, burning, stoning, and decapitation. The Mishnah organizes a vast amount of information on what sorts of capital crimes are punishable by which of the four modes of execution. That information is alleged to derive from Scripture. But the facts are many and the relevant verses few. What the Mishnah clearly contributes to this exercise is a first-rate piece of organization and elucidation of available facts. Where the facts come from we do not know. The Mishnah tractate Sanhedrin further describes the way in which trials are conducted in both monetary and capital cases and pays attention to the possibilities of perjury. The matter of banishment brings the Mishnah to a rather routine restatement of flogging, and the application of that mode of punishment concludes the discussion. Our selection from the Mishnah derives from Mishnah-tractate Sanhedrin, because that is where the reward and punishment involved in eternal life, or life in the world to come, takes its place within the larger category of penalty for violating the law of the Torah.

The character and interests of the Division of Damages present probative evidence of the larger program of the philosophers of the Mishnah. Their intention is to create nothing less than a full-scale Israelite government, subject to the administration of sages. This government is fully supplied with a constitution and bylaws (Sanhedrin, Makkot). It makes provision for a court system and procedures (Shebuot, Sanhedrin, Makkot), as well as a full set of laws governing civil society (Baba Qamma, Baba Mesia, Baba Batra) and criminal justice (Sanhedrin, Makkot). This government, moreover, mediates between its own community and the outside ("pagan") world. Through its system of laws it expresses its judgment of the others and at the same time defines, protects, and defends its own society and social frontiers (Abodah Zarah). It even makes provision for procedures of remission to expiate its own errors (Horayot).

The Division of Holy Things presents a system of sacrifice and sanctuary: Matters concerning the praxis of the altar and maintenance of the sanctuary. The praxis of the altar, specifically, involves sacrifice and things set aside for sacrifice and so deemed consecrated. Eight tractates cover this topic: Zebahim and part of Hullin, Menahot, Temurah, Keritot, part of Meliah, Tamid, and Qinnim. The maintenance of the sanctuary (inclusive of the personnel) is dealt with in Bekhorot, Arakhin, part of Meliah, Middot, and part of Hullin. Viewed from a distance, therefore, the Division's tractates divide themselves up into the following groups (in parentheses are tractates containing relevant materials): (1) rules for the altar and the praxis of the cult—Zebahim, Menahot, Hullin, Keritot, Tamid, Qinnim (Bekhorot, Meilah); (2) rules for the altar and the animals set aside for the cult—Arakhin, Temurah, Meilah (Bekhorot); and (3) rules for the altar and support of the Temple staff and buildings—Bekhorot, Middot (Hullin, Arakhin, Meilah, Tamid). In a word, this Division speaks of the sacrificial cult and the sanctuary in which the cult is conducted. The law pays special attention to the altar and the sanctuary, and to both materials to be utilized in the actual sacrificial rites and property, the value of which supports the cult and sanctuary in general. Both are deemed to be sanctified, that is, "Holy Things." The Division of Holy Things centers upon the rules always applicable to the cult.

The Division of Purities presents a very simple system of three principal parts: sources of uncleanness, objects and substances susceptible to uncleanness, and modes of purification from uncleanness. It tells the story of what makes a given sort of object unclean and what makes it clean. The tractates on these several topics are as follows: (1) sources of uncleanness—Ohalot, Negaim, Niddah, Makhshirin, Zabim, and Tebul Yom; (2) objects and substances susceptible to uncleanness—Kelim, Tohorot, and Uqsin; and (3) modes of purification—Parah, Miqvaot, Yadayim. Viewed as a whole, the Division of Purities treats the interplay of persons, food, and liquids. Dry inanimate objects or foods are not susceptible to uncleanness. What is wet is susceptible, so liquids activate the system. What is unclean, moreover, emerges from uncleanness through the operation of liquids, specifically, through immersion in fit water of requisite volume and in natural condition. Liquids thus also deactivate the system. Water in its natural condition is what concludes the process by removing uncleanness. Water in its unnatural condition, that is, deliberately affected by human agency, is what imparts susceptibility to uncleanness to begin with. The uncleanness of persons, furthermore, is signified by body liquids or flux in the case of the menstruating woman (Niddah) and the *zab* (Zabim, Leviticus 15). Corpse uncleanness is conceived to be a kind of effluent, a viscous gas, that flows like liquid. Utensils, for their part, receive uncleanness when they form receptacles able to contain liquid.

In sum, we have a system in which the invisible flow of fluidlike substances or powers serves to put food, drink, and receptacles into the status of uncleanness and to remove those things from that status. Whether or not we call the system "metaphysical," it certainly has no material base but is conditioned upon highly abstract notions. Thus, in material terms, the effect of liquid is upon food, drink, utensils, and man. The consequence has to do with who may eat and drink what food and liquid, and what food and drink may be consumed from which pots and pans. These loci are specified by tractates on utensils (Kelim) and on food and drink (Tohorot and Usqin).

We now make the abrupt move from the linguistic traits and topical program of the document, which frame and express the system, to the crisis precipitated by the destruction of the Second Temple. To the founders of the Mishnah, the aftermath of the first defeat brought to an end the orderly life of the villages and the land, the reliable relationship of calendar and crop with cult, all joined at the movement of moon, sun, and fixed stars. The problematic of the age, therefore, was located in that middle range of life between the personal tragedy of individuals who live and die and the national catastrophe of the history of Israel. The pivot had wobbled; everything organized around it and in relationship to it had quaked. What moved the world on its axis, the ball of the earth in its majesty? The answer is self-evident: seventy years of wars and the tumult of wars. There was, then, the generative problematic, framed at a moment of utter despair. Can we discern the answer, out of which the full outline of the question emerges?

Insofar as the Mishnah is a document about the holiness of Israel in its land, it expresses that conception of sanctification and theory of its modes that will have been shaped among those to whom the Temple and its technology of joining heaven and holy land through the sacred place defined the core of being: the caste of priests. Insofar as the Mishnah takes up the way in which transactions are conducted among ordinary folk and takes the position that it is through documents with a supernatural consequence that transactions are embodied and expressed (surely the position of the relevant tractates in the Divisions of Women and Damages), the Mishnah expresses what is self-evident to scribes. Just as, to the priest, there is a correspondence between the table of the Lord in the Temple and the locus of the divinity in the heavens, so, to the scribe, there is a correspondence between the documentary expression of the human will on earth, in writs of all sorts, in the orderly provision of courts for the predictable and just disposition of exchanges of persons and property, and heaven's judgment of these same matters. When a woman becomes sanctified to a particular man on earth through the appropriate document governing the transfer of her person and property, the woman is deemed truly sanctified to that man in heaven as well. A violation of the writ, therefore, is not merely a crime. It is a sin. That is why the Temple rite involving the wife accused of adultery is integral to the system of the division of Women.

So there are these two social groups, not categorically symmetrical with each other, the priestly caste and the scribal profession, for whom the Mishnah makes self-evident statements. We know, moreover, that in time to come the scribal profession would become a focus of sanctification, too. The scribe would be transformed into the rabbi, locus of the holy through what he knew, just as the priest had been and would remain locus of the holy through what he could claim for genealogy. The tractates of special interest to scribes-become-rabbis and to their governance of Israelite society, those of Women and Damages, together with certain others particularly relevant to utopian Israel beyond the system of the land—those tractates would grow and grow. Others would remain essentially as they were with the closure of the Mishnah. So we must notice that the Mishnah, for its part, speaks for the program of topics important to the priests. It takes up the persona of the scribes, speaking through their voice and in their manner.

Now, what we do not find, which becomes astonishing in the light of these observations, is sustained and serious attention to the matters of the caste of the priests and the profession of the scribes. True, scattered through the tractates are exercises, occasionally sustained and important exercises, on the genealogy of the priestly caste, their marital obligations and duties, and the things priests do and do not do in the cult in collecting and eating their sanctified food. Indeed, it would be no exaggeration to say that the Mishnah's system seen whole is not a great deal more than a handbook of how the priestly caste wished to design its life in Israel and the world. And yet in the fundamental structure of the document, its organization into divisions and tractates, there is no place for a Division of the Priesthood, no room even for a complete tractate on the rules of the priesthood, except, as we have seen, for the pervasive way of life of the priestly caste, which is everywhere. This absence of sustained attention to the priesthood is striking when we compare the way in which the priestly code at Leviticus 1–15 spells out its concerns: the priesthood, the cult, the matter of cultic cleanness. Since we do have divisions for the cult (the Division of Holy Things) and for cleanness (the Division of Purities), we are surprised that we do not have a Division of the Priesthood.

We must, moreover, be equally surprised that for a document so rich in the attention lavished upon petty matters of how a writ is folded and where the witnesses sign, so obsessed with the making of long lists and the organization of all knowledge into neat piles of symmetrically arranged words, the scribes who know how to make lists and match words nowhere come to the fore. They speak through the document, but they stand behind the curtains. They write the script, arrange the sets, design the costumes, situate the players in their places on the stage, raise the curtain—and play no role themselves at all. We have no division or tractate on such matters as how a person becomes a scribe, how a scribe conducts his work, who forms the center of the scribal profession and how authority is gained therein, the rights and place of the scribe in the system of governance through courts, the organization and conduct of schools or circles of masters and disciples through which the scribal arts are taught and perpetuated. This absence of even minimal information on the way in which the scribal profession takes shape and does its work is stunning when we realize that, within a brief generation, the Mishnah as a whole would fall into the hands of scribes, to be called rabbis, both in the Land of Israel and in Babylonia. These rabbis would make of the Mishnah exactly what they wished. Construed from the perspective of the makers of the Mishnah, the priests and the scribes who provide contents and form, substance and style, the Mishnah turns out to omit all reference to actors, when laying out the world that is their play.

The metaphor of the theater for the economy of Israel, the household of holy land and people, space and time, cult and home, leads to yet another perspective. When we look out upon the vast drama portrayed by the Mishnah, lacking as it does an account of the one who wrote the book and the one about whom

the book was written, we notice yet one more missing
component. In the structure of the Mishnah (that is, at the
foundations of Judaism), we find no account of that other
necessary constituent: the audience. To whom the document
speaks is never specified. What group ("class") generates the
Mishnah's problems is not at issue. True, it is taken for granted
that the world of the Mishnah expresses the sanctified being of
Israel in general. So the Mishnah speaks about the generality of
Israel, the people. But to whom, within Israel, the Mishnah
addresses itself and what groups are expected to want to know
what the Mishnah has to say, are matters that never come to full
expression.

And that brings us to the critical and inescapable question that
requires an answer: what can a person now do? Let me frame the
question in social terms. The building block of Mishnaic
discourse, the circumstance addressed whenever the issues of
concrete society and material transactions are taken up, is the
householder and his context. The Mishnah knows about all sorts
of economic activities. But for the Mishnah, the center and focus
of interest lies in the village. The village is made up of
households, each a unit of production in farming. The
households are constructed by and around the householder,
father of an extended family, including his sons and their wives
and children, his servants, his slaves (bondsmen), and the
craftsmen to whom he entrusts tasks he does not choose to do.
The concerns of householders are in transactions in land. Their
measurement of value is expressed in acreage of top, middle,
and bottom grade. Through real estate critical transactions are
worked out. The marriage settlement depends upon real
property. Civil penalties are exacted through payment of real
property. The principal transactions to be taken up are those of
the householder who owns beasts that do or suffer damage; who
harvests his crops and must set aside and sanctify them for use by
the castes scheduled from on high; who uses or sells his crops
and feeds his family; and who, if he is fortunate, will acquire still
more land. It is to householders that the Mishnah is addressed:
the pivot of society and its bulwark, the units of which the village
is composed, the corporate component of the society of Israel in
the limits of the village and the land. The householder is the
building block of the house of Israel, of its economy in the classic
sense of the word.

The one thing the Mishnah does not want to tell us is about change, about how things came to be what they are. That is why there can be no sustained attention to the priesthood and its rules, the scribal profession and its constitution, the class of householders and its interests. The Mishnah's pretense is that all of these have come to rest. They compose a world in stasis, made holy because it is complete and perfect. It is an economy—again in the classic sense of the word—awaiting the divine act of sanctification which, as at the creation of the world, would set the seal of holy rest upon an again-complete creation, just as in the beginning. There is no place for the actors when what is besought is no action whatsoever but only perfection, which is unchanging. There is room only for a description of how things are: the present tense, the sequence of completed statements and static problems. All the action lies within, in how these statements are made. Once they come to full expression, with nothing left to say, there also is nothing left to do, no need for actors, whether scribes, priests, or householders.

So the components of the system at the very basis of things are the social groups to whom the system refers. These groups obviously are not comparable to one another. They are not three species of the same social genus. One is a caste; the second, a profession; the third, a class. What they have in common is, first, that they do form groups and, second, that the groups are social in foundation and collective in expression. That is not a sizable claim. The priesthood is a social group; it coalesces. Priests see one another as part of a single caste, with whom, for example, they will want to intermarry. The scribes are a social group because they practice a single profession following a uniform set of rules. They coalesce in the methods by which they do their work. The householders are a social group, the basic productive unit of society, around which other economic activity is perceived to function. In an essentially agricultural economy, it is quite reasonable to regard the householder, the head of a basic unit of production, as part of a single class.

It remains to state, in a few words, the principal point expressed by the coalition of scribe, priest, and householder, for whom the Mishnah speaks. The Mishnah's principal message, which makes the Judaism of this document and of its social components distinctive and cogent, is that man is at the center of creation, the head of all creatures upon earth, corresponding to God in heaven, in whose image man is made. The way in which the Mishnah makes this simple and fundamental statement is to impute power to man to inaugurate and initiate those corresponding processes as sanctification and uncleanness, which play so critical a role in the Mishnah's account of reality. The will of man, expressed through the deed of man, is the active power in the world. Will and deed constitute those actors of creation that work upon neutral realms, subject to either sanctification or uncleanness: the Temple and table, the field and family, the altar and hearth, woman, time, space, transactions in the material world and in the world above as well. An object, a substance, a transaction, even a phrase or a sentence, is inert but may be made holy when the interplay of the will and deed of man arouses or generates its potential to be sanctified.

Just as the entire system of uncleanness and holiness awaits the intervention of man, which imparts the capacity to become unclean upon what was formerly inert or which removes the capacity to impart cleanness from what was formerly in its natural and puissant condition, so in the other ranges of reality, man is at the center on earth, just as is God in heaven. Man is counterpart and partner and creation, in that, like God he has power over the status and condition of creation, putting everything in its proper place, calling everything by its rightful name. So, stated briefly, the question taken up by the Mishnah and answered by Judaism is, *What can a man do?* And the answer laid down by the Mishnah is, man, through will and deed, is master of this world, the measure of all things. Since when the Mishnah thinks of man, it means the Israelite, who is the subject and actor of its system, the statement is clear. This man is Israel, who can do what he wills. In the aftermath of the two wars, the message of the Mishnah cannot have proved more pertinent— or poignant and tragic.

The method that has produced this result appeals to obvious and established facts, namely, on the one hand, events of the age in which the document came to closure, on the other, rhetorical, logical, and topical traits of the document itself. When the method can do its work, it is because we can locate correspondences between context and text, politics and proposition, social circumstance and substantive conviction. The obsessive quality of the language, with its interest in order, responds to the chaos beyond the context of the text. The profound inwardness of thought, the insistence that as things seem, as we want them to seem, so things are, just as we insist—these traits of mind make much of the little that the framers could, in fact, sort out. Making the best of a difficult circumstance, the system-builders addressed the critical problem of chaos and offered the self-evidently valid solution of that inner order that the mind alone perceives but that changes everything. The Mishnah's system is the work of philosopher-sages, joining priests and householders, all of them leftovers of an earlier age, in setting forth such social order and political structure as, in mind and imagination at least, seemed plausible. The continuators and successors, who received the writing and the religious system contained therein, changed everything but the main thing. But that judgment rests on studies not set forth and summarized here; for the present purpose, seeing the method in action suffices.

To conclude: in c.e. 66 a Jewish rebellion in the land of Israel against Rome's rule of the country broke out in Jerusalem. Initially successful, the rebels in the end were pushed back into the holy city, which fell in August 70. The Temple, destroyed in 586 b.c.e. and rebuilt three generations later, by the time of its second destruction had stood for five hundred years. In it the commandments of God to Moses concerning sacrifice reached fulfillment. With its destruction the foundations of Israel's national and social life in the land of Israel were shaken. The Temple had constituted one of the primary, unifying elements in that common life. The structure not only of political life and of society but also of the imaginative life of the country, depended upon the Temple and its worship and cult. It was there that people believed they served God. At the Temple the lines of structure—both cosmic and social—had converged. The Temple, moreover, had served as the basis for those many elements of autonomous self-government and political life left in the Jews' hands by the Romans. Consequently, the destruction of the Temple meant not merely a significant alteration in the cultic or ritual life of the Jewish people but also a profound and far-reaching crisis in their inner and spiritual existence. A viable cultural-religious existence was reconstructed during the next century and a half. What exactly happened? Between circa 70 and circa 200 a number of elements of the religious-cultural structure of the period before 70 were put together into a new synthesis. In response to the disaster of the destruction, Rabbinic Judaism took shape, and its success was in its capacity to claim things had not changed at all.

The Mishnah, therefore, portrays a system, a Judaism composed of (to the believers) self-evidently valid answers to critical and urgent questions. The system represents the response of those prepared once and for all to transcend historical events and to take their leave of wars and rumors of wars, of politics and public life. These persons undertook to construct a new reality beyond history, one that focused on the meaning of humdrum everyday life. After 70 there was no mere craven or exhausted passivity in the face of world-shaking events. We witness in particular among the sages after 70 ultimately represented in the Mishnah the beginnings of an active construction of a new mode of being. Their decision was to exercise freedom uncontrolled by history, to reconstruct the meaning and ultimate significance of events—to seek a world not outside this one formed by ordinary history, but a different and better world. This approach was a quest for eternity in the here and now, an effort to form a society capable of abiding amid change and stress. Indeed, it was a fresh reading of the meaning of history. The nations of the world suppose that they make "history," and think that their actions matter. But these sages in Israel knew that it is God who makes history, and that it is the reality formed in response to God's will that counts as history: God is the King of kings of kings.

EPILOGUE

The purpose in moving from writing to religion, the goal of my documentary method for the study of Judaism, is to investigate through the case of Judaism what I call the ecology of religion, that is, the interplay between a religious system and the social world that gives shape and meaning to this system. When we understand a religious system in the context of the social order, we grasp whatever in this world we are likely to understand about the role of religion in the shaping of the civilization of humanity. And no other generative force in civilization has exceeded in power and effect the formative force of religion. Accordingly, in this method I have meant to exemplify in a very particular setting the larger problem of how to relate the content of a religion to its context, of social culture to religious conviction, and, above all, of social change, which is public and general, to symbol change, which is particular and invariably distinctive to its setting. At stake in the study of the ecology of religion is whether and how religion forms an independent variable in the shaping of civilization, the point at which we started in chapter 1.

In the framing of my method, I draw upon a metaphor from natural sciences for the study of religion. My inquiry, then, concerns whether, in the analysis of the interrelated components of civilization, religion constitutes a singular constituent of the whole. Ecology is a branch of science concerned with the interrelationships of organisms and their environments. By "ecology of" I mean the study of the interrelation-

271

ship between a particular, religious way of viewing the world and living life, and the historical, social, and especially political situation of the people who view the world and live their lives in accord with the teaching have formed on-going groups, existing over time in various analyzing, and interpreting in context a Judaism does not conclude the work of studying ecology of Judaism as exemplar of the ecology of religion. An on-going social entity, after all, yields more than a single system, but the ecology of the social entity in its indicative traits requires attention not only for its changes but also for its enduring qualities.

But what can we say of the ecology of not a Judaism but of Judaism, now meaning all Judaisms? I see two fundamental traits to that ecology, one social and political, the other fundamentally autonomous of the material realities of society altogether. The former is the political, the latter, the religious fact of the ecosystem encompassing all Judaisms. The former—the politics that will affect all Judaisms—is readily identified. The Jewish people form a very small group, spread over many countries. One fact of their natural environment is that they form a distinct group in diverse societies. A second fact is that they constitute solely a community of faith and, for many, of fate, in that they have few shared social or cultural traits. A third is that they do not form a single political entity. A fourth is that they look back upon a very long and exceptionally painful history. A world view suited to the Jews' social ecology must make sense of their unimportance and explain their importance. It must define an ethos that will sustain and not only explain the continuing life of the group but also persuade people that their forming a distinct and distinctive community is important and worth carrying on. The interplay between the political, social, and historical life of the Jews and their conceptions of themselves in this world and the next—that is, their world view, contained in their canon, their way of life, explained by the teleology of the system and the symbolic structure that encompasses the two and stands for the whole all at once and all together—these define the focus for the inquiry into the political side of the ecology of the religion at hand, that is, the ecology of Judaism.

But if I claim that when we study religion, we deal with what I believe to be the single most important force in the formation of the life of civilization, I have also to ask about the religious component of the enduring ecology of the social entity. What we want to know about religion, as exemplified by the ecology of Judaism, therefore, is not only how religion forms a force in society and politics. In asking about the political and social problem addressed by matters of belief, we cannot treat religion as a contingent or merely instrumental, for the fundamental allegation of my method is that religion stands at the center of the world of humanity in society. I do claim that when we study the ecology of religion, we study written evidence about how through religious systems—ethos, ethnics, ethnos—humanity in society responded to challenge and change, mediated between the received tradition of politics and social life and the crisis of the age and circumstance. Religion is not trivial, not private, not individual, not a matter of the heart. Religion is public, political, social, economic. The religious component of the ecosystem in which a Judaism finds its place derives from the fundamental and generative religious structure to which all Judaisms have conformed, a religious structure that persists and applies ubiquitously because, under diverse circumstances, that deep structure both precipitates a crisis and resolves it.

Every Judaism finds its indicative trait as a Judaism in its appeal to a single part of Scripture, the Pentateuch in particular. And it is—for reasons that pertain to its very structuring of the consciousness of all Israel in relationship to their diverse circumstances—the Pentateuch that forms the other eco-system for a Judaism. Accordingly, we have now to take account of the ongoing, inherited realities that frame any given Judaic system and that invariably for all Judaisms define the setting for the systemic authorships that produce the writings. A religious system, a Judaism seen as a subset of Judaism, takes a place within a larger set of affirmed religious systems. In the present context *a* Judaism can be shown to relate to prior Judaisms, all Judaisms forming a diachronic fact, one framed as much by matters of attitude and conviction as by (for a given moment) a synchronic fact. True enough, there is not now and never has been a single Judaism. There have been only Judaisms, each with its distinctive system and new beginning, all resorting to available antecedents and claiming they are precedents, but in fact none with a history prior to its birth. Each system begins on its own, in response to a circumstance that strikes people as urgent and a question they find ineluctable. But all Judaisms address not only a single socio-ecological system, that of the Jews, but also respond to an on-going premise: that of the initial Torah, the Pentateuch.

Specifically, the Pentateuch, framed in 450 B.C.E. out of inherited materials, set forth certain attitudes and viewpoints that would define for all Judaisms to follow a single structure of experience and expectation. And that structure stood autonomous of the social and political facts of any given group of Jews to whom, and for whom, a Judaism was meant to speak. Accordingly, while we identify one ecosystem of the religion, Judaism, as social and political, the other, in my view, must be classified as religious: the religious ecosystem for a religion, a Judaism. Specifically, all Judaisms have addressed resentments in their respective "Israels," and these resentments are precipitated by the pentateuchal theory of its "Israel," that is, the social entity of the pentateuchal Judaism, and by the concommitant world view and way of life of that same system. All Judaisms have not only dealt with but also have resolved those resentments. All Judaisms in one way or another sorted out whatever social experience their "Israels" proposed to explain by appeal to the tension of exile and the remission of return. That singular and indicative appeal formed an ecological fact for all Judaisms, as much as the Jews' minority status and utopian aspirations defined issues to be addressed by any Judaism.

The original reading of the Jews' existence as exile and return derives from the Pentateuch, the five books of Moses, which were composed as we now have them (out of earlier materials, to be sure) in the aftermath of the destruction of the Temple in 586 B.C.E. and in response to the exile to Babylonia, which means that the experience selected and addressed by the authorship of the document is that of exile and restoration. As a matter of fact, that framing of events into the pattern at hand represents an act of powerful imagination and interpretation. It is an experience that is invented because no one person or group both went into "exile" and also "returned home." Diverse experiences have been sorted out, various persons have been chosen, and the whole has been worked into a system by those who selected history out of happenings and models out of masses of persons. So, to begin with, Scripture does not record a particular person's experience, yet it also is not an account of a whole nation's story. The reason is that the original exile encompassed mainly the political classes of Jerusalem and some useful populations alongside. Many Jews in the Judea of 586 never left. And, as is well known, a great many of those who ended up in Babylonia stayed there. Only a minority went back to Jerusalem. Consequently, the story of exile and return to Zion encompasses what happened to only a few families, who identified themselves as the family of Abraham, Isaac, and Jacob, and their genealogy as the history of Israel. Those families that stayed and those that never came back would have told a different normative and paradigmatic tale altogether had they written the Torah.

That experience of the few that formed the paradigm for Israel beyond the restoration, taught as normative, in fact generated profound alienation. Let me state with emphasis the lessons people claimed to learn out of the events they had chosen for their history: *The life of the group is uncertain, subject to conditions and stipulations. Nothing is set and given; all things are a gift: land and life itself.* But what actually did happen in that uncertain world—exile but then restoration—marked the group as special, different, select. There were other ways of seeing things, and the pentateuchal picture was no more compelling than any other. Those Jews who did not go into exile, and those who did not "come home" had no reason to take the view of matters that characterized the authorship of Scripture. The life of the group need not have appeared more uncertain, more subject to contingency and stipulation, than the life of any other group. The land did not require the vision that imparted to it the enchantment, the personality, that in Scripture it received: "The land will vomit you out as it did those who were here before you" (Lev. 18:28). And the adventitious circumstance of Iranian imperial policy—a political happenstance—did not have to be recast into return. So nothing in the system of Scripture—exile for reason, return as redemption—followed necessarily and logically. Everything was invented; everything was interpreted.

That experience of the uncertainty regarding the life of the group a century or so from the destruction of the First Temple of Jerusalem by the Babylonians in 586 to the building of the Second Temple of Jerusalem by the Jews, with Persian permission and sponsorship returned from exile, formed the paradigm. With the promulgation of the "Torah of Moses" under the sponsorship of Ezra, the Persians' viceroy, at ca. 450 B.C.E., all future Israels would then refer to that formative experience as it had been set down and preserved as the norm for Israel in the mythic terms of that "original" Israel, the Israel not of Genesis and Sinai and the end at the moment of entry into the promised land but the "Israel" of the families that recorded as the rule and the norm the story of both the exile and the return. In that minority genealogy, that story of exile and return, alienation and remission, imposed on the received stories of pre-exilic Israel, adumbrated time and again in the five books of Moses, and addressed by the framers of that document in their work over all, we find that paradigmatic statement in which every Judaism, from then to now, found its structure and deep syntax of social existence, the grammar of its intelligible message.

That experience (in theological terms) rehearsed the conditional moral existence of sin and punishment, suffering and atonement and reconciliation, and (in social terms) the uncertain and always conditional national destiny of disintegration and renewal of the group. The moment captured within the five books of Moses, that is to say, the judgment of the generation of the return to Zion, led by Ezra, about its extraordinary experience of exile and return, would inform the attitude and viewpoint of all the Judaisms and all the Israels beyond. Accordingly, we identify as a fact of the diachronic ecology of all Judaisms that generative and definitive moment precisely as all Judaisms have done, that is, by looking into that same Scripture. All

Judaisms identify the Torah or the five books of Moses as the written-down statement of God's will for Israel, the Jewish people (which, as a matter of fact, every Judaism also identifies as its own social group). I suppose that on the surface, we should specify that formative and definitive moment, recapitulated by all Judaisms, with the story of Creation down to Abraham and the beginning of his family, the children of Abraham, Isaac, and Jacob. Or perhaps we are advised to make our way to Sinai and hold that this original point of definition descends from heaven. But allowing ourselves merely to retell the story deprives us of the required insight. Recapitulating the story of the religion does not help us understand the religion. Identifying the point of origin of the story, by contrast, does. For the story tells not what happened on the occasion to which the story refers (the creation of the world, for instance) but how (long afterward and for their own reasons) people want to portray themselves. The tale, therefore, recapitulates that resentment, that obsessive and troubling point of origin, that the group wishes to explain, transcend, transform.

Every Judaism found as its task the recapitulation of the original Judaism: exile and return, resentment of circumstance and reconciliation with the human condition of a given "Israel." That is to say, each made its own distinctive statement of the generative and critical resentment contained within that questioning of the given, that deep understanding of the uncertain character of the existence of the group in its normal location and under circumstances of permanence that (so far as the Judaic group understood things) characterized the life of every other group but Israel. What for everyone else (so it seemed to the Judaisms addressed to the Israels through time) was given for Israel was a gift. What all the nations knew as how things *must* be, Israel understood as how things *might not be:* exile and loss, alienation and resentment, but, instead of annihilation, renewal, restoration, reconciliation, and (in theological language) redemption. So that paradigmatic experience, the one beginning in 586 and ending in circa 450, written down in that written Torah of Moses, made its mark. That pattern, permanently inscribed in the Torah of God to Moses at Sinai, would define for all Israels over all time that matter of resentment demanding recapitulation: leaving home, coming home.

What is the one systemic trait that marks all Judaisms and sets them apart from all other religious systems, viewed jointly and severally? The religious ecology of Judaisms is dictated by that perpetual asking of the question, who are we? That trait of self-consciousness, that incapacity to accept the group and its data—way of life, world view—as a given is the one thing which draws together Judaisms from beginning to end. The Jews' persistent passion for self-definition characterizes all of the Judaisms they have made for themselves. What others take for granted, the Jews perceive as the received, the special, the extraordinary. And that perception of the remarkable character of what to other groups is the absolute datum of all being requires explanation.

Since the formative pattern imposed that perpetual, self-conscious uncertainty, treating the life of the group as conditional and discontinuous, Jews have asked themselves who they are and invented Judaisms to answer that question. Accordingly, on account of the definitive paradigm—ecology in an intellectual form—affecting their group-life in various contexts, no circumstances have permitted Jews to take for granted their existence as a group. Looking back on Scripture and its message, Jews have ordinarily treated as special, subject to conditions, and therefore uncertain what (in their view) other groups enjoyed as unconditional and simply given. Why the paradigm renewed itself is clear: This particular view of matters generated expectations that could not be met and hence created resentment—and then provided comfort and hope that made it possible to cope with that resentment. Specifically, each Judaism retells in its own way and with its distinctive emphases the tale of the five books of Moses, the story of a no-people that becomes a people, that has what it has only on condition and that can lose it all by virtue of its own sin. That is a terrifying, unsettling story for a social group to tell of itself because it imposes acute self-consciousness, chronic insecurity, upon what should the be level plane and firm foundation of society. That is to say, the collection of diverse materials, joined into a single tale on the occasion of the original exile and restoration because of the repetition in age succeeding age, also precipitates the recapitulation of the interior experience of exile and restoration—always because of sin and atonement. To conclude at the point at which we began, then, the power of religion to form an independent variable, alongside politics, economics, and the facts of social organization and structure, derives from its capacity (in the case at hand) to form a permanent paradigm and to perpetuate a single attitude and experience. And how was and is this done? Promising what could not be delivered, then providing solace for the consequent disappointment, the system at hand precipitated in age after age the very conditions necessary for its own replication. Precipitating resentment and then remitting the consequent anguish, religion itself forms a self-perpetuating fact of the ecology of religion. Religion is not only a category of the life of society, politics, economics. As an irreducible fact of humanity, religion is unique in its social power.

Defining a Judaism, Introducing Rabbinic Literature

By a Judaism, I mean a religious system that appeals to the Hebrew Scriptures or Old Testament in setting forth a world view and describing a way of life addressed to a particular "Israel." There have been many Judaisms, past and present. Any identification of a single, normative Judaism requires theological judgments that rest upon conviction. Description, rather than conviction, begins in the recognition of the variety of Judaic systems known not only in today's world but also in the past. Seen descriptively, diverse Judaisms have flourished over time, from the completion of the Pentateuch, the five books of Moses in circa 500 B.C.E., to our own day. All of them have identified an "Israel," meaning God's holy people, and all have appealed to passages of Scripture, particularly the Pentateuch, for justification for the respective systems that they have set forth. The symbolic system of each Judaism, however, rests upon a structure particular to itself. One Judaism may appeal for its generative symbol to "the Torah," meaning not only the five books of Moses but a much larger heritage of divine revelation in the media of both writing and oral formulation and transmission. Another Judaism may identify as its principal mode of expression a way of life centered upon cultic holiness realized within the community, as with the Essenes in general and the Qumran Essenes in particular. The symbol of that Judaism will be not the Torah but the table at which everyday food was consumed in a state of cultic cleanness. A third Judaism, Orthodoxy of the Zionist sort, in our own time, may utilize the Messiah-theme and identify the formation of a Jewish state with the beginning of the attainment of the Messianic age.

These and other examples of Judaisms point both to the diversity of the religious systems that identify themselves as "Judaism" and commonalities among them. These commonalities are, first, appeal to Scripture (but each to its own florilegium of verses as prooftexts for preselected propositions), second, address to "Israel" (but each with its own identification of its devotees with "Israel" or, at least, "the true Israel"), and, third, a program of concrete actions in the workaday world for the realization of the faith (but every Judaism has its own notion of the essential or required actions). The theological definition of Judaism yields only diversity, therefore, and a comparison of ideas about God or the definition of the Torah held among several Judaisms would yield equivalent diversity (just as comparisons among Christianities' Christologies or ecclesiologies present considerable points of disagreement). Defining all Judaisms within a single structure, rather than through a search for common points of theology, by contrast, produces a clear picture of shared and fundamental traits.

When we state in general terms the pentateuchal story that is shared among all Judaisms, we find ourselves retelling in the setting of mythical ancestors the experience of exile and return, alienation and redemption, that actually characterized the Jews' history from the destruction of the temple of Jerusalem in 586 B.C.E. to the return to Jerusalem (Zion) and the rebuilding of the temple about a century and a half later. While not all Jews were sent into exile in 586 by the Babylonian conquerors (and among those who did go away, still fewer came back from 540 onward, under the new masters of the Middle East, the Iranians under Cyrus of the Persian dynasty of Iran), the compilers of the Pentateuch treated as normative the experience of being sent away from the land and returning to the land, hence, exile and redemption. Thus, Abraham was commanded to leave Ur of the Chaldees, in the general vicinity of the Babylonia to which the exiles had been sent, and to wander to the land. His "children" (within the theory of "Israel" as one big family) gained the land but lost it to Egypt, then underwent wanderings in the desert until they regained the land. The land was held not permanently and as a settled fact of life but only on condition of obeying God's Torah, or, revelation, including the law for the conduct of everyday life, and so living up the covenant made by God with successive progenitors of "Israel."

This pentateuchal story set forth the stipulative quality of possession of the land and treated the life of the people Israel as subject to qualifications and conditions, not as a given. Setting forth not only the conditionality of Israel's existence but also the promise of reward for obedience to God's covenant, the Pentateuch laid out a fundamental structure that thereafter defined the generative experience of all Judaisms. Each would set forth an account of its "Israel" that treated the given as subject to conditions but also defined those conditions that would provide security and resolve doubt. A Judaism, in general, therefore not only provoked resentment and doubt but also resolved the doubt and provided remission for resentment, and that fundamental structural pattern, expressed as (in political and this-worldly terms) exile and redemption, characterizes every known Judaism.

Among Judaisms, a single one predominated from late antiquity to modern times and remains a powerful influence among Jews even today, and that is the Judaism that finds its definitive statement in the myth that when Moses received the Torah as a revelation from God at Mount Sinai, God gave the Torah through two media, writing and also memory. The written Torah of this Judaism of the dual Torah is represented by Scripture or the Old Testament. The other Torah, formulated orally and transmitted only in memory, was handed on for many generations, from Moses down to the great sages of the early centuries of the Common Era when it finally reached writing in documents produced by sages, who bore the honorific title "rabbi," "my lord." This kind of Judaism bears several titles, one rabbinic, because of the character of its leadership, and another talmudic, because of its principal document. Talmudic Judaism may best be traced through the unfolding of its writings, because it was in writing, in study in academies, through the teaching of holy men (in contemporary times, women as well) qualified for saintliness by learning (specifically, mastery of the Torah through discipleship) that the Judaism took shape. Just as one may write the history of Roman Catholic Christianity by tracing the story of the papacy, though that history would not be complete, and the history of Protestant Christianity through telling the story of the Bible in the world since the Reformation, so the history of the Judaism of the dual Torah takes shape in the tale of its holy books. Since in this book I have set forth on the basis of a particular set of documents the methods I have worked out for turning a religion's writings into an account of that religion, let me define the writings of the Judaism that serve as exemplary.

A review of the written evidence for the Judaism of the dual Torah makes the leap from the Pentateuch, circa 450 B.C.E., to the end of the second century and the groups of writings that begin with the Mishnah, a philosophical law book brought to closure at circa C.E. 200, later on called the first statement of the oral Torah. In its wake the Mishnah drew tractate Abot, circa C.E. 250, a statement concluded a generation after the Mishnah on the standing of the authorities of the

Mishnah; Tosefta, circa c.e. 300, a compilation of supplements of various kinds to the statements in the Mishnah; and three systematic exegeses of books of Scripture or the written Torah, Sifra to Leviticus, Sifré to Numbers, and another Sifré to Deuteronomy, of indeterminate date but possibly concluded by c.e. 300. These books overall form one stage in the unfolding of the Judaism of the dual Torah, in which emphasis is put on the issues of sanctification of the life of Israel in the aftermath of the destruction of the Temple of Jerusalem in c.e. 70, in which, it was commonly held, Israel's sanctification came to full realization in the bloody rites of sacrifice to God on high. I call this system a Judaism without Christianity, because the issues found urgent in the documents representative of this phase address questions not pertinent to the Christian challenge to Judaism at all.

The second set of the same writings—the writings of the Judaism despite Christianity—begins with the Talmud of the Land of Israel, or Yerushalmi, generally supposed to have come to a conclusion at circa c.e. 400; Genesis Rabbah, assigned to about the next half century; Leviticus Rabbah, circa c.e. 450, Pesiqta deRab Kahana, circa c.e. 450–500; and, finally, the Talmud of Babylonia or Bavli, assigned to the late sixth or early seventh century. The two Talmuds systematically interpret passages of the Mishnah, and the other documents, as is clear, do the same for books of the written Torah. The interpretation of Scripture in the Judaism of the dual Torah is collected in documents that bear the title of Midrash (pl., midrashim), meaning "exegesis." The single striking trait of Midrash as produced by the Judaism of the dual Torah is the persistent appeal, in interpreting a verse or a theme of Scripture, to some other set of values or considerations than those contained within the verse or topic at hand. On that account rabbinic Midrash compares something to something else, as does a parable, or it explains something in terms of something else, as does allegory. Rabbinic Midrash reads Scripture within the principle that things never are what they seem. In late antiquity, rabbinic Midrash-compilation mainly attended to the pentateuchal books of Genesis, Exodus, Leviticus, Numbers, and Deuteronomy. Some other treatments of biblical books important in synagogue liturgy, particularly the Five Scrolls (Lamentations Rabbati, Esther Rabbah, and the like) are also supposed to have reached closure at this time. This second set of writings introduces, alongside the paramount issue of Israel's sanctification, the matter of Israel's salvation, with doctrines of history, on the one side, and of the Messiah, on the other, given prominence in the larger systemic statement.

Let me briefly expand upon this skeletal account of the documents that define the problem solved by the documentary method of the study of Judaism. Between circa C.E. 200, when autonomous government was well established again, and circa 600, the continuous and ongoing movement of sages, holding positions of authority in the Jewish governments recognized by Rome and Iran as political leaders of the Jewish communities of the land of Israel (to just after C.E. 400) and of Babylonia (to about C.E. 500), respectively, wrote two types of books. One type of book extended, amplified, systematized, and harmonized components of the legal system laid forth in the Mishnah. The work of Mishnah-exegesis produced four principal documents as well as an apologia for the Mishnah. This last—the rationale or apologia—came first in time, about a generation or so beyond the publication of the Mishnah itself. It was tractate Abot, circa C.E. 250, a collection of sayings attributed to both authorities whose names occur also in the Mishnah, and to some sages who flourished after the conclusion of the Mishnah. These later figures, who make no appearance in that document, stand at the end of the compilation. The other three continuators of the Mishnah were the Tosefta, the Talmud of the land of Israel (the Yerushalmi), and the Bavli. The Tosefta, containing a small proportion of materials contemporaneous with those presently in the Mishnah and a very sizable proportion secondary to and dependent on the Mishnah, reached conclusion some time between circa 300 and 400. The Yerushalmi closed at circa 400. The Bavli, as I said, was completed by circa 600. All these dates, of course, are rough guesses, but the sequence in which the documents made their appearance is not. The Tosefta addresses the Mishnah; its name means "supplement," and its function was to supplement the rules of the original documents. The Yerushalmi mediates between the Tosefta and the Mishnah, commonly citing a paragraph of the Tosefta in juxtaposition with a paragraph of the Mishnah and commenting on both, or so arranging matters that the paragraph of the Tosefta serves, just as it should, to complement a paragraph of the Mishnah. The Bavli, following the Yerushalmi by about two centuries, pursues its own program, which, as I said, was to link the two Torahs and restate them as one.

The stream of exegesis of the Mishnah and the exploration of its themes of law and philosophy flowed side by side with a second. This other river coursed up out of the deep wells of the written Scripture. But it surfaced only long after the work of Mishnah-exegesis was well under way and followed the course of that exegesis, now extended to Scripture. The exegesis of the Hebrew Scriptures, a convention of all systems of Judaism from before the conclusion of Scripture itself, obviously occupied sages from the very origins of their group. No one began anywhere but in the encounter with the written Torah. But the writing down of exegeses of Scripture in a systematic way, signifying also the formulation of a program and a plan for the utilization of the written Torah in the unfolding literature of the Judaism taking shape in the centuries at hand, developed in a quite distinct circumstance.

Specifically, one fundamental aspect of the work of Mishnah-exegesis began with one ineluctable question. How does a rule of the Mishnah relate to, or rest upon, a rule of Scripture? That question demanded an answer so that the status of the Mishnah's rules, and, right alongside, of the Mishnah itself, could find a clear definition. Standing by itself, the Mishnah bore no explanation of why Israel should obey its rules and accept its vision. Brought into relationship to Scriptures, in mythic language, viewed as part of the Torah, the Mishnah gained access to the source of authority operative in Israel. Accordingly, the work of relating the Mishnah's rules to those of Scripture got under way alongside the formation of the Mishnah's rules themselves. Collecting and arranging exegeses of Scripture as these related to passages of the Mishnah first reached literary form in the Sifra to Leviticus and in Sifré, to Numbers and Sifré to Deuteronomy. Even at that early stage, exegeses of passages of Scripture in their own context and not only for the sake of Mishnah-exegeses attracted attention. But a principal motif in all three books concerned the issue of Mishnah-Scripture relationships.

A still more fruitful path also emerged from the labor of Mishnah-exegesis. As the work of Mishnah-exegesis got under way in the third century, exegetes of the Mishnah and others alongside undertook a parallel labor. It was to work through verses of Scripture in exactly the same way—word for word, phrase for phrase, line for line—in which, to begin with, the exegetes of the Mishnah pursued the interpretation and explanation of the Mishnah. To state matters simply, precisely the types of exegesis that dictated the way in which sages read the Mishnah now guided their reading of Scripture as well. And as people began to collect and organize comments in accord with the order of sentences and paragraphs of the Mishnah, they found the stimulation to collect and organize comments on clauses and verses of Scripture. This kind of work got under way in the Sifra and the two Sifrés. It reached massive and magnificent fulfillment in Genesis Rabbah, which, as its name tells us, presents a line-for-line reading of the book of Genesis.

Let me give an account of what we find in Genesis Rabbah, which will show us how the sages of Judaism wrote with and through Scripture.

To begin with, the sages in Genesis Rabbah take for granted that Scripture speaks to the life and condition of Israel, the Jewish people. God repeatedly says exactly that to Abraham and to Jacob. The entire narrative of Genesis is so formed as to point toward the sacred history of Israel, the Jewish people: its slavery and redemption; its coming Temple in Jerusalem; its exile and salvation at the end of time. The powerful message of Genesis proclaims that the world's creation commenced a single, straight line of events, leading in the end to the salvation of Israel and, through Israel, to that of all humanity. Therefore, a given story will bear a deeper message about what it means to be Israel, on the one hand, and what in the end of days will happen to Israel, on the other. Sages invariably searched the stories of Genesis for evidence of the origins not only of creation and of Israel, but also of Israel's cosmic way of life, its understanding of how, in the passage of nature and the seasons, humanity worked out its relationship with God. The holy way of life that Israel lived through the seasons of nature would therefore make its mark upon the stories of the creation of the world and the beginning of Israel. At the time at which Genesis Rabbah reached closure, the Roman empire in general, and the Land of Israel in particular, went from pagan to Christian rule. The political situation of the Jews, and of the Judaism as presented by the sages of the document at hand and of the canon of which it forms a part, radically works its way through Adam's sin, Noah, and, especially, the founding family of Israel in its first four generations, Abraham, Isaac, Jacob, and Joseph. The sages systematically applied the history of the people of Israel to the lives and deeds of the founders, the fathers and the mothers of this book of the Torah. Authorships of other Midrash-compilations accomplished the same important task.

Let us now return to the description of the rabbinic literature, having considered how the sages read the Mishnah, on the one hand, and Scripture, on the other. Beyond these two modes of exegesis and the organization of exegesis in books, lies yet a third mode. To understand it, we once more turn back to the Mishnah's great exegetes, represented first in the Yerushalmi. While the original exegesis of the Mishnah in the Tosefta addressed the document under study through a line-by-line commentary, responding only in discrete and self-contained units of discourse, the authors of the Yerushalmi developed yet another mode of discourse entirely. They treated not phrases or sentences but principles and large scale conceptual problems. They dealt not only with a given topic, a subject and its rule, but also with an encompassing problem, a principle and its implications for a number of topics and rules. This more discursive and philosophical mode of thought produced for Mishnah-exegesis, in somewhat smaller volume but in much richer contents, sustained essays on principles cutting across specific rules. The work of sustained and broad-ranging discourse resulted in a type of exegetical work beyond that which was focused on words, phrases, and sentences.

Discursive exegesis is represented in Leviticus Rabbah, a document generally supposed to have reached closure sometime after Genesis Rabbah, circa 400–500. Leviticus Rabbah presents not phrase-by-phrase systematic exegesis of verses in the book of Leviticus but a set of thirty-seven topical essays. These essays, syllogistic in purpose, take the form of citations and comments on verses of Scripture, to be sure. But the compositions range widely over the far reaches of the Hebrew Scriptures, although focusing narrowly upon a given theme. More-over, they make quite distinctive points about that theme. The essays constitute compositions, not merely composites. Whether devoted to God's favor to the poor and humble or to the dangers of drunkenness, the essays, exegetical in form, discursive in character, correspond to the equivalent legal essays amply represented in the Yerushalmi.

So in this other mode of Scripture interpretation, too, the framers of the exegeses of Scripture accomplished in connection with Scripture what the Yerushalmi's exegetes of the Mishnah were doing in the same way at the same time. Yet another mode of scriptural exegesis is one in which the order of Scripture's verses is left far behind, and in which topics, not passages of Scripture, take over as the mode of organizing thought. Represented by Pesiqta deRab. Kahana, Lamentations Rabbati, and some other collections conventionally assigned to the sixth and seventh centuries, these entirely discursive compositions move in their own direction, only marginally relating in mode of discourse to any counterpart types of composition in the Yerushalmi (or in the Bavli).

At the end of this extraordinary creative age of Judaism, the authors of units of discourse collected in the Bavli drew together the two, up-to-then distinct, modes of organizing thought, either around the Mishnah or around Scripture. They treated both Torahs, oral and written, as equally available in the work of organizing large-scale exercises of sustained inquity. So we find in the Bavli a systematic treatment of some tractates of the Mishnah. And within the same aggregates of discourse, we also find (in somewhat smaller proportion to be sure, roughly 60 to 40 percent in the sample I made of three tractates) a second principle of organizing and redaction. That principle dictates that ideas be laid out in line with verses of Scripture, themselves dealt with in cogent sequence, one by one, just as the

Mishnah's sentences and paragraphs come under analysis in cogent order and one by one. So much for the written evidence that forms the arena of inquiry.

There are three distinct modes of organizing sustained discourse in the canon of the Judaism of the dual Torah. These cogent statements are (1) those built around the exegesis of the oral Torah, the Mishnah, hence the Tosefta and two Talmuds; (2) those that serve to amplify the written Torah, the Midrash-compilations; and (3) those that find cogency in the life and teaching of a given sage or group of sages. No collection of stories and sayings about sages emerged in the formative age, as counterparts to the Gospels, for example. To spell this out, let me explain further three modes of organizing large-scale discourse in the Judaism of the dual Torah. One was to make use of books or verses or themes of Scripture. A second was to follow the order of the Mishnah and to compose a systematic commentary and amplification of that document. This was the way, for example, of those who created the Talmud of the Land of Israel a century or so before. A third was to organize stories about and sayings of sages. These were framed around twin biographical principles, either as strings of stories about great sages of the past or as collections of sayings and comments drawn together solely because the same name stands behind the sayings.

The Midrash-compilations served a distinctive task in the formation of the Judaism of the dual Torah. The Midrash produced by the Judaism of the dual Torah from the fourth century onward, in particular Genesis Rabbah and Leviticus Rabbah, took as its set of urgent questions the issue defined by Christianity as it assumed control of the Roman empire and provided, as self-evidently valid answers, a system deriving its power from the Torah, read by sages, embodied by sages, exemplified by sages, as the reply. In this enormous intellectual enterprise we confront the counterpart to the evangelists' rereading of Scripture so as to answer the urgent question facing first-century Christians: Who is it that people say I am? In both cases an extraordinary experience, the one in the encounter with a man beyond time, the other in the meeting of an age beyond all expectation, required the rereading of Scripture in the light of what—in each circumstance—people grasped as the ultimate issue of eternity.

Through Midrash, the rabbinic sages mediated between Israel's perceived condition in an uncertain world and Israel's vivid faith in the God who chooses Israel and reveals the Torah. Faced with an unredeemed world, sages read Scripture as an account of how things are meant to be. To them, things are not what they seem, and that was a judgment made not only about this world but also about Scripture.

This world does not testify to God's wish and plan, and Scripture does not record merely the stories and sayings that we read there. This world serves as a metaphor for Scripture's reality, and Scripture provides a metaphor for Israel's as well. Reading one thing in terms of something else, the rabbinic exegetes produced in Midrash a powerful instrument of theological renewal through Scripture.

The verses that are quoted in rabbinic Midrash ordinarily shift from the meanings they convey to the implications they contain, so they speak about something, anything, other than what they seem to be speaking about. This as-if frame of mind renews Scripture, with the sage seeing everything with fresh eyes. And the result of the new vision was a reimagining of the social world envisioned by the document at hand, that is, the everyday world of Israel in its land in that difficult time. For what the sages now proposed was a reconstruction of existence along the lines of the ancient design of Scripture as they read it. What that meant was that, from a sequence of one-time and linear events, everything that happened was turned into a repetition of known and already experienced paradigms, hence, once more, a mythic being. The source and core of the myth, of course, derive from Scripture—Scripture reread, renewed, reconstructed along with the society that revered Scripture.

Reading one thing in terms of something else, the builders of the document systematically adopted for themselves the reality of the Scripture, its history and doctrines. They transformed that history from a sequence of one-time events, leading from one place to some other, into an ever-present mythic world. No longer was there one Moses, one David, one set of happenings of a distinctive and never-to-be-repeated character. Now whatever happened of which the thinkers propose to take account must enter and be absorbed into that established and ubiquitous pattern and structure founded in Scripture. It is not that biblical history repeats itself. Rather, biblical history no longer constitutes history as a story of things that happened once, long ago, and pointed to some one moment in the future. But it becomes an account of things that happen every day—hence, an ever-present mythic world. That is why, in Midrash in the Judaism of the dual Torah, Scripture as a whole does not dictate the order of discourse, let alone its character. In this document, a verse here, a phrase there is chosen. In the more mature Midrash-compilations, such as Leviticus Rabbah and Pesiqta deRab Kahana, these then presented the pretext for propositional discourse commonly quite out of phase with the cited passage.

Since biblical events exemplify recurrent happenings—sin and redemption, forgiveness and atonement—they lose their one-time character. At the same time and in the same way, current events find a place within the ancient, but eternally present, paradigmatic scheme. So no new historical events, other than exemplary episodes in lives of heroes, demand narration because, through what is said about the past, what was happening in the times of the framers of Midrash in the Judaism of the dual Torah would also come under consideration. This mode of dealing with biblical history and contemporary events produces two reciprocal effects. The first is the mythicization of biblical stories, their removal from the framework of ongoing, unique patterns of history and sequences of events and their transformation into accounts of things that happen all the time. The second is that contemporary events lose all their specificity and enter the paradigmatic framework of established mythic existence. So (1) the Scripture's myth happens every day, and (2) every day produces reenactment of the Scripture's myth.

This brings us to the final and authoritative statement of the Judaism of the dual Torah, the Talmud of Babylonia or Bavli. A tripartite corpus of inherited materials awaiting composition in a cogent composite document found its way into the Bavli. Prior to that time, the framers of documents had tended to resort to a single principle of organization, whether scriptural, mishnaic, or biographical. The authorship of the Bavli took up materials, in various states of completion, that were pertinent to the Mishnah or to the principles of laws that the Mishnah had originally brought to articulation. It had in hand received materials, again in various conditions, pertinent to the Scripture, both as the Scripture related to the Mishnah and also as the Scripture laid forth its own narratives. The authorship also collected and arranged sayings of and stories about sages. But this third principle of organizing discourse took a subordinate position with regard to the other two. The framers of the Bavli organized the Bavli around the Mishnah. But they also adapted and included vast tracts of antecedent materials organized as scriptural commentary. These they inserted whole and complete, not at all in response to the Mishnah's program. And, finally, while making provision for compositions built upon biographical principles, preserving both strings of sayings from a given master (and often a given tradent of a given master) as well as tales about authorities of the preceding half millennium, they did nothing new. That is to say, the ultimate authorships of the canonical documents never created redactional compositions of a sizable order that focused upon given authorities, even though sufficient materials lay at hand to allow doing so. God's will reached Israel through Scripture, Mishnah, sage—that is, by the evidence and testimony of each of these three media equally. That is the premise of the Judaism of the entire rabbinic canon, of each of the stories that appeal to a verse of Scripture, a phrase or sentence of the Mishnah, or a teaching or action of a sage. Recognizing the three components of the single canon, the written Torah, the oral Torah, and the sage as the living Torah, leads us deep into the investigation at hand.

A brief word on the history of the formation of the Judaism at hand is in order. That history may be narrated through traits of the two distinct stages in which the writings took shape. The first of the two stages in the formation of the Judaism of the dual Torah exhibits no sign of interest in or response to the advent of Christianity. The second, from the Yerushalmi forward, lays stress upon points that, in retrospect, appear to respond to and to counter the challenge of Christianity. The point of difference, of course, is that from the beginning of the legalization of Christianity in the early fourth century to the establishment of Christianity at the end of that same century, Jews in the land of Israel found themselves facing a challenge that, prior to Constantine, they had found no compelling reason to consider. The specific crisis came when the Christians pointed to the success of the church in the politics of the Roman state as evidence that Jesus Christ was king of the world and that his claim to be Messiah and King of Israel had now found vindication. When the Emperor Julian, 361–363, apostatized and renewed state patronage of paganism, he permitted the Jews to begin to rebuild the Temple as part of his large plan of humiliating Christianity. His prompt death on an Iranian battlefield supplied further evidence for heaven's choice of the Christian church and the truth of the church's allegations concerning the standing and authority of Jesus as the Christ. The Judaic documents that reached closure in the century after these events attended to those questions of salvation, for example, doctrine of history and of the Messiah, authority of the sages' reading of Scripture as against the Christians' interpretation, and the like, that had earlier not enjoyed extensive consideration. In all, this second Judaism, which I characterize as a Judaism despite Christianity, met the challenge of the events of the fourth century. The Judaic system of the dual Torah, expressed in its main outlines in the Yerushalmi and in associated compilations of biblical exegeses concerning Genesis, Leviticus, and some other scriptural books, culminated in the Bavli, which emerged as the authoritative document of the Judaism of the dual Torah from then to now.

The Judaism of the dual Torah from the seventh century onward flourished within Christian and Islamic contexts. Its success in both worlds derived from its capacity to explain for the Jews the condition of the Israel that they unanimously concurred they constituted. The dual Torah explained the present and accounted for a worthwhile future. In the context of Christianity, it addressed the Christian challenge to Judaism, with its claim that the Messiah had already come and "Israel after the flesh" had had its redemption when the Second Temple was built; that "Israel" was now another Israel, after the spirit; that history focused not upon holy Israel but upon Jesus Christ. The answer of the dual Torah, from its documents in the fourth century (the Yerushalmi) onward, was that the Messiah would come when Israel obeyed the Torah; that Israel after the flesh was the true and only family of Abraham, Isaac, and Jacob; and that what happened in all of history responded to the moral condition of Israel and God's judgment of Israel. Islam, later on, posed a less acute, because less specific, challenge, since it did not claim to supersede but only to succeed and form the seal of the revelation of God to Moses (and Jesus). The subordination of Israel to Islam found ample explanation in the apologia already composed in response to the triumph of Christianity in the time of Constantine, in the fourth century.

That is why in medieval times the Judaism of the dual Torah prevailed from Morocco to India, from France to Hungary and Rumania, Lithuania, Poland, and the Ukraine, and from Algeria to England. In the nineteenth and twentieth centuries, through the migration of many Jewish families, it became also predominant in the Western hemisphere, Africa, and Australasia. This single Judaism, appealing to its well-defined canon of writings, absorbed within itself an extraordinarily varied range of spiritual impulses, mystical and philosophical alike, and existed in many different variations, such as Reform Judaism, Orthodoxy, Conservative Judaism. And, so far as Jews seek to work out a religious system for the explanation of their existence as a social group, it is defined by the Judaism of the dual Torah. Evidence for that fact derives from the character of heresies in medieval and modern times. In every instance, the heresy denied a principle critical to the Judaism of the dual Torah or affirmed a belief denied by it. An example of the former is Karaism, from the ninth century, which denied the belief that there was an oral as well as a written Torah revealed at Sinai. An example of the latter is Sabbateanism from the seventeenth and eighteenth centuries, which affirmed that the Messiah had come and was not an observer of the laws of the Torah at all. The first important Judaic system to stand wholly outside of the symbolic system and mythic structure of the Judaism of the dual Torah is the Judaism of Holocaust and Redemption, which has taken shape since 1967. The influence of this Judaism is presently considerable, but no one now knows its future history.

I. INTRODUCTION

The bibliography of part of my writing, which follows, requires an explanation in the larger context of my intellectual biography and autobiography. Let me therefore introduce the bibliography with an account of the *oeuvre* that it represents. My field of study is religion, and the shape of my method finds outline and definition in that academic subject. Now, religions form social worlds and do so through the power of their rational thought, that is, their capacity to explain data in a (to an authorship) self-evidently valid way. The framers of religious documents answer urgent questions, framed in society and politics to be sure, in a manner deemed self-evidently valid by those addressed by the authorships at hand. At stake in my *oeuvre*, now in print in more than two hundred books of various classifications and serving diverse purposes and audiences, are striking examples of how people in writing explain to themselves who they are as a social entity. Religion as a powerful force in human society and culture is realized in society, not only or mainly theology; religion works through the social entity that embodies that religion. Religions form social entities—"churches" or "peoples" or "holy nations" or monasteries or communities—that, in the concrete, constitute the "us," as against "the nations" or merely "them." And religions carefully explain, in deeds and in words, who that "us" is—and they do it every day. To see religion in this way is to take religion seriously as a way of realizing, in classic documents, a large concept of the world. But how do we describe, analyze, and interpret a religion, and how do we relate the contents of a religion to its context? These issues of method are worked out through the reading of texts, and, I underline, through taking seriously and in their own terms the particularity and specificity of texts.

291

The formative writings of a particular Judaism serve as an example of how such work might be done. My *oeuvre* has concerned exemplary classics of Judaism and how they form a cogent statement. These classical writings, produced from the first to the seventh centuries C.E., form the canon of a particular statement of Judaism, the Judaism of the dual Torah, oral and written. That canon defined Judaism in both Christendom and Islam from the seventh century to the present. The circumstances of its formation, in the beginnings of Western civilization, the issues important to its framers, the kind of writings they produced, the modes of mediating change and responding to crisis—these form the center of interest. To expound my method for systemic description, analysis, and interpretation on the basis of written evidence, I wrote this book. But the larger context in which my method has taken shape requires explanation in its own terms. That is what I propose to explain concerning my *oeuvre,* now three decades in the making.

To undertake systemic analysis on the strength of written evidence, I have systemically reread the classic documents of the Judaism of the dual Torah. These documents—the Mishnah, Midrash-compilations, the two Talmuds—represent the collective statement and consensus of authorships (none is credibly assigned to a single author and all are preserved because they are deemed canonical and authoritative) and show us how those authorships proposed to make a statement to their situation—and, I argue, upon the human condition.

That brings us to the systemic approach to the reading of the formative documents of Judaism, which I have invented. Spelling it out is not difficult. Writings such as those we read have been selected by the framers of a religious system, and, read all together, those writings are deemed to make a cogent and important statement of that system, hence the category, "canonical writings." I call this encompassing canonical picture a "system" when it is composed of three necessary components: an account of a world view, a prescription of a corresponding way of life, and a definition of the social entity that finds definition in the one and description in the other. When those three fundamental components fit together, they sustain one another in explaining the whole of a social order, hence constituting the theoretical account of a system. Systems defined in this way work out a cogent picture, for those who make them up, of *how* things are correctly to be sorted out and fitted together, of *why* things are done in one way, rather than in some other, and of *who* they are that do and understand matters in this particular way. When, as is commonly the case, people invoke God as the foundation for their world view, maintaining that their way of life corresponds to what God wants of them, projecting their social entity in a particular relationship to God, then we have a religious system. When, finally, a religious system appeals as an important part of its authoritative literature or canon to the Hebrew Scriptures of ancient Israel or "Old Testament," we have a Judaism.

The movement from text to context and matrix is signaled by use of the word "system." For reading a text in its context and as a statement of a larger matrix of meaning, I propose to ask larger questions of systemic description of a religious system represented by the particular text and its encompassing canon. Colleagues who work on issues of religion and society will find familiar the program I am trying to work out. But, I underline, the success of that program is measured by its power to make the texts into documents of general intelligibility for the humanities, to read the text at hand in such a way as to understand its statement within, and of, the human condition. That seems to me not only the opposite of reductionism but also a profoundly rationalist mode of inquiry.

Systems begin in the social entity, whether one or two persons or two hundred or ten thousand—there and not in their canonical writings, which come only afterward, or even in their politics. The social group, however formed, frames the system, the system then defines its canon within, and addresses its politics to the larger setting, the *polis*, without. We describe systems from their end products, the writings. But we have then to work our way back from canon to system, not to imagine either that the canon is the system or that the canon creates the system. The canonical writings speak in particular to those who can hear, that is, to the members of the community who, on account of that perspicacity of hearing, constitute the social entity or systemic community. The community then comprises that social group, the system of which is recapitulated by the selected canon. The group's exegesis of the canon in terms of the everyday imparts to the system the power to sustain the community in a reciprocal and self-nourishing process. The community through its exegesis then imposes continuity and unity on whatever is in its canon.

While, therefore, we cannot account for the origin of a successful system, we can explain its power to persist. It is a symbolic transaction, as I said just now, in which social change comes to expression in symbol change. That symbolic transaction, specifically, takes place in its exegesis of the systemic canon, which, in literary terms, constitutes the social entity's statement of itself. So, once more, the texts recapitulate the system. The system does not recapitulate the texts. The system comes before the texts and defines the canon. The exegesis of the canon then forms that ongoing social action that sustains the whole. A system does not recapitulate its texts, it selects and orders them. A religious system imputes to them as a whole cogency, on to the next, that their original authorships have not expressed in and through the parts, and through them a religious system expresses its deepest logic, *and it also frames that just fit that joins system to circumstance.*

The whole works its way out through exegesis, and the history of any religious system is the exegesis of its exegesis. And the first rule of the exegesis of systems is the simplest, and the one with which I conclude: *The system does not recapitulate the canon. The canon recapitulates the system.* The system forms a statement of a social entity, specifying its world view and way of life in such a way that, to the participants in the system, the whole makes sound sense, beyond argument. So in the beginning are not words of inner and intrinsic affinity, but (as Philo Judaeus would want us to say) the Word: the transitive logic, the system, all together, all at once, complete, whole, finished—the word awaiting only that labor of exposition and articulation that the faithful, for centuries to come, will lavish at the altar of the faith. A religious system therefore presents a fact not of history but of immediacy, of the social present. So in this exercise we undertake first description, that is, the text, then analysis, that is, the context, and finally, interpretation, that is, the matrix in which a system has its being.

Let me now specify the discipline within which my method is meant to find its place. It is the history of religion, and my special area, history of Judaism in its formative period, the first six centuries C.E. I am trying to find out how to describe a Judaism in a manner consonant with the historical character of the evidence, therefore in the synchronic context of society and politics, and not solely or mainly in the diachronic context of theology, which until now has defined matters. The inherited descriptions of the Judaism of the dual Torah (or merely "Judaism") have treated as uniform the whole corpus of writing called "the oral Torah". The time and place of the authorship of a document played no role in our use of the allegations, as to fact, of the writers of that document. All documents have ordinarily been treated as part of a single coherent whole, so that anything we find in any writing held to be canonical might be cited as evidence of views on a given doctrinal or legal or ethical topic. "Judaism", then, was described by applying to all of the canonical writings the categories found imperative: e.g., beliefs about God, life after death, revelation, and the like. So far as historical circumstance played a role in that description, it was assumed that everything in any document applied pretty much to all cases, and historical facts derived from sayings and stories pretty much as the former were cited and the latter told.

Prior to the present time, ignoring the limits of documents and therefore the definitive power of historical context and social circumstance, all books on "Judaism" or "classical," "Rabbinic," "Talmudic" Judaism have promiscuously cited all writings deemed canonical in constructing pictures of the theology or law of that Judaism, severally and jointly, so telling us about Judaism, all at once and in the aggregate. That approach has lost all standing in the study of Christianity of the same time and place, for all scholars of the history of Christianity understand the diversity and contextual differentiation exhibited by the classical Christian writers. But, by contrast, ignoring the documentary origin of statements, the received pictures of Judaism have presented as uniform and unitary theological and legal facts that originated each in their own documents, (that is to say, in their distinctive time and place), and each as part of a documentary context, possibly also of a distinct system of its own. I have corrected that error by insisting that each of those documents be read in its own term, as a statement—if it constituted such a statement—*of* a Judaism or, at least, *to* and so in behalf of a Judaism. I maintained that each theological and legal fact was to be interpreted, to begin with, in relationship to the other theological and legal facts among which it found its original location.

The result of that reading of documents as whole but discrete statements, which I believe we can readily demonstrate defined their original character, is in such works of mine as *Judaism: The Evidence of the Mishnah, Judaism and Society: The Evidence of the Yerushalmi, Judaism and Scripture: The Evidence of Leviticus Rabbah,* as well as *Judaism and Story: The Evidence of The Fathers According to Rabbi Nathan.* At the conclusion of this last work, for reasons spelled out in its own logic, I stated that the documentary approach had carried me as far as it could. Having begun with the smallest whole units of the oral Torah, the received documents, and having moved onward to the recognition of the somewhat larger groups comprised by those documents, I reached an impasse. On the basis of literary evidence—shared units of discourse, shared rhetorical and logical modes of cogent statement, for example—I came to the conclusion that a different approach to the definition of the whole, viewed all together and all at once, was now required. Seeing the whole all together and all at once demanded a different approach. But—and I state with heavy emphasis—*It has to be one that takes full account of the processes of formation and grants full recognition to issues of circumstance and context, the layers and levels of completed statements.* That is what I propose to accomplish in the exercise of systemic analysis. My explanation of the movement from text to context to matrix now takes on, I believe, more concrete meaning.

I am trying to find out how to describe that "Judaism" beyond the specific texts—now beyond the text and the context and toward the matrix of all of the canonical texts—that each document takes for granted but no document spells out. And that research inquiry brings me to the matter of category-formation, which, in this context, requires me to specify the categorical imperative in the description of a Judaism. As I see it, there are three components of any Judaism, deriving their definition from the systemic model with which I began: world view, way of life, social entity. As is clear, "Israel" forms the social entity. The documents at hand, as I shall show, demand that we focus upon that same matter. So the category comes to me from the theoretical framework I have devised and from the inductive reading of the sources as I have now read the bulk of them. Two further categories that will occupy my attention in time to come may be stated in Judaic and also in abstract theoretical terms. The Judaic category, God "in our image", corresponds to the theoretical component of the world view, and the Judaic category of the human being "after our likeness" corresponds—though not so self-evidently—to the theoretical component of the way of life. The correspondence will strike the reader as a simple one, when it is recalled that in any Judaism "we" are what "we" do. To all Judaic systems known to me, one's everyday way of life forms a definitive element in the system, and if we wish to know how a Judaic system at its foundations defines in way of life, we do well to translate the details of the here and the now into the portrait of humanity "after our likeness." I have now spelled out in my studies the systemic social entity and the systemic world view in, respectively, *"Israel:" Judaism and its Social Metaphors* and *The Incarnation of God. The Character of Divinity in Formative Judaism.* My account of the systemic way of life in due course will be *In Our Image: Judaism and its Anthropological Metaphors.* My sense is that the planned study is full of self-evident propositions, which is why I have been reluctant to carry it out. What these studies set forth, then, are the systemic social entity, world view, and, in the anthropology, way of life.

To explain these two works and the anticipated completion of the project, I determined to pursue through the formative documents, as I had traced the stages of their unfolding, the formation and function of the principal systemic components of the world view of the Judaism at hand. Since any Judaism will make a statement concerning world view, way of life, and social entity or "Israel," I see three choices. "World view" begins with heaven, not earth, since it is the world up there upon which Judaic sages fix their gaze. So I wrote a work on the personality of God "in our image." "Social entity," of course, requires us to examine "Israel." As to "way of life," I see that category as representing, in a Judaic system, the systemic theory of humanity or anthropology. I identify as anthropological the metaphors through which the authorships of the documents of the dual Torah speak in concrete terms of that abstraction that is treated as a thing when we speak of "way of life."

There is a larger program for the study of religion. It concerns the social scientific setting for the academic study of religion, with special reference to the three principal components of a program of a social system, politics, economics, and philosophy. My most current work has called me to study the economics, politics, and philosophy of the Judaic systems in their successive unfolding in late antiquity. Let me set this present project forth. I have undertaken the development of the field of the political economy of religion, exemplified through the case of Judaism in its classical age.

Political economy joins the study of the institutions for the management of power that we know as the politics of a society with the analysis of the disposition of scarce resources that we know as economics. In prior ages, the ideas that governed collective life and conduct, that is, political ideas, encompassed issues of material life generally deemed economic, and in the interstices and interplay of both politics and economics, large-scale conceptions of the public interest and of society took shape. Plato's *Republic* and Aristotle's *Politics* (particularly the latter) pay ample attention to economics in the setting of politics, and in the case of Aristotle, what the system says about economics forms a chapter within the larger statement of the system as a whole. And that is the point at which religion becomes a matter of acute interest. For religious systems may make statements not only about matters we identify as theology but also about economics and political behavior.

Religions are today studied as modes of making social worlds, but that language very commonly veils considerable uncertainty about what we wish to know about the "making of a social world" that a religion proposes to accomplish (and may actually effect). In any event, one universal criterion for the differentiation and classification of religious systems is whether or not a religious system addresses, encompasses within its system, the realm of political economy. Some do, some don't. Christianity in late antiquity had virtually nothing to say about economics and cannot be said to have affected political economy at all, while in medieval times, with its encounter with Aristotle in particular, Christianity in the West worked out a political economy that predominated until the eighteenth century, when politics went its way and economics became disembedded from the political world. It is perfectly self-evident that from antiquity Judaism and, from its beginning in early medieval times, Islam, have taken as critical the issues of political economy and have assumed a powerful role in the organization of politics and the management of economics. And other religious systems do as well. That is why the political economy of religions and how it is to be described, analyzed, and interpreted, forms a central concern for anyone interested in how humanity in the past and the world today sorts out the issues of public policy for politics and economics alike.

Until World War I, considerable interest attached to generalizations about the political economy of religion. The field does not have to be invented, only renewed and reworked in light of things we have learned about religion and about the academic study of religion. For one major example, Weber's *Protestant Ethic and the Spirit of Capitalism* was only a chapter in public discussion, alongside Sombart's work on the theory that capitalism arose not from the Protestants but from the Jews. Weber worked on China, India, and ancient Israel as well, asking about the relationships between religious belief and the conduct of political economy, that is, rational economic action within a defined political framework of power relationships, all read against the backdrop of beliefs about "the sacred" or other religious concerns. So we may say that the political economy of religions is an old subject. But it has to be reworked, since we now realize that belief systems of religion form only one part of the whole and not, as even Weber posited, the centerpiece of interest. Since Weber we have learned much about religion and how to study religion, but we have not pursued Weber's questions. And that is why, through the reengagement with political economy as a dimension of religious systems and their construction of societies and world views, I have undertaken to renew a discipline that, well over half a century ago, proved its worth.

But political economy of religion assuredly requires renewal, and available work guides only as to goal, not as to method, and that is for two reasons. First, none of the inherited work accomplished the useful description of the religions under study. The ways in which religions are described have vastly changed. My work on systemic description, analysis, and interpretation of religions, focused on Judaism, shows in contrast with Weber's *Ancient Judaism* that we have made many steps forward since that time and has rendered utterly obsolete every word in Weber's book on the same subject. Second, while the issues of political economy in relationship to religion retain their urgency in Islam, Christendom, and the worlds of India and Southeast Asia, for example (so that we cannot speak of Latin America without its liberation theology, a vast statement upon issues of political economy), systematic and critical work is virtually unknown. In the range of theory and the accurate description, analysis, and interpretation of the political economy of a religious world, and in the comparison of the political economy of one religious system with that of another, scholarship in the study of religion has fallen silent. And yet, as we now recognize, there is simply no coping with the world today without the intellectual tools for understanding religion, not as a theory of another world but as a power and force in the shaping of this world. Fights about Islam in Iran and Afghanistan, about Roman Catholic Christianity in Poland, and about Judaism in the state of Israel and the USA only illustrate the simple fact that most (though not all) of humanity does what it does by reason of religious conviction. And since public policy falls silent before that fact, it is time to reenter discourse with issues long dormant on the relationship between religious systems and the world of politics and of economics.

But in universities, this is done in a way particular to scholarship, in full recognition that, beyond universities, what we learn will be put to good use by others in the framing of public policy, a partnership of learning. And that is the point at which my proposed five-year research program becomes pertinent. What we do is address not concrete and practical issues of the other but matters of theory that may guide those who do make policy. In my "Federal" career I have seen how much we in the bureaucracy (for our citizens' councils are part of the

Bibliography299

bureaucracy) depend upon research done on contract, and that involves not merely collecting and analyzing facts but gaining a long perspective and working out a useful theory that will guide our staff in collecting and analyzing facts and so working out the everyday policy that the bureaucracy effects. What we require is hypotheses and the testing of hypotheses against facts, and hypotheses emerge, to begin with, in the trial and error of particular cases: asking questions, attempting answers, testing hypotheses, explaining things. So long as a case is meant to exemplify, so long as we ask of a case "why this, not that?" with a sustained answer meant to generate a theory, the case is not the mere collecting and arranging of facts but an exercise in description, analysis, and interpretation.

I use as my case the Judaism of late antiquity, because that is one religious system that did, indeed, develop a large-scale conception of political economy; that is to say, it is a religious system that made its encompassing statement also through what it had to say about the household as the irreducible unit of production, about the market and its role in rationing scarce goods, and about wealth and its relationship to money (and to land, as a matter of fact). In this regard, that Judaism carried forward in a way so far as I know, unique in ancient times, the systematic thought of Aristotle, the only figure in antiquity who had anything important to say about economics. The system of that Judaism, further, paid ample attention also to the disposition of issues and institutions of power we know as political science—once again, a remarkable labor of large-scale social thought. The study, therefore, of the political economy of ancient Judaism, beginning in the law codes and other writings of that Judaism, seems to me a promising area in which to develop the intellectual tools—points of inquiry, modes of thought—that will serve as useful models in studying the political economy of Islam, in its varieties and rich diversity, as well as of Christianities of medieval and modern times. It goes without saying that the reading of the law for other than legal theory, so far as the study of antiquity is concerned, also is not a commonplace inquiry.

My own preparation for this work began with my study of the logical structures of the writings of ancient Judaism, yielding *The Making of the Mind of Judaism*. After I finished the latter, I turned to economics, which is now *The Economics of Judaism: The Initial Statement*. Reading for this work and conversations with colleagues here have broadened my conception and made me realize that Aristotle is the model for this system as a whole, combining as he did the issues of the material sustenance of society with the political organization of society and, of course, exercising a sustaining influence nearly down to the eighteenth century Physiocrats, founders of economics as we now know it. It was with my study of Plato and Aristotle in the setting of economics, as I looked for the affinities and influences on the thought of the writers of the formative documents of Judaism, that my notion of the "re-founding" of political economy of religion as a subfield of the academic study of religion came up. I now work on the next two studies of the initial system, which are *The Politics of Judaism* and *The Philosophy of Judaism*. When this systematic account of the economics, politics, and philosophy embedded in the initial system has been completed, I shall turn to the next system, connected to but not continuous or wholly symmetrical with the first, which is the system to which the Talmuds of the Land of Israel and Babylonia and related writings attest.

To conclude, in my *ouevre* I see two important results for the teaching of religion as an academic subject. First, I am trying to learn how to read a text in such a way as to highlight the human situation addressed by an authorship. If I can do so, I can show undergraduates of diverse origin what this text has to say to people in general, not only to Jews (of a quite specific order) in particular. In other words, my entire enterprise is aimed at a humanistic and academic reading of classics of Judaism, yet with full regard for their specific statements to their own world. People wrote these books as a way of asking and answering questions we can locate and understand—that is my premise—and when we can find those shared and human dimensions of documents, we can relate classic writings to a world we understand and share. That imputes a common rationality to diverse authorships and ages—theirs and ours—and, I believe, expresses the fundamental position of the academic humanities.

The second lesson draws us from text to context. Treating a religion in its social setting as something a group of people do together rather than as a set of beliefs and opinions prepares scholars and serious-minded students to make sense of a real world of ethnicity and political beliefs formed on the foundation of religious origins. Indeed, if they do not understand that religion constitutes one of the formative forces in the world today, they will not be able to cope with the future. But how to see precisely the ways in which religion forms social worlds? In the small case of Judaism, a set of interesting examples is set forth. Here they see that diverse Judaic systems responded to pressing social and political questions by setting forth cogent and (to the believers) self-evidently valid answers. That is one important aspect of the world-creating power of religion, and one nicely illuminated in the formation of Judaic systems.

The more critical academic issue should be specified. We are living in an age in which the old humanities are joined by new ones; women's studies (in their humanistic mode), black studies, Jewish studies, and a broad variety of other subjects have entered the curriculum. The universities require them because we now know that the humanities encompass a world beyond the European. But how are we to make our own and academic what appears at first encounter to be alien and incomprehensible? One solution accepts as special and particular the new humanities, treating as general and normal the old ones.

Hence—in the settlement accepted by some—Jews teach Jewish things to Jews and form a segregated intellectual community within the larger academic world. But I think that the subject matter at hand is too urgent and important—and altogether too interesting—to be left to the proprietors or to be permitted to be segregated. To deprive interested colleagues and students of access to the rich human experience and expression contained within the cultural artifacts of hitherto excluded parts of humanity diminishes the academic program and misrepresents the condition of humanity. But how to afford access to what is strange and perceived as abnormal is not readily explained. I have spent nearly thirty years trying to find appropriate access for colleagues and students alike to one of the new humanities. In the terms of Judaic studies I have insisted that the ghetto walls, once down, may not be reconstructed in the community of intellect. And in that same framework, I have spent my life trying to explore the dimensions of a world without walls. That is the context in which the entire program, now spelled out, finds its shape and motivation.

II. BIBLIOGRAPHY

1. The Pre-critical Stage

A Life of Yohanan ben Zakkai. Leiden: Brill, 1962. Awarded the Abraham Berliner Prize in Jewish History, Jewish Theological Seminary of America, 1962. Second edition, completely revised, 1970. Japanese translation by Yamamoto Shoten Publishing House, Tokyo, expected in 1990.

A History of the Jews in Babylonia. Leiden: Brill, 1965–1970. Vols. I–V.

I.   *The Parthian Period.* 1965. Second printing, revised, 1969. Third printing, Chico, Calif.: Scholars Press for Brown Judaic Studies, 1984.
II.   *The Early Sasanian Period.* 1966.
III.   *From Shapur I to Shapur II.* 1968.
IV.   *The Age of Shapur II.* 1969.
V.   *Later Sasanian Times.* 1970.

Aphrahat and Judaism. The Christian Jewish Argument in Fourth Century Iran. Leiden: Brill, 1971.

2. The Beginning of the Critical Enterprise

Development of a Legend. Studies on the Traditions Concerning Yohanan ben Zakkai. Leiden: Brill, 1970.

The Rabbinic Traditions about the Pharisees before 70. Leiden: Brill, 1971. Vols. I–III.

I.   *The Masters.*
II.   *The Houses.*
III.   *Conclusions.*

Eliezer ben Hyrcanus. The Tradition and the Man. Leiden: Brill, 1973. Vols. I–II.

I.   *The Tradition.*
II.   *The Man.*

3. Literature

The Work of Description of the Sources: Describing the Canon, Document by Document; the Stage of Translation, Form-Analysis, and Exegesis

A History of the Mishnaic Law of Purities. Leiden: Brill, 1974–1977. Vols. I–XX.

I.   *Kelim. Chapters One through Eleven.* 1974.
II.   *Kelim. Chapters Twelve through Thirty.* 1974.
III.   *Kelim. Literary and Historical Problems.* 1974.
IV.   *Ohalot. Commentary.* 1975.
V.   *Ohalot. Literary and Historical Problems.* 1975.
VI.   *Negaim. Mishnah-Tosefta.* 1975.
VII.   *Negaim. Sifra.* 1975.
VIII.   *Negaim. Literary and Historical Problems.* 1975.
IX.   *Parah. Commentary.* 1976.
X.   *Parah. Literary and Historical Problems.* 1976.
XI.   *Tohorot. Commentary.* 1976.
XII.   *Tohort. Literary and Historical Problems.* 1976.
XIII.   *Miqvaot. Commentary.* 1976.
XIV.   *Miqvaot. Literary and Historical Problems.* 1976.
XV.   *Niddah. Commentary.* 1976.
XVI.   *Niddah. Literary and Historical Problems.* 1976.
XVII.   *Makhshirin.* 1977.
XVIII.   *Zabim.* 1977.
XIX.   *Tebul Yom. Yadayim.* 1977.
XX.   *Uqsin. Cumulative Index, Parts I–XX.* 1977.

The Tosefta. Translated from the Hebrew. New York: Ktav, 1977–1980. Vols. II–VI.

II.   *Second Division. Moed.*
III.   *Third Division. Nashim.*
IV.   *Fourth Division. Neziqin.*
V.   *Fifth Division. Qodoshim.*
VI.   *Sixth Division. Tohorot.*

The Tosefta. Translated from the Hebrew. I. The First Division (Zeraim). New York: Ktav, 1985. Edited.

The Tosefta: Its Structure and its Sources. Atlanta: Scholars Press for Brown Judaic Studies, 1986. Reprise of pertinent results in *Purities*, Vols. I–XXI.

A History of the Mishnaic Law of Holy Things. Leiden: 1979, Brill. Vols. I–V.

I.   *Zebahim. Translation and Explanation.*
II.   *Menahot. Translation and Explanation.*
III.   *Hullin, Bekhorot. Translation and Explanation.*
IV.   *Arakhin, Temurah. Translation and Explanation.*
V.   *Keritot, Meilah, Tamid, Middot, Qinnim. Translation and Explanation.*

Form Analysis and Exegesis: A Fresh Approach to the Interpretation of Mishnah. Minneapolis: The University of Minnesota Press, 1980.

A History of the Mishnaic Law of Women. Leiden: Brill, 1979–1980. Vols. I–IV.

I.   *Yebamot. Translation and Explanation.*
II.   *Ketubot. Translation and Explanation.*
III.   *Nedarim, Nazir. Translation and Explanation.*
IV.   *Sotah, Gittin, Qiddushin. Translation and Explanation.*

A History of the Mishnaic Law of Appointed Times. Leiden: Brill, 1981–1983. Vols. I–IV.

I.   *Shabbat. Translation and Explanation.*
II.   *Erubin, Pesahim. Translation and Explanation.*
III.   *Sheqalim, Yoma, Sukkah. Translation and Explanation.*
IV.   *Besah, Rosh Hashshanah, Taanit, Megillah, Moed Qatan, Hagigah. Translation and Explanation.*

A History of the Mishnaic Law of Damages. Leiden: Brill, 1983–1985. Vols. I–IV.

I.   *Baba Qamma. Translation and Explanation.*
II.   *Baba Mesia. Translation and Explanation.*
III.   *Baba Batra, Sanhedrin, Mallot. Translation and Explanation.*
IV.   *Shebuot, Eduyyot, Abodah Zarah, Abot, Horayyot. Translation and Explanation.*

The Mishnah. A New Translation. New Haven and London: Yale University Press, 1987.
The Talmud of the Land of Israel. A Preliminary Translation and Explanation. Chicago: The
    University of Chicago Press, 1982–1989. Vols. IX–XII, XIV–XV, XVII–XXXIV.

XXXIV.	*Horayot. Niddah.* 1982.
XXXIII.	*Abodah Zarah.* 1982.
XXXII.	*Shebuot.* 1983.
XXXI.	*Sanhedrin. Makkot.* 1984.
XXX.	*Baba Batra.* 1984.
XXIX.	*Baba Mesia.* 1984.
XXVIII.	*Baba Qamma.* 1984.
XXVII.	*Sotah.* 1984.
XXVI.	*Qiddushin.* 1984.
XXV.	*Gittin.* 1985.
XXIV.	*Nazir.* 1985.
XXIII.	*Nedarim.* 1985.
XXII.	*Ketubot.* 1985.
XXI.	*Yebamot.* 1986.
XX.	*Hagigah. Moed Qatan.* 1986.
XIX.	*Megillah.* 1987.
XVIII.	*Besah. Taanit.* 1987.
XVII.	*Sukkah.* 1987.
XV.	*Sheqalim.* 1988.
XIV.	*Yoma.* 1989.
XII.	*Erubin.* 1989.
XI.	*Shabbat.* 1990.
X.	*Orlah. Bikkurim.* 1990.
IX.	*Hallah.* 1991.

In the Margins of the Yerushalmi. Notes on the English Translation. Chico, Calif.: Scholars
    Press for Brown Judaic Studies, 1983. Edited.
Torah from Our Sages: Pirke Avot. A New American Translation and Explanation. Chappaqua:
    Rossel, 1983. Paperback edition, 1987.
The Talmud of Babylonia. An American Translation. Chico, Calif.: Scholars Press for Brown
    Judaic Studies, 1984–1985. For Leviticus Rabbah, see below: *Judaism and Scripture:
    The Evidence of Leviticus Rabbah.*

I.	*Tractate Berakhot.*
VI.	*Tractate Sukkah.*
XVII.	*Tractate Sotah.*
XXIII.A.	*Tractate Sanhedrin. Chapters I–III.*
XXIII.B.	*Tractate Sanhedrin. Chapters IV–VIII.*
XXIII.C.	*Tractate Sanhedrin. Chapters IX–XI.*
XXXII.	*Tractate Arakhin.*

Genesis Rabbah. The Judaic Commentary on Genesis. A New American Translation. Atlanta:
    Scholars Press for Brown Judaic Studies, 1985. Vols. I–III.

I.	*Parashiyyot One through Thirty-Three. Genesis 1:1–8:14.*
II.	*Parashiyyot Thirty-Four through Sixty-Seven. Genesis 8:15–28:9.*
II.	*Parashiyyot Sixty-Eight through One Hundred. Genesis 28:10–50:26.*

*Sifra. The Judaic Commentary on Leviticus. A New Translation. The Leper. Leviticus
    13:1–14:57.* Chico: Scholars Press for Brown Judaic Studies, 1985. With a section by
    Roger Brooks. Based on *A History of the Mishnaic Law of Purities. VI. Negaim. Sifra.*
Sifré to Numbers. An American Translation. Atlanta: Scholars Press for Brown Judaic
    Studies, 1986. Vols. I–II.

I.   1–58.
II.   59–115.
The Fathers According to Rabbi Nathan. An Analytical Translation and Explanation. Atlanta: Scholars Press for Brown Judaic Studies, 1986.
Pesiqta deRab Kahana. An Analytical Translation and Explanation. Atlanta: Scholars Press for Brown Judaic Studies, 1987. Vols. I–II. For Pesiqta Rabbati, see below: *From Tradition to Imitation. The Plan and Program of Pesiqta deRab Kahana and Pesiqta Rabbati.*
I.   1–14.
II.   15–28.
Sifré to Deuteronomy. An Analytical Translation. Atlanta: Scholars Press for Brown Judaic Studies, 1987. Vols. I–II.
I.   *Pisqaot One through One Hundred Forty-Three. Debarim, Waethanan, Eqeb, Re'eh.*
II.   *Pisqaot One Hundred Forty-Four through Three Hundred Fifty-Seven. Shofetim, Ki Tese, Ki Tabo, Nesabim, Ha'azinu, Zot Habberakhah.*
Sifré to Deuteronomy. An Introduction to the Rhetorical, Logical, and Topical Program. Atlanta: Scholars Press for Brown Judaic Studies, 1987.
Sifra. An Analytical Translation. Atlanta: Scholars Press for Brown Judaic Studies, 1988. Vols. I–III. I. *Introduction*
I.   *Introduction, Vayyiqra Dibura Denedabah, Vayiqqra Dibura Dehobah.*
II.   *Sav, Shemini, Tazria, Negaim, Mesora, Zabim.*
III.   *Aharé Mot, Qedoshim, Emor, Behar, Behuqotai.*
Sifra in Perspective. The Documentary Comparison of the Midrashim of Ancient Judaism. Atlanta: Scholars Press for Brown Judaic Studies, 1988.
Mekhilta Attributed to R. Ishmael. An Analytical Translation. Atlanta: Scholars Press for Brown Judaic Studies, 1988. Vols. I–II.
I.   *Pisha, Beshallah, Shirata, Vayassa.*
II.   *Amalek, Bahodesh, Neziqin, Kaspa, Shabbata.*
Mekhilta Attributed to R. Ishmael. An Introduction to Judaism's First Scriptural Encyclopaedia. Atlanta: Scholars Press for Brown Judaic Studies, 1988.
Forthcoming:
Uniting the Dual Torah: Sifra and the Problem of the Mishnah. Cambridge and New York: Cambridge University Press, 1990.
Planned:
In the Margins of Sifra. Notes on the English Translation. Atlanta: Scholars Press for Brown Judaic Studies, 1992. Edited.

4. History

The Stage of Analytical Comparison and Contrast Among the Components of the Canon of Formative Judaism

A History of the Mishnaic Law of Purities. Leiden: Brill, 1977. Vols. XXI–XXII.
XXI.   *The Redaction and Formulation of the Order of Purities in the Mishnah and Tosefta.*
XXII.   *The Mishnaic System of Uncleanness. Its Context and History.*
The Mishnah before 70. Atlanta: Scholars Press for Brown Judaic Studies, 1987. Reprise of pertinent results of *A History of the Mishnah Law of Purities,* Vols. III, V, VIII, X, XII, XIV, XVI, XVII, XVIII.
A History of the Mishnaic Law of Holy Things. Leiden: Brill, 1979. Vol. VI. *The Mishnaic System of Sacrifice and Sanctuary.*
A History of the Mishnaic Law of Women. Leiden: Bill, 1980. Vol. V. *The Mishnaic System of Women.*
A History of the Mishnaic Law of Appointed Times. Leiden: Brill, 1981. Vol. V. *The Mishnaic System of Appointed Times.*

A History of the Mishnaic Law of Damages. Leiden: Brill, 1985. Vol. V. *The Mishnaic System of Damages.*

The Talmud of the Land of Israel. A Preliminary Translation and Explanation. Chicago: The University of Chicago Press, 1983. Vol. XXXV. *Introduction. Taxonomy.*

The Integrity of Leviticus Rabbah. The Problem of the Autonomy of a Rabbinic Document. Chico, Calif.: Scholars Press for Brown Judaic Studies, 1985.

Comparative Midrash: The Plan and Program of Genesis Rabbah and Leviticus Rabbah. Atlanta: Scholars Press for Brown Judaic Studies, 1986.

From Tradition to Imitation. The Plan and Program of Pesiqta deRab Kahana and Pesiqta Rabbati. Atlanta: Scholars Press for Brown Judaic Studies, 1987. With a fresh translation of Pesiqta Rabbati *Pisqaot* 1–5, 15.

Canon and Connection: Intertextuality in Judaism. Lanham, M.D.: University Press of America, 1986. Studies in Judaism series.

Midrash as Literature: The Primacy of Documentary Discourse. Lanham, M.D.: University Press of America, 1987. Studies in Judaism series.

The Bavli and Its Sources: The Question of Tradition in the Case of Tractate Sukkah. Atlanta: Scholars Press for Brown Judaic Studies, 1987.

Invitation to Midrash: The Working of Rabbinic Bible Interpretation. A Teaching Book. San Francisco: Harper & Row, 1988.

What Is Midrash? Philadelphia: Fortress Press, 1987. Dutch translation, Hilversum: Gooi & Sticht, 1989.

5. Religion
Reconstructing and Interpreting the History of the Formation of Judaism

Invitation to the Talmud. A Teaching Book. New York: Harper & Row, 1973. Second printing, 1974. Paperback edition, 1975. Reprinted, 1982. Second edition, completely revised, San Francisco: Harper & Row, 1984. Japanese translation, Tokyo: Yamamoto Shoten, 1989.

Judaism. The Evidence of the Mishnah. Chicago: The University of Chicago Press, 1981. *Choice* "Outstanding Academic Book List," 1982–1983. Paperback edition, 1984. Second printing, 1985. Third printing, 1986. Second edition, augmented, Atlanta: Scholars Press for Brown Judaic Studies, 1987. Hebrew translation *(Hayyahadut le'edut hammishnah),* Tel Aviv: Sifriat Poalim, 1987. Italian translation, Torino: Editrice Marietti, 1989.

Judaism without Christianity. An Introduction to the System of the Mishnah. Hoboken, N.J.: Ktav, 1989. Abbreviated version of *Judaism: The Evidence of the Mishnah.*

Judaism in Society: The Evidence of the Yerushalmi. Toward the Natural History of a Religion. Chicago: The University of Chicago Press, 1983. *Choice* "Outstanding Academic Book List," 1984–1985.

Judaism and Scripture: The Evidence of Leviticus Rabbah. Chicago: The University of Chicago Press, 1986. Fresh translation of Margulies's text and systematic analysis of problems of composition and redaction. Jewish Book Club selection, 1986.

Judaism: The Classical Statement. The Evidence of the Bavli. Chicago: The University of Chicago Press, 1986. *Choice* "Outstanding Academic Book List," 1987.

Judaism and Story: The Evidence of The Fathers According to Rabbi Nathan. Chicago: The University of Chicago Press, 1989.

Ancient Israel after Catastrophe. The Religious World-View of the Mishnah. The Richard Lectures for 1982. Charlottesville, N.C.: The University Press of Virginia, 1983.

The Foundations of Judaism. Method, Teleology, Doctrine. Philadelphia: Fortress Press, 1983–1985. Vols. I–III.

I.   *Midrash in Context. Exegesis in Formative Judaism.* Second printing, Alanta:
            Scholars Press for Brown Judaic Studies, 1988.

II.   *Messiah in Context. Israel's History and Destiny in Formative Judaism.* Second
            printing, Lanham, M.D.: University Press of America, 1988. Studies in
            Judaism series. Italian translation, Casale Monferrato: Editrice
            Marietti, 1989.

III.   *Torah: From Scroll to Symbol in Formative Judaism.* Second printing, Atlanta:
            Scholars Press for Brown Judaic Studies, 1988.

The Foundations of Judaism. Philadelphia: Fortress Press, 1988. Abridged edition of the
     foregoing trilogy. Dutch translation, Hilversum: Gooi & Sticht, 1989.

The Oral Torah. The Sacred Books of Judaism. An Introduction. San Francisco: Harper & Row,
     1985. Bnai Brith Jewish Book Club selection, 1986. Paperback, 1987.

Scriptures of the Oral Torah. Sanctification and Salvation in the Sacred Books of Judaism. San
     Francisco: Harper & Row, 1987. Editor. Jewish Book Club selection, 1988.

Vanquished Nation, Broken Spirit. The Virtues of the Heart in Formative Judaism. New York:
     Cambridge University Press, 1987. Jewish Book Club selection, 1987.

"To See Ourselves as Others See Us." Jews, Christians, "Others" in Late Antiquity. Chico, Calif.:
     Scholars Press, 1985. Edited with Ernest S. Frerichs. Studies in Humanities.

Judaic Perspectives on Ancient Israel. Philadelphia: Fortress Press, 1987. Edited with
     Baruch A. Levine and Ernest S. Frerichs.

Judaisms and Their Messiahs in the Beginning of Christianity. New York: Cambridge
     University Press, 1987. Edited with William Scott Green and Ernest S. Frerichs.

Goodenough's Jewish Symbols. An Abridged Edition. Princeton: Princeton University Press,
     1988. Editor.

Judaism in the Beginning of Christianity. Philadelphia: Fortress Press, 1983. British edition,
     London: SPCK, 1984. French translation *(Le judaisme a l'aube du christianisme),* Paris:
     Editions du Cerf, 1986. German translation *(Judentum in frühchristlicher Zeit),*
     Stuttgart: Calwerverlag, 1988. Dutch translation *(De Joodse wieg van het Christendom),*
     Kampen: J. H. Kok, 1987. Norwegian translation *(Jødedommen i den første kirstne tid;*
     translated by Johan B. Hygen), Trondheim: Tapir Publishers, University of
     Trondheim, 1987. Italian translation, Torino: Editrice Marietti, 1989. Japanese
     translation, Tokyo: Kyo Bun Kwan, 1990.

Judaism in the Matrix of Christianity. Philadelphia: Fortress Press, 1986. British edition,
     Edinburgh: T & T Collins, 1988. Dutch translation, Hilversum: Gooi & Sticht, 1989.
     Italian translation, Torino: Editrice Marietti, 1989.

Judaism and Christianity in the Age of Constantine. Issues of the Initial Confrontation. Chicago:
     The University of Chicago Press, 1987.

*Death and Birth of Judaism. The Impact of Christianity, Secularism, and the Holocaust on Jewish
     Faith.* New York: Basic Books, 1987.

Self-Fulfilling Prophecy: Exile and Return in the History of Judaism. Boston: Beacon Press,
     1987.

Goodenough on History of Religion and on Judaism. Atlanta: Scholars Press for Brown Judaic
     Studies, 1986. Edited with Ernest S. Frerichs.

*Science, Magic, and Religion in Concert and in Conflict. Judaic, Christian, Philosophical, and
     Social Scientific Perspectives.* New York: Oxford University Press, 1988. Edited with
     Ernest S. Frerichs and Paul V. Flesher.

The Enchantments of Judaism. Rites of Transformation from Birth Through Death. New York:
     Basic Books, 1987. Judaic Book Club selection, 1987. Jewish Book Club selection,
     1987.

Judaism and Its Social Metaphors. New York: Cambridge University Press, 1988.

The Incarnation of God: The Character of Divinity in Formative Judaism. Philadelphia: Fortress
     Press, 1988.

Writing with Scripture: The Authority and Uses of the Hebrew Bible in the Torah of Formative Judaism. Philadelphia: Fortress Press, 1989.

The Making of the Mind of Judaism. Atlanta: Scholars Press for Brown Judaic Studies, 1987.

The Economics of Judaism. The Initial Statement. Chicago: The University of Chicago Press, 1989.

The Formation of the Jewish Intellect. Making Connections and Drawing Conclusions in the Traditional System of Judaism. Atlanta: Scholars Press for Brown Judaic Studies, 1988.

The Essential Mishnah. The Social, Theological and Philosophical Vision of the Mishnah. Northvale, N.J.: Jason Aronson, 1990.

Forthcoming:

The Politics of Judaism. The Formative Age. Dealing with the systemic description of the Mishnah's political theory and comparison with Plato's *Republic* and Aristotle's *Politics.* To be submitted to the University of Chicago Press for publication in 1990.

Planned:

The Philosophy of Judaism. The Initial Statement. Monographs followed by a book dealing with the Second Sophistic and the Mishnah.

6. Explaining the Enterprise
Exposition of Problems of Method

The Formation of the Babylonian Talmud. Studies on the Achievements of Late Nineteenth and Twentieth Century Historical and Literary-Critical Research. Leiden: Brill, 1970. Editor.

The Modern Study of the Mishnah. Leiden: Brill, 1973. Editor.

Soviet Views of Talmudic Judaism. Five Papers by Yu. A. Solodukho. Leiden: Brill, 1973. Editor.

From Mishnah to Scripture. The Problem of the Unattributed Saying. Chico, Calif.: Scholars Press for Brown Judaic Studies, 1984. Reprise and reworking of materials in *A History of the Mishnaic Law of Purities.*

In Search of Talmudic Biography. The Problem of the Attributed Saying. Chico, Calif.: Scholars Press for Brown Judaic Studies, 1984. Reprise and reworking of materials in *Eliezer ben Hyrcanus. The Tradition and the Man.*

The Peripatetic Saying: The Problem of the Thrice-Told Tale in Talmudic Literature. Chico, Calif.: Scholars Press for Brown Judaic Studies, 1985. Reprise and reworking of materials in *Development of a Legend; Rabbinic Traditions about the Pharisees before 70,* vols. I–III.

The Memorized Torah. The Mnemonic System of the Mishnah. Chico, Calif.: Scholars Press for Brown Judaic Studies, 1985. Reprise and reworking of materials in *Rabbinic Traditions about the Pharisees before 70,* vols. I and III, and *A History of the Mishnaic Law of Purities,* vol. XXI.

Oral Tradition in Judaism: The Case of the Mishnah. New York: Garland Publishing, 1987. Albert Bates Lord Monograph Series of the journal, *Oral Tradition.* Restatement of results in various works on the Mishnah, together with a fresh account of the problem.

The Study of Ancient Judaism. New York: Ktav, 1981. Vols. I–II. Editor.

    I.   *Mishnah, Midrash, Siddur.*

    II.   *The Palestinian and Babylonian Talmuds.* Second printing, 1988.

Take Judaism, for Example. Studies toward the Comparison of Religions. Chicago: The University of Chicago Press, 1983. Editor.

Method and Meaning in Ancient Judaism. Missoula, Mont.: Scholars Press for Brown Judaic Studies, 1979. Second printing, 1983.

Method and Meaning in Ancient Judaism. Second Series. Chico, Calif.: Scholars Press for Brown Judaic Studies, 1980.

Method and Meaning in Ancient Judaism. Third Series. Chico, Calif.: Scholars Press for Brown Judaic Studies, 1980.

Ancient Judaism. Disputes and Debates. Chico, Calif.: Scholars Press for Brown Judaic Studies, 1984.

The Public Side of Learning. The Political Consequences of Scholarship in the Context of Judaism. Chico, Calif.: Scholars Press for the American Academy of Religion, 1985. Studies in Religion series.

Reading and Believing: Ancient Judaism and Contemporary Gullibility. Atlanta: Scholars Press for Brown Judaic Studies, 1986.

Ancient Judaism and Modern Category-Formation. "Judaism," "Midrash," "Messianism," and Canon in the Past Quarter-Century. Lanham, M.D.: University Press of America, 1986. Studies in Judaism series.

Struggle for the Jewish Mind. Debates and Disputes on Judaism Then and Now. Lanham, M.D.: University Press of America, 1987. Studies in Judaism series.

First Principles of Systemic Analysis. The Case of Judaism in the History of Religion. Lanham, M.D.: University Press of America, 1980. Studies in Judaism series.

The Systemic Analysis of Judaism. Atlanta: Scholars Press for Brown Judaic Studies, 1988.

From Description to Conviction. Essays on the History and Theology of Judaism. Atlanta: Scholars Press for Brown Judaic Studies, 1987.

Why No Gospels in Talmudic Judaism? Atlanta: Scholars Press for Brown Judaic Studies, 1988.

Paradigms in Passage: Patterns of Change in the Contemporary Study of Judaism. Lanham, M.D.: University Press of America, 1988. Studies in Judaism series.

Wrong Ways and Right Ways in the Study of Formative Judaism. Critical Method and Literature, History, and the History of Religion. Atlanta: Scholars Press for Brown Judaic Studies, 1988.

Forthcoming:

Religious Writings and Religious Systems. Systemic Analysis of Holy Books in Christianity, Islam, and Judaism. Atlanta: Scholars Press for Brown Judaic Studies, 1989. Edited. Papers from NEH Summer Seminar for College Teachers on the Documentary Method for the Study of Religion.

7. Restatement of Results
Systematic *Haute Vulgarisation* for the Wider Scholarly World

Early Rabbinic Judaism. Historical Studies in Religion, Literature, and Art. Leiden: Brill, 1975.

The Academic Study of Judaism. Essays and Reflections. New York: Ktav, 1975. Second printing, Chico, Calif.: Scholars Press for Brown Judaic Studies, 1982.

The Academic Study of Judaism. Second Series. New York: Ktav, 1977.

The Academic Study of Judaism. Third Series. Three Contexts of Jewish Learning. New York: Ktav, 1980.

Talmudic Judaism in Sasanian Babylonia. Essays and Studies. Leiden: Brill, 1976.

Judaism in the American Humanities. Chico, Calif.: Scholars Press for Brown Judaic Studies, 1981.

Judaism in the American Humanities. Second Series. Jewish Learning and the New Humanities. Chico, Calif.: Scholars Press for Brown Judaic Studies, 1983.

Das pharisäische und talmudische Judentum. Tuebingen: J.C.B. Mohr (Paul Siebeck), 1984. Edited by Hermann Lichtenberger. Foreword by Martin Hengel. Italian translation under way.

Formative Judaism. Religious, Historical, and Literary Studies. First Series. Chico, Calif.: Scholars Press for Brown Judaic Studies, 1982.

Formative Judaism. Religious, Historical, and Literary Studies. Second Series. Chico, Calif.: Scholars Press for Brown Judaic Studies, 1983.

Formative Judaism. Religious, Historical, and Literary Studies. Third Series. Torah, Pharisees, and Rabbis. Chico, Calif.: Scholars Press for Brown Judaic Studies, 1983.
Formative Judaism. Religious, Historical, and Literary Studies. Fourth Series. Problems of Classification and Composition. Chico, Calif.: Scholars Press for Brown Judaic Studies, 1984.
Formative Judaism. Religious, Historical, and Literary Studies. Fifth Series. Revisioning the Written Records of a Nascent Religion. Chico, Calif.: Scholars Press for Brown Judaic Studies, 1985.
Major Trends in Formative Judaism. First Series. Society and Symbol in Political Crisis. Chico, Calif.: Scholars Press for Brown Judaic Studies, 1983.
Major Trends in Formative Judaism. Second Series. Texts, Contents, and Contexts. Chico, Calif.: Scholars Press for Brown Judaic Studies, 1984.
Major Trends in Formative Judaism. Third Series. The Three Stages in the Formation of Judaism. Chico, Calif.: Scholars Press for Brown Judaic Studies, 1985. Italian translation, Casale Monferrato: Editrice Marietti, 1989.
The Religious Study of Judaism. Description, Analysis, Interpretation. Vol. I. Lanham, M.D.: University Press of America, 1986. Studies in Judaism series.
The Religious Study of Judaism. Description, Analysis, Interpretation. Vol. II. *The Centrality of Context.* Lanham, M.D.: University Press of America, 1986. Studies in Judaism series.
The Religious Study of Judaism. Description, Analysis, Interpretation. Vol. III. *Context, Text, and Circumstance.* Lanham, M.D.: University Press of America, 1987. Studies in Judaism series.
The Religious Study of Judaism. Description, Analysis, Interpretation. Vol. IV. *Ideas of History, Ethics, Ontology, and Religion in Formative Judaism.* Lanham, M.D.: University Press of America, 1988. Studies in Judaism series.
Understanding Seeking Faith. Essays on the Case of Judaism. Atlanta: Scholars Press for Brown Judaic Studies, 1986–1989. Vols. I–III.
I.   *Debates on Method, Reports of Results.*
II.   *Literature, Religion, and the Social Study of Judaism.*
II.   *Society, History, and the Political and Philosophical Uses of Judaism.*
The Pharisees. Rabbinic Perspectives. New York: Ktav, 1985. Reprise of *Rabbinic Traditions about the Pharisees before 70,* vols. I–III.
Israel and Iran in Talmudic Times. A Political History. Lanham, M.D.: University Press of America, 1986. Studies in Judaism series. Reprise of materials in *A History of the Jews in Babylonia,* parts of chapter 1 of vols. II–V. Jewish Book Club selection, 1988.
Judaism, Christianity, and Zoroastrianism in Talmudic Babylonia. Lanham, M.D.: University Press of America, 1986. Studies in Judaism series. Reprise of materials in *A History of the Jews in Babylonia,* parts of chapter 1 of vols. II–V and of *Aphrahat and Judaism.*
Israel's Politics in Sasanian Iran. Jewish Self-Government in Talmudic Times. Lanham, M.D.: University Press of America, 1986. Studies in Judaism series. Reprise of materials in *A History of the Jews in Babylonia,* parts of chapter 2 of vols. I–V.
The Wonder-Working Lawyers of Talmudic Babylonia. The Theory and Practice of Judaism in Its Formative Age. Lanham, M.D.: University Press of America, 1987. Studies in Judaism series. Reprise of materials in *A History of the Jews in Babylonia,* vols. II–V.
School, Court, Public Administration: Judaism and Its Institutions in Talmudic Babylonia. Atlanta: Scholars Press for Brown Judaic Studies, 1987. Reprise of materials in *A History of the Jews in Babylonia,* vols. III–V.
A Religion of Pots and Pans? Modes of Philosophical and Theological Discourse in Ancient Judaism. Essays and a Program. Atlanta: Scholars Press for Brown Judaic Studies, 1989.

8. Toward the Creation of a New Academy
Scholarly Books Organized and Edited

Report of the 1965–1966 Seminar on Religions in Antiquity. Hanover: Dartmouth College
   Comparative Studies Center, 1966. Reprinted, 1984.
Religions in Antiquity. Essays in Memory of Erwin Ramsdell Goodenough. Leiden: Brill, 1968.
   Supplements to *Numen.* Vol. XIV. Second printing, 1970. Third printing, 1972.
Christianity, Judaism, and Other Greco-Roman Cults. Studies for Morton Smith at Sixty. Leiden:
   Brill, 1975. Vols. I–IV.
I.   *New Testament.*
II.   *Early Christianity.*
III.   *Judaism before 70.*
IV.   *Judaism after 70. Other Greco-Roman Cults.*
Essays in Honor of Yigael Yadin. Edited with Geza Vermes. Special issue of *Journal of Jewish
   Studies,* 1982.
The New Humanities and Academic Disciplines. The Case of Jewish Studies. Madison: The
   University of Wisconsin Press, 1984.
New Perspectives on Ancient Judaism. I. *Contents and Contexts in Judaic and Christian
   Interpretation. Formative Judaism.* Lanham, M.D.: University Press of America, 1987.
   Studies in Judaism series. Edited with Ernest S. Frerichs, Richard Horsley, and
   Peder Borgen. Vols. I–III.
I.   *Contents and Context in Judaic and Christian Interpretation. Formative Judaism.*
II.   *Contents and Contexts in Judaic and Christian Interpretation. Ancient Israel.
         Formative Christianity.*
III.   *Judaic and Christian Interpretation of Texts: Contents and Contexts.* Edited with
         Ernest S. Frerichs.
Religion and Society in Ancient Times. Essays in Honor of Howard Clark Kee. Philadelphia:
   Fortress Press, 1988. Edited with Richard Horsley, Peder Borgen, and Ernest S.
   Frerichs.
Forthcoming:
The Marvin Fox Festschrift on the History of Ideas in Judaism. Vols. I–IV. Edited with Ernest S.
   Frerichs, Nahum Sarna. Planned for 1990.

Providing Textbooks for Undergraduate Instruction and Popular Works for the Public at Large

Fellowship in Judaism. The First Century and Today. London: Valentine, Mitchell, 1963.
History and Torah. Essays on Jewish Learning. London: Valentine, Mitchell, 1965. New
   York: Schocken Books, 1964. Paperback, 1967.
Judaism in the Secular Age. Essays on Fellowship, Community, and Freedom. London:
   Valentine, Mitchell, 1970. New York: Ktav, 1970.
The Way of Torah. An Introduction to Judaism. Encino, Calif.: Dickenson Publishing, 1970.
   In Living Religion of Man series. Edited by Frederick Streng. Second printing, 1971.
   Third printing, 1971. Second edition, revised, 1973. Third printing, 1976. Third
   edition, thoroughly revised, Belmont: Wadsworth Publishing, 1979. Third printing,
   1980. Fourth printing, 1982. Fifth printing, 1983. Sixth printing, 1985. Seventh
   printing, 1986. Fourth edition, completely revised and rewritten, 1988. Second
   printing, 1988. Italian translation, Torino: Editrice Marietti, 1989.
Life of Torah. Readings in the Jewish Religious Experience. Encino, Calif.: Dickenson
   Publishing, 1974. Editor. Third printing, Belmont, Calif.: Wadsworth

Publishing, 1980. Sixth printing, 1984. Seventh printing, 1987.

There We Sat Down. Talmudic Judaism in the Making. Nashville: Abingdon Press, 1972. Second printing, New York: Ktav, 1978.

American Judaism. Adventure in Modernity. Englewood Cliffs, N.J.: Prentice-Hall, 1972. Second printing, 1973. Third printing, 1976. Fourth printing, New York: Ktav, 1978.

From Politics to Piety. The Emergence of Pharisaic Judaism. Englewood Cliffs, N.J.: Prentice-Hall, 1973. Second printing, New York: Ktav, 1978. Japanese translation *(Parisai Ha towa Nanika—Seifi Kara Keiken e),* Tokyo: Kyo Bun Kwan, 1988.

Contemporary Judaic Fellowship. In Theory and in Practice. New York: Ktav, 1972. Editor.

Understanding Jewish Theology. Classical Themes and Modern Perspectives. New York: Ktav, 1973. Editor.

Understanding Rabbinic Judaism. From Talmudic to Modern Times. New York: Ktav, 1974. Editor. Second printing, 1977. Fourth printing, 1985.

First Century Judaism in Crisis. Yohanan ben Zakkai and the Renaissance of Torah. Nashville: Abingdon Press, 1975. Second printing, New York: Ktav, 1981.

Between Time and Eternity. The Essentials of Judaism. Encino, Calif.: Dickenson Publishing, 1976. Fifth printing, Belmont, Calif.: Wadsworth Publishing, 1983. Sixth printing, 1987.

Understanding American Judaism. Toward the Description of a Modern Religion. New York: Ktav, 1975. Vols. I–II. Editor.

I.   *The Synagogue and the Rabbi.*

II.   *The Sectors of American Judaism: Reform, Orthodoxy, Conservatism, and Reconstructionism.*

Stranger at Home. Zionism, "The Holocaust," and American Judaism. Chicago: The University of Chicago Press, 1980. Paperback edition, 1985. Second printing, 1985. Third printing, 1988.

Tsedakah. Can Jewish Philanthropy Buy Jewish Survival? Chappaqua: Rossel, 1982. Second printing, 1983. Fourth printing, 1988.

Our Sages, God, and Israel. An Anthology of the Yerushalmi. Chappaqua: Rossel, 1984. Jewish Book Club selection, 1985.

The Jewish War against the Jews. Reflections on Golah, Shoah, and Torah. New York: Ktav, 1984.

How to Grade Your Professors and Other Unexpected Advice. Boston: Beacon Press, 1984. Second printing, 1984.

Israel in America. A Too-Comfortable Exile? Boston: Beacon Press, 1985. Paperback edition, 1986.

Genesis and Judaism: The Perspective of Genesis Rabbah. An Analytical Anthology. Atlanta: Scholars Press for Brown Judaic Studies, 1986.

Christian Faith and the Bible of Judaism. Grand Rapids, Mich.: Wm. B. Eerdmans, 1987.

Reading Scriptures: An Introduction to Rabbinic Midrash. With Special Reference to Genesis Rabbah. New York: Rossel/Behrman House, 1987.

From Testament to Torah: An Introduction to Judaism in Its Formative Age. Englewood Cliffs, N.J.: Prentice-Hall, 1987.

Heschel Speaks! An Anthology of Abraham Joshua Heschel. New York: Madison, 1989. Edited with Noam M. M. Neusner.

Social Foundations of Judaism. Case-Studies of Religion and Society in Classical and Modern Times. Englewood Cliffs, N.J.: Prentice-Hall, 1989. Edited with Calvin Goldscheider.

Who, Where, and What Is "Israel"? Zionist Perspectives on Israeli and American Judaism. Lanham, M.D.: University Press of America, 1989. Studies in Judaism series.

Forthcoming:

A Priest and a Rabbi Read the Bible Together. New York: Warner Books, 1990. With Andrew M. Greeley.